D1321361

MICHIGAN STATE UNIVERSITY
LIBRARY

OCT 23 2017

WITHDRAWN

Refereed and Nonrefereed Economic Journals

Refereed and Nonrefereed Economic Journals

A Guide to Publishing Opportunities

Compiled by
A. Carolyn Miller
and
Victoria J. Punsalan

With the assistance of Kenneth G. Rohm

Greenwood Press
New York • Westport, Connecticut • London

Library of Congress Cataloging-in-Publication Data

Miller, A. Carolyn.
  Refereed and nonrefereed economic journals.

  Bibliography: p.
  Includes indexes.
  1. Economics—Periodicals—Directories.
  2. Economics—Authorship—Marketing—Directories.
  I. Punsalan, Victoria J. II. Rohm, Kenneth G.
  III. Title.
  HB63.M54 1988   016.33'005   87-25158
  ISBN 0-313-25857-0 (lib. bdg. : alk. paper)

British Library Cataloguing in Publication Data is available.

Copyright © 1988 by A. Carolyn Miller and Victoria J. Punsalan

All rights reserved. No portion of this book may be
reproduced, by any process or technique, without the
express written consent of the publisher.

Library of Congress Catalog Card Number: 87-25158
ISBN: 0-313-25857-0

First published in 1988

Greenwood Press, Inc.
88 Post Road West, Westport, Connecticut 06881

Printed in the United States of America

The paper used in this book complies with the
Permanent Paper Standard issued by the National
Information Standards Organization (Z39.48-1984).

10 9 8 7 6 5 4 3 2 1

Contents

Preface

This directory is designed to aid prospective authors seeking publication opportunities in economic journals. Besides providing manuscript submission information for over two hundred academic and professional economic journals accepting manuscripts in English, this guide includes specific information on reviewing practices and clearly identifies refereed and nonrefereed economic journals. In addition, refereed journals are classified by levels of refereeing according to type of reviewer and author anonymity or nonanonymity.

Information for the journals was obtained from a survey conducted in May 1986 of 244 editors of journals currently indexed in the Journal of Economic Literature. Survey forms were also sent to the top twenty-four journals listed in eight prestige studies [See References 1, 3, 6, 8, 9, 12, 13, 14], all but three of which--Management Science, Problems of Communism, and Soviet Studies--are also indexed in JEL. Excluded from the population were journals that do not publish articles in English, those that consist entirely of translations into English or of conference proceedings, those that publish only invited articles or those written by in-house staff, and annuals. Two of the journals replied that they had ceased, reducing the total to 242 surveys. After numerous follow-ups by mail and by telephone, 218 questionnaires were finally completed, a 90% rate of response. Three of these, however, were found to publish only invited articles, and were eliminated. Ninety-six of the final 215 journals surveyed, or approximately 45%, are from outside the United States.

Entries for each journal, listed alphabetically by title, are comprised of three parts. The first provides brief bibliographical information about the age and affiliation of the journal, frequency of publication, circulation and audience. A concise statement of the journal's editorial policy is included to help the author select a journal for publication. As a further aid to journal selection, the percentage of unsolicited manuscripts published in an average issue is included; journals that devote 100% of their space to unsolicited manuscripts will obviously provide greater publishing opportunities. The International Standard Serial Number (ISSN) is provided as an aid to identification of the journal.

Part two, "Review Information," is unique to this guide in that it identifies refereed and nonrefereed journals, classifies refereed journals by levels of refereeing, and provides other specific details about the reviewing process. From this section prospective authors will receive additional information about space availability--the number of articles published in an average issue of the journal--and further information to aid in selection of a journal: the journal's acceptance rate, the average review time and publication time lag, and the return of the manuscript with reviewers' comments. The number of reviewers for each manuscript, excluding in-house editors, and the type of reviewer (board, external, or board and external) are specified. For journals using blind review, the stages of the reviewing process in which the author's name and identification are removed are provided. (It should be noted that a number of nonrefereed journals, as well as refereed journals, use blind review.) The reviewing criteria used by the journal are also included in this section and are discussed in detail under "Refereeing," below.

Information the author needs before submitting the manuscript is found in part three, "Manuscript Information." If the journal's guidelines and style requirements are published in the journal, specific issues and/or dates are given; if they are not published, information is given as to their availability on request. Preferred topics for articles, the style manual used by the journal, and information concerning query and cover letters, number of manuscript copies and manuscript length, abstract, fee requirements, and other submission details are included. The complete address for submission of manuscripts is listed at the end of each entry.

REFEREEING

Despite the critical role of refereed journals in academic publishing, little is known about the criteria of a refereed journal, the qualities or characteristics that separate the refereed journal from the nonrefereed journal. Prospective authors seeking publication outlets and administrators seeking to verify faculty publications in promotion and tenure dossiers often have difficulty determining whether a journal is refereed. Prestige studies have ranked many journals by discipline but cannot be used to classify or rank other journals, particularly the newer journals; prestige alone, moreover, may not guarantee that a journal is refereed. Guides and directories offer only brief information about reviewing practices and appear to have unclear and conflicting standards for classifying journals as refereed. Information in individual journals also varies, and consulting individual journal issues is both time consuming and limited to journals in easily accessible collections. This lack of agreed-upon, published criteria for a refereed journal is surprising in light of evidence that administrators and members of promotion and tenure committees often do not read a candidate's publications but judge the quality of a journal article by the quality or reputation of the journal in which it appeared [10, p. 673].

Although widespread criticism of reviewing practices has appeared in scholarly journals, few studies include a definition of a refereed journal. Definitions that have appeared refer to the type of reviewer--"an expert or experts (none of whom are on the editorial staff), who are specialists in the subject field covered by the paper" [7, p. 178]--or to "professional scholars of the discipline" [11, p. 155]. Two definitions specify two reviewers, but only one of them specifies that the reviewer will be "independent" and that the author will not be identified [11, p. 155; 5, p. 3]. Two of the three agree that the reviewer will be anonymous [11, p. 155; 7, p. 178]. A survey of deans of business schools and of journal editors reveals disagreement in the use of external and in-house reviewers and in the use of blind and non-blind review; curiously, the number of reviewers was not a criterion in the survey except for unilateral review, a category of refereeing supported by only a small percentage of both deans and editors [15, pp. 47-48].

Defining a refereed journal is difficult not only because of the lack of agreed-upon criteria but also because of the varying reviewing practices of scholarly journals.

Agreement apparently exists that refereed journals use reviewers (referees) who are experts (peers) to evaluate unsolicited manuscripts and advise the editor; agreement does not exist on the number or type of reviewer or on other editorial and reviewing practices. Based upon a previous study of reviewing practices [10] and a recent survey of the literature, the definition of a refereed journal in this guide is as follows:

> A refereed journal has a structured reviewing system in which at least two reviewers, excluding in-house editors, evaluate each unsolicited manuscript and advise the editor as to acceptance or rejection.

References to two reviewers appear often in the literature of scholarly communication [10, p. 680]. Journals vary, however, in the type of reviewer they use, and even within journals, selection of reviewers may vary by individual manuscript. Editorial board members may be the reviewers the editor most often asks to evaluate manuscripts or, depending on the expertise of the reviewer and the subject of the manuscript, an editor may seek advice from both a board member and an external reviewer. For some journals (37% of the refereed journals in this survey), reviewers are most often external, members of neither an in-house staff nor an editorial or advisory board. Critics believe that the use of external reviewers may reduce bias by eliminating the "dynastic tendency" [11, p. 163], "Establishment" [4, p. 940], or "old-boy and old-girl connections" [2, p. 367] of the editorial or advisory boards (by whatever names they are called). In order to distinguish between journals that use two external reviewers for the most part and journals that use other types of reviewers, refereed journals are classified into three groups: I, those that use two or more external reviewers; II, those that use one or more external reviewers and one or more board members; and III, those that use two or more board members to evaluate manuscripts.[1]

Although controversial, blind review has been suggested frequently as another obvious and simple method of reducing editorial and reviewer bias. In this guide, journals are defined as using blind review if an author's name and identification are removed during any stage of the reviewing process: in preliminary screening, in board review, in external review, and in final selection of the manuscript. Because of its importance as an aid to reducing bias in the reviewing process, blind review is used as an additional method of classifying refereed journals. The three categories of refereed journals, I, II, and III, are divided into subclasses "A" and "B" according to the journal's practice of having the author unknown ("A") or known ("B") to the reviewer. A journal, thus, that uses two external reviewers and blind review is classified as I-A; a journal that uses two board members and does not use blind review is classified as III-B. The three classes and subclasses, ranked in order according to the journal's use of these two bias safeguards (external reviewers and blind review), are as follows:

Class I   Journals that use two or more external reviewers
           A.   Author is unknown (blind review)
           B.   Author is known

Class II   Journals that use one or more external reviewers and one or more board reviewers
           A.   Author is unknown
           B.   Author is known

Class III   Journals that use two or more board reviewers
                 A.   Author is unknown
                 B.   Author is known

    In addition to identifying and classifying refereed journals, this guide provides information about a journal's use of specific reviewing procedures that (1) aid the author in selecting a journal for submission of a manuscript, and (2) guard against bias in the editorial and reviewing processes. Based on the criteria recommended in "Criteria for Identifying a Refereed Journal" [10], these reviewing procedures, some admittedly controversial, represent an attempt to identify a standard for journal refereeing. If agreed-upon and established across disciplines, the suggested criteria will become specific characteristics that objectively identify the refereed and nonrefereed journal.

    For each entry, the reviewing procedures used by the journal are listed by number under "Reviewing Criteria Used," subdivided by sections "Manuscript Submission Aids" and "Bias Safeguards." The ten reviewing criteria, some of which have been discussed in detail, are described in the following listing. For all criteria, editors were asked to indicate their practices for the most part or in most cases.

MANUSCRIPT SUBMISSION AIDS:

1.   Guidelines published in journal. The selection of a journal for submission of a manuscript is more precise if the journal publishes guidelines concerning its purpose, scope, and audience, either in each issue or in stated issues.

2.   Style requirements published in journal. Although style requirements may be deduced from examination of the journal, an author is aided if the journal publishes style information, either in each issue or in stated issues. (Note: For both style requirements and guidelines, the availability on request is not included in the criteria.)

BIAS SAFEGUARDS:

3.   Author's name removed from manuscript. As previously discussed, blind review is seen as an important means of reducing bias. Journals are listed as using blind review if the author's name and identification are removed from the manuscript during any stage in the reviewing process: in preliminary screening, in board review, in external review, and in final selection of the manuscript. (Note: Some journals may indicate that they use blind review in both board and external review, while the reviewers for the journal are listed only as external. This apparent inconsistency exists because the editor was asked to list the reviewers used in most cases.)

4.   Two or more do preliminary screening. Editors acknowledge that they or a managing editor do the preliminary screening of manuscripts. Numerous manuscripts are rejected on this initial reading. This criterion was designed to assure that more than one person is involved in the initial decision about manuscript review.

5. Outside experts who are not board members review manuscripts. As discussed, the use of external reviewers, members of neither the editorial nor advisory board nor other formally organized group associated with the publication of the journal, is another means of reducing bias in the reviewing process.

6. One or more, in addition to the editor, select external reviewers. To reduce bias, at least one person in addition to the editor helps select reviewers.

7. Two or more external reviewers evaluate each manuscript. Soliciting at least two reviews from experts not on an editorial or advisory board is another important bias safeguard. (Note: Review by board members is not included in this criterion.)

8. Reviewers use evaluation criteria form. As a means of reducing reviewer bias and improving interreviewer reliability, editors send reviewers evaluation criteria or manucript rating forms. Forms are defined as evaluation criteria forms if they contain at least three criteria as guides to the evaluation of manuscripts. (Examples from submitted forms: importance of the contribution, originality, research design and methodology, literature review, documentation, writing style and readability, organization and presentation, relevance, etc.) Forms that ask only for judgment as to acceptance or rejection of manuscripts are excluded, as are instructions that contain criteria but are not on a standardized form. Journals that reported that they use evaluation criteria forms but refused to send copies for examination and comparison are also excluded from this criterion.

9. Reviewers' comments sent automatically (on form or not). Critics of the reviewing process recommend that reviewers' comments should be sent to authors as a matter of course. Respondents who qualified their answers with "Editor's discretion" are reported as "9*."

10. Signed reviewers' comments sent. Although controversial, the identification of reviewers is seen by many critics as essential to open discourse and responsible evaluation. Journals are also included if they provide signed reviews as an option of the referee or of the editor.

(Note: Two of the original criteria, the publication of the evaluation criteria form in the journal and the sending of the completed form to the author, have been omitted from the list because of poor responses to the survey questions.)

At the end of the guide is a table entitled "Journals' Reviewing Criteria." An "x" under the individual criterion indicates that the editorial or reviewing procedure is currently used by the journal, as reported by the editor or other editorial staff member. An asterisk (*) before the journal title indicates that the journal is refereed.

Also at the end of the guide is a list of refereed journals, classified by levels of refereeing, a list of nonrefereed journals, a Geographical Index of all journals in the guide, and an Affiliations and Keywords Index. A section entitled "Key to Journal Information," with brief explanations, a table of abbreviations, and a bibliography of style manual publishers precede the alphabetical listing of journals.

Carolyn Miller began the research for this guide while on sabbatical leave from The Pennsylvania State University and, with Victoria Punsalan, continued preparing the manuscript while both served as reference librarians at Heindel Library, The Capital College, The Pennsylvania State University at Harrisburg, Middletown, Pennsylvania. Journals that were not locally available we examined at the University Libraries of The Pennsylvania State University, University Park, and at the Library of Congress and the Melvin Gelman Library of George Washington University. We personally examined at least one issue of the 215 titles in this guide.

We are grateful to our library director, Dr. Charles Townley, for his support and encouragement while we were preparing the manuscript. We were also helped immeasurably by our colleagues in the reference department, librarians Nancy Dewald and Margaret Dewey, who located information, cajoled by telephone, verified, proofread, and cheered us on during our quest for accuracy and completeness. Ruth Runion-Slear, interlibrary loan clerk, Heindel Library, verified and located journals by computer and completed innumerable photocopy requests. At University Park, our friends in the University Libraries' Interlibrary Loan Department--Linda Schreck, Terry Burris, and Debra Shelow--and Pat Scott, former Heindel Library colleague, responded to our requests with speed and good humor. To all of these, our sincere appreciation.

Our special thanks to graduate student Kenneth Rohm for his invaluable help with the coding, data entry and computer analysis, copyediting and proofreading, to Hope Hamill for her skilled and cheerful typing of the manuscript, and to Gerald Phibbs for his expert composition--across a continent--on the Macintosh. Carolyn Miller also expresses her appreciation to The Pennsylvania State University for granting her sabbatical leave to begin the research for this project.

Most of all, we are indebted to the editors who answered our survey questionnaires, letters, and telephone calls. Our appreciation for their patience, courtesy, and cooperation. We have done our best to insure that the information in this guide is accurate and complete.

A. Carolyn Miller
Victoria J. Punsalan

NOTE

1. Some scholars may limit the term "refereed" to those journals that use only external reviewers. Since at present no published, agreed-upon standards exist for a refereed journal, it has seemed appropriate in this guide to designate as refereed all journals that use at least two reviewers in addition to in-house editors.

REFERENCES

1. Bennett, J. T. , M. H. Johnson, and P. Germanis. "An Abstract Approach to the Relative Ranking of Economics Journals." Nebraska Journal of Economics and Business, 19 (Spring 1980), 52-64.

2. Bernard, H. R. "Report from the Editor." Human Organization, 39 (Winter 1980), 366-69.

3. Billings, B. B., and G. J. Viksnins. "The Relative Quality of Economics Journals: An Alternative Rating System." Western Economic Journal, 10 (December 1972), 467-69.

4. Brackbill, Y., and F. Korten. "Journal Reviewing Practices: Authors' and APA Members' Suggestions for Revision." American Psychologist, 25 (October 1970), 937-40.

5. Gazda, G. M. et al. "Continuation with a New Phase." Journal of Group Psychotherapy, Psychodrama and Sociometry, 34 (1981), 1-6.

6. Hawkins, R. G., L. S. Ritter, and I. Walter. "What Economists Think of Their Journals." Journal of Political Economy, 81 (July/August 1973), 1017-32.

7. Juhasz, S. et al. "Acceptance and Rejection of Manuscripts." IEEE Transactions on Professional Communication, PC-18 (September 1975), 177-85.

8. Liebowitz, S. J., and J. P. Palmer. "Assessing the Relative Impacts of Economics Journals." Journal of Economic Literature, 22 (March 1984), 77-88.

9. McDonough, C. C. "The Relative Quality of Economics Journals Revisited." Quarterly Review of Economics and Business, 15 (Spring 1975), 91-97.

10. Miller, A. C., and S. L. Serzan. "Criteria for Identifying a Refereed Journal." Journal of Higher Education, 55 (November/December 1984), 673-99.

11. Mohan, R. P., and G. S. Kowalski. "Refereed Journals and Professional Respectability." International Journal of Contemporary Sociology, 16 (January & April 1979), 154-67.

12. Moore, W. J. "The Relative Quality of Economics Journals: A Suggested Rating System." Western Economic Journal, 10 (June 1972), 156-69.

13. Niemi, A. W. "Journal Publication Performance During 1970-1974: The Relative Output of Southern Economics Departments." Southern Economic Journal, 42 (July 1975), 97-106.

14. Skells, J. W., and R. A. Taylor. "The Relative Quality of Economics Journals: An Alternative Rating System." Western Economic Journal, 10 (December 1972), 470-73.

15. Wooten, B. E., A. F. Steiert, and J. A. Ryan. "Refereed Journals: A Survey of Deans and Editors." Collegiate News and Views, 38 (Fall-Winter 1984), 47-49.

Key to Journal Information

JOURNAL TITLE: Correct, current title(s) of the journal.

FIRST PUBLISHED: Year of first publication of the journal.

FREQUENCY: Number of times a year the journal is published.

CIRCULATION: Latest annual circulation as supplied by the editor or found in reference works.

AFFILIATION: Name and current address of college, university, professional organization, learned society, or agency that is associated with the publication of the journal.

AUDIENCE: Readers for whom the journal is intended.

PERCENT OF UNSOLICITED ARTICLES/ISSUE: Number of unsolicited articles relative to the total number of articles published in an average issue of the journal, expressed in percent.

ISSN: International Standard Serial Number.

EDITORIAL POLICY: Journal's goals and areas of interest as written or approved by the editor or quoted from the journal's published statements.

REFEREED: Yes/No, according to definition in Preface.

ACCEPTANCE RATE: Number of unsolicited manuscripts accepted for publication relative to the total number of unsolicited manuscripts submitted to the journal, expressed in percent. (Data is for 1985.)

NUMBER OF REVIEWER(S)/MS., EXCLUDING IN-HOUSE EDITOR(S): The average number of persons who evaluate each manuscript in addition to the in-house editors.

REVIEWER(S): Persons who evaluate each unsolicited manuscript.
(Note: Practices may vary. Reviewers listed are the editor's indication of the journal's practice in most cases.)

ARTICLES/AVG. ISSUE: The number of articles in an average issue of the journal.

REVIEWING CRITERIA USED:

MANUSCRIPT SUBMISSION AIDS, BIAS SAFEGUARDS: Reviewing procedures used (1) to aid in the selection of a journal for submission of a manuscript, and (2) to guard against bias in the editorial and reviewing processes. Refer to Preface for explanation of reviewing criteria.

BLIND REVIEW: Yes/No, indicating if the author's name and identification are removed from the manuscript at any stage in the reviewing process. If the journal uses blind review, reviewing stages are indicated. See Preface.

AVERAGE REVIEW TIME: Average length of time between submission of a manuscript and notification to the author of its acceptance or rejection.

PUBLICATION TIME LAG: Average length of time between acceptance and publication of a manuscript.

MANUSCRIPT RETURNED WITH COMMENTS: Yes/No, indicating if the manuscript with the reviewers' comments is returned to the author. "SASE Required" indicates that a self-addressed, stamped envelope is required for return of the manuscript.

GUIDELINES PUBLISHED: Yes/No, indicating publication date(s) of guidelines concerning purpose, scope, and audience of the journal. Availability on request is also indicated.

STYLE REQUIREMENTS PUBLISHED: Yes/No, indicating publication date(s) of style requirements of the journal. Availability on request is also indicated.

STYLE MANUAL USED: The style manual that authors should use in preparing a manuscript for the journal.

PREFERRED TOPICS: Editor's listing of preferred topics for submitted manuscripts.

QUERY LETTER: Yes/No, indicating if, before submission, the author should query the editor about the suitability of the manuscript.

SIMULTANEOUS SUBMISSION: Yes/No, indicating if submission of a manuscript to more than one journal at the same time is permitted.

ABSTRACT WITH MANUSCRIPT: Yes/No, indicating if an abstract should be included when the manuscript is submitted. If an abstract is required, the number of words is indicated.

COVER LETTER: Yes/No, indicating if a cover letter should be included with the manuscript.

NUMBER OF MANUSCRIPT COPIES: Number of copies of the manuscript, including original if appropriate, that should be submitted.

MANUSCRIPT LENGTH: Preferred number of words/pages of manuscript.

SUBMISSION FEE: Yes/No, indicating if a fee, including amount, is required when a manuscript is submitted.

PAGE CHARGES: Yes/No, indicating if, after acceptance of the manuscript, a fee is charged to help subsidize the publication of the article. The amount given is the fee per page of the published article.

MANUSCRIPT ACKNOWLEDGED: Yes/No, indicating if the editorial staff sends the author an acknowledgment of receipt of the manuscript. "SASE req." indicates that a self-addressed, stamped envelope is required for acknowledgment.

EARLY PUBLICATION OPTION: Yes/No, indicating if the journal will publish an article earlier than scheduled. A fee is usually required for this option.

COPYRIGHT OWNER: Indicates author, journal, publisher, institution or organization that holds the copyright to the published article.

REPRINTS: Yes/No, indicating if reprints are available and, if so, whether purchase is optional or required.

AUTHOR COMPENSATION: Fee paid, if any, number of reprints/tear sheets, journal copies in which the article appeared, or subscription given to the author for the published article.

MANUSCRIPT ADDRESS: Correct address to use when submitting a manuscript to the journal. (Note: Because of space constraints, for the most part only the U. S. address is given for international journals with more than one manuscript submission address.)

Abbreviations

adm	administration	rev	review
assoc	association	revrs	reviewers
Aus$	Australian dollar	SASE	self-addressed,
avg	average		stamped envelope
auto	automatically	seln	selection
Can$	Canadian dollar	sevl	several
excl	excluding	two(+)	two or more
ext	external	wds	words
inst	institute	wks	weeks
ISSN	International Standard		
	Serial Number		
max	maximum		
mgt	management		
mo(s)	month(s)		
mss	manuscripts		
nat	national	Frequency of Publication	
N.R.	no response		
/MS	per manuscript	M	Monthly
/page	per page	Q	Quarterly
pp	pages	Bi-M	Every 2 months
pref	preferred		(Bimonthly)
prel	preliminary	S-A	Twice a year
pub	published		(Semiannually)
req	required	3/Yr	3 times a year
reqts	requirements	6/Yr	6 times a year
res	research	Irreg	Irregularly

Style Manual Publishers

AEA   American Economic Association. <u>Style Instructions</u>.
Nashville, TN, The Association, 1986. 3 pp.

APSA   American Political Science Association. <u>Style Manual</u>.
Washington, D. C., The Association, 1985. 4 pp.

ASA   American Sociological Association. <u>Style Manual</u>.
Washington, D. C., The Association, 1986. 1 p.

AUSTRALIA   Australia. Commonwealth Printing Office. <u>Style Manual</u>.
Canberra, Australian Government Publishing Service.

CHICAGO   <u>The Chicago Manual of Style</u>. 13th ed. Chicago,
University of Chicago Press, 1982. 738 pp.

ELSEVIER   Elsevier Science Publishing Co., Inc. <u>Instructions for Authors</u>.
New York, The Publisher. 3 pp.

GPO   United States. Government Printing Office. <u>Style Manual</u>.
Washington, D. C., Government Printing Office, 1984. 479 pp.
(Stock No. 021-000-00121-0)

HARVARD   Harvard Law Review Association. <u>A Uniform System of
Citation</u>. 14th ed. Cambridge, MA, The Association,
1986. 255 pp.

MLA   Achtert, Walter S., and Joseph Gibaldi. <u>The MLA Style
Manual</u>. New York, Modern Language Association of
America, 1985. 271 pp.

UN   United Nations. <u>UN Editorial Manual</u>. New York, United
Nations, 1983. 525 pp. (Publication E.83.I.16)

ALPHABETICAL LIST
OF JOURNALS

The Accounting Review

FIRST PUBLISHED: 1926   FREQUENCY: Q   CIRCULATION: 16,000

AFFILIATION: American Accounting Association, 5717 Bessie Drive,
  Sarasota, FL 33583

AUDIENCE: Academic/Professional

PERCENT OF UNSOLICITED ARTICLES/ISSUE: 100%   ISSN: 0001-4826

EDITORIAL POLICY: To publish the results of deductive and inductive
  research in all areas of accounting.

REVIEW INFORMATION

REFEREED: Yes (II-A)   ACCEPTANCE RATE: 12%

NUMBER OF REVIEWER(S)/MS., EXCLUDING IN-HOUSE EDITOR(S): 2

REVIEWER(S): Board and external   ARTICLES/AVG. ISSUE: 10

REVIEWING CRITERIA USED: BLIND REVIEW: Yes (Board and
  MANUSCRIPT SUBMISSION AIDS: 1, 2   external review)

  BIAS SAFEGUARDS: 3, 5, 8, 9

AVERAGE REVIEW TIME: 2-3 mos.   PUBLICATION TIME LAG: 6 mos.

MANUSCRIPT RETURNED WITH COMMENTS: Yes

MANUSCRIPT INFORMATION

GUIDELINES PUBLISHED: April issue

STYLE REQUIREMENTS PUBLISHED: Each issue

STYLE MANUAL USED: In-house

PREFERRED TOPICS: All areas of accounting

QUERY LETTER: No   SIMULTANEOUS SUBMISSION: No

ABSTRACT WITH MANUSCRIPT: 200 wds.   COVER LETTER: Yes

NUMBER OF MANUSCRIPT COPIES: 3   MANUSCRIPT LENGTH: 25 pp.

SUBMISSION FEE: $25.   PAGE CHARGES: No

MANUSCRIPT ACKNOWLEDGED: Yes   EARLY PUBLICATION OPTION: No

COPYRIGHT OWNER: Journal   REPRINTS: Optional purchase

AUTHOR COMPENSATION: None

MANUSCRIPT ADDRESS: Prof. William R. Kinney, Jr., Editor, The Accounting
  Review, Graduate School of Business Administration, University of
  Michigan, Ann Arbor, MI 48109

Acta Oeconomica

FIRST PUBLISHED: 1966   FREQUENCY: 8/Yr.   CIRCULATION: 1,000

AFFILIATION: Hungarian Academy of Sciences, 1051 Budapest, Roosevelt-
ter 9, Hungary

AUDIENCE: Academic/Professional; Government

PERCENT OF UNSOLICITED ARTICLES/ISSUE: 0-10%   ISSN: 0001-6373

EDITORIAL POLICY: To inform foreign readers on economic policy and
related research in Hungary; theoretical and methodological aspects
are included. Topicality, comprehensibility for foreign readers
and novelty are preferred. Possibility for contributions by foreign
authors on planned economies. Text mostly in English; rarely in
French, German or Russian.

REVIEW INFORMATION

REFEREED: No   ACCEPTANCE RATE: 30%

NUMBER OF REVIEWER(S)/MS., EXCLUDING IN-HOUSE EDITOR(S): 1

REVIEWER(S): Board   ARTICLES/AVG. ISSUE: 10

REVIEWING CRITERIA USED: BLIND REVIEW: No

  MANUSCRIPT SUBMISSION AIDS: 0

  BIAS SAFEGUARDS: 4, 5, 6, 9, 10

AVERAGE REVIEW TIME: 1-2 mos.   PUBLICATION TIME LAG: 12 mos.

MANUSCRIPT RETURNED WITH COMMENTS: No

MANUSCRIPT INFORMATION

GUIDELINES PUBLISHED: No; not available

STYLE REQUIREMENTS PUBLISHED: No; not available

STYLE MANUAL USED: In-house

PREFERRED TOPICS: Centrally planned economies, East-West trade,
  international economics

QUERY LETTER: No   SIMULTANEOUS SUBMISSION: Yes

ABSTRACT WITH MANUSCRIPT: 100-200 wds.   COVER LETTER: Yes

NUMBER OF MANUSCRIPT COPIES: 2   MANUSCRIPT LENGTH: 30-40 pp.

SUBMISSION FEE: No   PAGE CHARGES: No

MANUSCRIPT ACKNOWLEDGED: Yes   EARLY PUBLICATION OPTION: Yes

COPYRIGHT OWNER: Author and journal   REPRINTS: Optional purchase

AUTHOR COMPENSATION: 70 free reprints

MANUSCRIPT ADDRESS: Tamàs Földi, Managing Editor, Acta Oeconomica,
  H-1112 Budapest, Budaorsi ùt 45, Hungary

Agricultural Economics Research

FIRST PUBLISHED: 1949   FREQUENCY: Q   CIRCULATION: 2,500

AFFILIATION: U.S. Department of Agriculture, Economic Research Service. Address same as journal's.

AUDIENCE: Academic/Professional; Business/Industrial; Government

PERCENT OF UNSOLICITED ARTICLES/ISSUE: 61-80%   ISSN: 0021-1423

EDITORIAL POLICY: Publishes articles reporting results of economic research supported by USDA, describing new methods or critically evaluating methods still in use, describing new or expanding areas of research or statistics. Authors are restricted to USDA employees or those individuals who have done the work described in the manuscript on contract with USDA.

REVIEW INFORMATION

REFEREED: Yes (I-A)   ACCEPTANCE RATE: 60%

NUMBER OF REVIEWER(S)/MS., EXCLUDING IN-HOUSE EDITOR(S): 2

REVIEWER(S): External   ARTICLES/AVG. ISSUE: 3

REVIEWING CRITERIA USED: BLIND REVIEW: Yes (External review and final selection)
  MANUSCRIPT SUBMISSION AIDS: 1, 2
  BIAS SAFEGUARDS: 3, 5, 7, 9

AVERAGE REVIEW TIME: 4 mos.   PUBLICATION TIME LAG: 3 mos.

MANUSCRIPT RETURNED WITH COMMENTS: Yes

MANUSCRIPT INFORMATION

GUIDELINES PUBLISHED: Each issue

STYLE REQUIREMENTS PUBLISHED: Each issue

STYLE MANUAL USED: In-house; GPO

PREFERRED TOPICS: Agricultural economics

QUERY LETTER: No   SIMULTANEOUS SUBMISSION: No

ABSTRACT WITH MANUSCRIPT: No   COVER LETTER: Yes

NUMBER OF MANUSCRIPT COPIES: 3   MANUSCRIPT LENGTH: 25 pp.

SUBMISSION FEE: No   PAGE CHARGES: No

MANUSCRIPT ACKNOWLEDGED: Yes   EARLY PUBLICATION OPTION: No

COPYRIGHT OWNER: None claimed   REPRINTS: Not available

AUTHOR COMPENSATION: 2 free journals

MANUSCRIPT ADDRESS: Gerald Schluter, Economics Editor, Agricultural Economics Research, Economic Research Service, USDA, Room 1140, 1301 New York Avenue, N.W., Washington, D.C. 20005-4788

The American Economic Review

FIRST PUBLISHED: 1911   FREQUENCY: Q   CIRCULATION: 28,000

AFFILIATION: American Economic Association, 1313 21st Avenue South, Nashville, TN 37212-2786

AUDIENCE: Academic/Professional; Business/Industrial; Government

PERCENT OF UNSOLICITED ARTICLES/ISSUE: 81-100%   ISSN: 0002-8282

EDITORIAL POLICY: To publish the results of outstanding scientific research in economics.

REVIEW INFORMATION

REFEREED: Yes (I-B)   ACCEPTANCE RATE: 13%

NUMBER OF REVIEWER(S)/MS., EXCLUDING IN-HOUSE EDITOR(S): 2

REVIEWER(S): External   ARTICLES/AVG. ISSUE: 14

REVIEWING CRITERIA USED: BLIND REVIEW: No

  MANUSCRIPT SUBMISSION AIDS: 0

  BIAS SAFEGUARDS: 5, 6, 7, 9

AVERAGE REVIEW TIME: 2 mos.   PUBLICATION TIME LAG: 6 mos.

MANUSCRIPT RETURNED WITH COMMENTS: Yes

MANUSCRIPT INFORMATION

GUIDELINES PUBLISHED: No; not available

STYLE REQUIREMENTS PUBLISHED: No; available on request

STYLE MANUAL USED: In-house

PREFERRED TOPICS: No preference

QUERY LETTER: No   SIMULTANEOUS SUBMISSION: No

ABSTRACT WITH MANUSCRIPT: No   COVER LETTER: Yes

NUMBER OF MANUSCRIPT COPIES: 4   MANUSCRIPT LENGTH: 50 pp.

SUBMISSION FEE: $25. for members/   PAGE CHARGES: No
  subscribers; $50. for others

MANUSCRIPT ACKNOWLEDGED: Yes   EARLY PUBLICATION OPTION: No

COPYRIGHT OWNER: Journal   REPRINTS: Optional purchase

AUTHOR COMPENSATION: None

MANUSCRIPT ADDRESS: Orley Ashenfelter, Managing Editor, The American Economic Review, 209 Nassau Street, Princeton, NJ 08542-4607

The American Economist

FIRST PUBLISHED: 1960　　　FREQUENCY: S-A　　　CIRCULATION: 8,500

AFFILIATION: Omicron Delta Epsilon, P.O. Drawer AS, University of
　Alabama, AL　35486

AUDIENCE: Academic/Professional

PERCENT OF UNSOLICITED ARTICLES/ISSUE: 61-80%　　　ISSN: 0002-8290

EDITORIAL POLICY: The purpose is twofold. First, to provide an out-
　let for essays and papers written by young economists. Second, to
　provide them with current developments in pure and applied economics.

REVIEW INFORMATION

REFEREED: No　　　　　　　　　ACCEPTANCE RATE: 20%

NUMBER OF REVIEWER(S)/MS., EXCLUDING IN-HOUSE EDITOR(S): 1

REVIEWER(S): External　　　　　ARTICLES/AVG. ISSUE: 13

REVIEWING CRITERIA USED:　　　BLIND REVIEW: No

　MANUSCRIPT SUBMISSION AIDS: 0

　BIAS SAFEGUARDS: 5, 9

AVERAGE REVIEW TIME: 6 mos.　　PUBLICATION TIME LAG: 12 mos.

MANUSCRIPT RETURNED WITH COMMENTS: No

MANUSCRIPT INFORMATION

GUIDELINES PUBLISHED: No; available on request

STYLE REQUIREMENTS PUBLISHED: No; available on request

STYLE MANUAL USED: Chicago

PREFERRED TOPICS: Various areas of economics

QUERY LETTER: No　　　　　　　　SIMULTANEOUS SUBMISSION: No

ABSTRACT WITH MANUSCRIPT: Yes　　COVER LETTER: Yes

NUMBER OF MANUSCRIPT COPIES: 3　MANUSCRIPT LENGTH: 15 pp.

SUBMISSION FEE: No　　　　　　　PAGE CHARGES: No

MANUSCRIPT ACKNOWLEDGED: Yes　　EARLY PUBLICATION OPTION: No

COPYRIGHT OWNER: Publisher　　　REPRINTS: Not available

AUTHOR COMPENSATION: None

MANUSCRIPT ADDRESS: Michael Szenberg, Editor-in-Chief, The American
　Economist, Lubin Graduate School of Business, Pace University,
　Pace Plaza, New York, NY　10038

American Historical Review

FIRST PUBLISHED: 1895   FREQUENCY: 5/Yr.   CIRCULATION: 16,000

AFFILIATION: American Historical Association, 400 A Street, SE,
  Washington, D.C.   20003

AUDIENCE: Academic/Professional; Government

PERCENT OF UNSOLICITED ARTICLES/ISSUE: 90%   ISSN: 0002-8762

EDITORIAL POLICY: Historical articles of broad scope are invited,
  including economic history and demographics. Prefer 30-35 pages,
  fully documented. See October 1970 issue.

REVIEW INFORMATION

REFEREED: Yes (I-A)   ACCEPTANCE RATE: 17%

NUMBER OF REVIEWER(S)/MS., EXCLUDING IN-HOUSE EDITOR(S): 4

REVIEWER(S): External   ARTICLES/AVG. ISSUE: 4

REVIEWING CRITERIA USED: BLIND REVIEW: Yes (External
  MANUSCRIPT SUBMISSION AIDS: 1, 2   review only)

  BIAS SAFEGUARDS: 3, 4, 5, 7, 8, 9*, 10

AVERAGE REVIEW TIME: 3-4 mos.   PUBLICATION TIME LAG: 6-8 mos.

MANUSCRIPT RETURNED WITH COMMENTS: Yes

MANUSCRIPT INFORMATION

GUIDELINES PUBLISHED: Vol. 75, No. 6 (1970)

STYLE REQUIREMENTS PUBLISHED: Each issue

STYLE MANUAL USED: In-house; Chicago

PREFERRED TOPICS: History of all varieties of approaches and subject
  areas throughout the world and from ancient times to the present

QUERY LETTER: No   SIMULTANEOUS SUBMISSION: No

ABSTRACT WITH MANUSCRIPT: No   COVER LETTER: Yes

NUMBER OF MANUSCRIPT COPIES: 4   MANUSCRIPT LENGTH: 30-35 pp.

SUBMISSION FEE: No   PAGE CHARGES: No

MANUSCRIPT ACKNOWLEDGED: Yes   EARLY PUBLICATION OPTION: No

COPYRIGHT OWNER: Journal and author   REPRINTS: Optional purchase

AUTHOR COMPENSATION: None

MANUSCRIPT ADDRESS: David L. Ransel, Editor, American Historical
  Review, Indiana University, 914 Atwater, Bloomington, IN 47405

American Journal of Agricultural Economics

FIRST PUBLISHED: 1919   FREQUENCY: 5/Yr.   CIRCULATION: 6,000

AFFILIATION: American Agricultural Economics Association, Department
  of Economics, 180 Heady Hall, Iowa State University, Ames, IA 50011

AUDIENCE: Academic/Professional; Government

PERCENT OF UNSOLICITED ARTICLES/ISSUE: 81-100%   ISSN: 0002-9092

EDITORIAL POLICY: "To provide a forum for creative and scholarly
  work in agricultural economics."

REVIEW INFORMATION

REFEREED: Yes (I-A)   ACCEPTANCE RATE: 25%

NUMBER OF REVIEWER(S)/MS., EXCLUDING IN-HOUSE EDITOR(S): 3

REVIEWER(S): 1 board, 2 external   ARTICLES/AVG. ISSUE: 15-20

REVIEWING CRITERIA USED: BLIND REVIEW: Yes (External
  MANUSCRIPT SUBMISSION AIDS: 1, 2   review only)

  BIAS SAFEGUARDS: 3, 4, 5, 6, 7, 9

AVERAGE REVIEW TIME: 3 mos.   PUBLICATION TIME LAG: 1-3 mos.

MANUSCRIPT RETURNED WITH COMMENTS: Yes

MANUSCRIPT INFORMATION

GUIDELINES PUBLISHED: Each issue

STYLE REQUIREMENTS PUBLISHED: Each issue

STYLE MANUAL USED: Chicago

PREFERRED TOPICS: Farm management, development, econometrics,
  marketing, extension, policy, labor, resources, international

QUERY LETTER: No   SIMULTANEOUS SUBMISSION: Yes

ABSTRACT WITH MANUSCRIPT: 100 wds.   COVER LETTER: Yes

NUMBER OF MANUSCRIPT COPIES: 4   MANUSCRIPT LENGTH: 30 pp.

SUBMISSION FEE: No   PAGE CHARGES: $45. per page

MANUSCRIPT ACKNOWLEDGED: Yes   EARLY PUBLICATION OPTION: No

COPYRIGHT OWNER: Journal   REPRINTS: Purchase required

AUTHOR COMPENSATION: 100 free reprints/tear sheets

MANUSCRIPT ADDRESS: Peter J. Barry, Editor, American Journal of
  Agricultural Economics, University of Illinois, 305 Mumford Hall,
  1301 West Gregory Drive, Urbana, IL 61801

The American Journal of Economics and Sociology

FIRST PUBLISHED: 1941   FREQUENCY: Q   CIRCULATION: 2,142

AFFILIATION: Sponsored by the Francis Neilson Fund and the Robert Schalkenbach Foundation. Address same as journal's.

AUDIENCE: Academic/Professional

PERCENT OF UNSOLICITED ARTICLES/ISSUE: 80%   ISSN: 0002-9246

EDITORIAL POLICY: Promotion of the interdisciplinary approach to the analysis and solution of the economic, social, political and moral problems of American democratic capitalism.

REVIEW INFORMATION

REFEREED: Yes (II-B)   ACCEPTANCE RATE: 25%

NUMBER OF REVIEWER(S)/MS., EXCLUDING IN-HOUSE EDITOR(S): 2-4

REVIEWER(S): Board and external   ARTICLES/AVG. ISSUE: 10

REVIEWING CRITERIA USED: BLIND REVIEW: No

  MANUSCRIPT SUBMISSION AIDS: 0

  BIAS SAFEGUARDS: 4, 5, 9

AVERAGE REVIEW TIME: 1-3 mos.   PUBLICATION TIME LAG: 12 mos.

MANUSCRIPT RETURNED WITH COMMENTS: Yes

MANUSCRIPT INFORMATION

GUIDELINES PUBLISHED: No; available on request

STYLE REQUIREMENTS PUBLISHED: No; not available

STYLE MANUAL USED: MLA

PREFERRED TOPICS: All the social sciences and social philosophy

QUERY LETTER: No   SIMULTANEOUS SUBMISSION: No

ABSTRACT WITH MANUSCRIPT: No   COVER LETTER: Yes

NUMBER OF MANUSCRIPT COPIES: 4   MANUSCRIPT LENGTH: 5,000 wds. max.

SUBMISSION FEE: No   PAGE CHARGES: No

MANUSCRIPT ACKNOWLEDGED: Yes   EARLY PUBLICATION OPTION: No

COPYRIGHT OWNER: Journal   REPRINTS: Optional purchase

AUTHOR COMPENSATION: 2 free journals, 100 free reprints/tear sheets

MANUSCRIPT ADDRESS: Will Lissner, Editor-in-Chief, The American Journal of Economics and Sociology, 5 East 44th Street, New York, NY 10017

The American Political Science Review

FIRST PUBLISHED: 1906   FREQUENCY: Q   CIRCULATION: 12,000

AFFILIATION: American Political Science Association, 1527 New Hampshire
Avenue, NW, Washington, D.C. 20036

AUDIENCE: Academic/Professional

PERCENT OF UNSOLICITED ARTICLES/ISSUE: 100%   ISSN: 0003-0554

EDITORIAL POLICY: "Aims to publish scholarly research and writing of
exceptional merit. . . . Contributors must demonstrate how their
analysis or exposition illuminates a significant research problem,
or answers an important research question, of general interest in
political science."

REVIEW INFORMATION

REFEREED: Yes (I-A)   ACCEPTANCE RATE: 9%

NUMBER OF REVIEWER(S)/MS., EXCLUDING IN-HOUSE EDITOR(S): 2

REVIEWER(S): External   ARTICLES/AVG. ISSUE: 10-12

REVIEWING CRITERIA USED: BLIND REVIEW: Yes (Board and
  MANUSCRIPT SUBMISSION AIDS: 0   external review)

  BIAS SAFEGUARDS: 3, 5, 7, 9

AVERAGE REVIEW TIME: 3 mos.   PUBLICATION TIME LAG: 10 mos.

MANUSCRIPT RETURNED WITH COMMENTS: No

MANUSCRIPT INFORMATION

GUIDELINES PUBLISHED: No; not available

STYLE REQUIREMENTS PUBLISHED: No; available on request

STYLE MANUAL USED: APSA

PREFERRED TOPICS: All fields of political science

QUERY LETTER: No   SIMULTANEOUS SUBMISSION: No

ABSTRACT WITH MANUSCRIPT: 150 wds. max. COVER LETTER: Yes

NUMBER OF MANUSCRIPT COPIES: 4   MANUSCRIPT LENGTH: 30 pp.

SUBMISSION FEE: No   PAGE CHARGES: No

MANUSCRIPT ACKNOWLEDGED: Yes   EARLY PUBLICATION OPTION: No

COPYRIGHT OWNER: Joint   REPRINTS: Optional purchase

AUTHOR COMPENSATION: None

MANUSCRIPT ADDRESS: Samuel Patterson, Managing Editor, The American
Political Science Review, Department of Political Science, Ohio
State University, Columbus, OH 43210-1373

The Antitrust Bulletin

FIRST PUBLISHED: 1955   FREQUENCY: Q   CIRCULATION: 1,500
AFFILIATION: None

AUDIENCE: Academic/Professional
PERCENT OF UNSOLICITED ARTICLES/ISSUE: 61-80%   ISSN: 0003-603X
EDITORIAL POLICY: Publication of scholarly articles dealing with
  domestic and foreign competition laws and industrial organization
  economics.

REVIEW INFORMATION

REFEREED: No   ACCEPTANCE RATE: N.R.
NUMBER OF REVIEWER(S)/MS., EXCLUDING IN-HOUSE EDITOR(S): 1
REVIEWER(S): Board   ARTICLES/AVG. ISSUE: 8
REVIEWING CRITERIA USED: BLIND REVIEW: Yes (Board and
  MANUSCRIPT SUBMISSION AIDS: 0   external review)
  BIAS SAFEGUARDS: 3, 5, 6
AVERAGE REVIEW TIME: 2 mos.   PUBLICATION TIME LAG: 6 mos.
MANUSCRIPT RETURNED WITH COMMENTS: No

MANUSCRIPT INFORMATION

GUIDELINES PUBLISHED: No; available on request
STYLE REQUIREMENTS PUBLISHED: No; available on request
STYLE MANUAL USED: Harvard
PREFERRED TOPICS: Antitrust laws, domestic and foreign

QUERY LETTER: No   SIMULTANEOUS SUBMISSION: No
ABSTRACT WITH MANUSCRIPT: No   COVER LETTER: Yes
NUMBER OF MANUSCRIPT COPIES: 1   MANUSCRIPT LENGTH: Not specified

SUBMISSION FEE: No   PAGE CHARGES: No

MANUSCRIPT ACKNOWLEDGED: Yes   EARLY PUBLICATION OPTION: No
COPYRIGHT OWNER: Publisher   REPRINTS: Optional purchase

AUTHOR COMPENSATION: 50 free reprints/tear sheets
MANUSCRIPT ADDRESS: William J. Curran III, Esq., Editor-in-Chief,
  The Antitrust Bulletin, 421 Hemlock Court, Pittsburgh, PA 15237

Applied Economics

FIRST PUBLISHED: 1969   FREQUENCY: M   CIRCULATION: 1,000
AFFILIATION: None

AUDIENCE: Academic/Professional; Business/Industrial; Government
PERCENT OF UNSOLICITED ARTICLES/ISSUE: 100%   ISSN: 0003-6846
EDITORIAL POLICY: "The primary purpose of Applied Economics is to
  encourage the application of economic analysis to specific problems
  in both the public and private sector. It particularly hopes to
  foster quantitative studies."

REVIEW INFORMATION

REFEREED: No   ACCEPTANCE RATE: 41-50%
NUMBER OF REVIEWER(S)/MS., EXCLUDING IN-HOUSE EDITOR(S): 1
REVIEWER(S): External   ARTICLES/AVG. ISSUE: 8
REVIEWING CRITERIA USED: BLIND REVIEW: No
  MANUSCRIPT SUBMISSION AIDS: 1, 2
  BIAS SAFEGUARDS: 5, 9
AVERAGE REVIEW TIME: 4 mos.   PUBLICATION TIME LAG: 12 mos.
MANUSCRIPT RETURNED WITH COMMENTS: Yes

MANUSCRIPT INFORMATION

GUIDELINES PUBLISHED: Each issue
STYLE REQUIREMENTS PUBLISHED: Each issue
STYLE MANUAL USED: In-house
PREFERRED TOPICS: Applied economics

QUERY LETTER: No   SIMULTANEOUS SUBMISSION: No
ABSTRACT WITH MANUSCRIPT: Yes   COVER LETTER: Yes
NUMBER OF MANUSCRIPT COPIES: 3   MANUSCRIPT LENGTH: No limit

SUBMISSION FEE: No   PAGE CHARGES: No

MANUSCRIPT ACKNOWLEDGED: Yes   EARLY PUBLICATION OPTION: No
COPYRIGHT OWNER: Publisher   REPRINTS: Purchase required

AUTHOR COMPENSATION: One free journal
MANUSCRIPT ADDRESS: Prof. Maurice Peston, Editor, Applied Economics,
  Queen Mary College, Economics Department, University of London,
  Mile End Road, London E1 4NS, U.K.

Applied Statistics / Journal of the Royal Statistical Society, Series C

FIRST PUBLISHED: 1952   FREQUENCY: 3/Yr.   CIRCULATION: 5,000

AFFILIATION: Royal Statistical Society. Address same as journal's.

AUDIENCE: Academic/Professional; Business/Industrial; Government

PERCENT OF UNSOLICITED ARTICLES/ISSUE: 81-100%   ISSN: 0035-9254

EDITORIAL POLICY: "Aims to publish papers giving a simple presentation of new or recent methodology. Reviews or comparisons of
existing methodology are acceptable providing these highlight novel
aspects of practical use. Practical examples should normally be
included . . . and extended algebraic developments of abstract
mathematics should be avoided."

REVIEW INFORMATION

REFEREED: Yes (I-B)   ACCEPTANCE RATE: 20%

NUMBER OF REVIEWER(S)/MS., EXCLUDING IN-HOUSE EDITOR(S): 2

REVIEWER(S): External   ARTICLES/AVG. ISSUE: 10-12

REVIEWING CRITERIA USED: BLIND REVIEW: No

  MANUSCRIPT SUBMISSION AIDS: 1, 2

  BIAS SAFEGUARDS: 5, 6, 7, 8, 9

AVERAGE REVIEW TIME: 4 mos.   PUBLICATION TIME LAG: 6 mos.

MANUSCRIPT RETURNED WITH COMMENTS: Yes

MANUSCRIPT INFORMATION

GUIDELINES PUBLISHED: Each issue

STYLE REQUIREMENTS PUBLISHED: Vol. 32, No. 3 (1983)

STYLE MANUAL USED: In-house

PREFERRED TOPICS: Statistics applied in many disciplines

QUERY LETTER: No   SIMULTANEOUS SUBMISSION: No

ABSTRACT WITH MANUSCRIPT: Yes   COVER LETTER: Yes

NUMBER OF MANUSCRIPT COPIES: 3   MANUSCRIPT LENGTH: No limit

SUBMISSION FEE: No   PAGE CHARGES: No

MANUSCRIPT ACKNOWLEDGED: Yes   EARLY PUBLICATION OPTION: No

COPYRIGHT OWNER: Author   REPRINTS: Optional purchase

AUTHOR COMPENSATION: None

MANUSCRIPT ADDRESS: The Executive Secretary, Royal Statistical
Society, 25 Enford Street, London W1H 2BH, U.K.

AREUEA / American Real Estate and Urban Economics Association Journal

FIRST PUBLISHED: 1973   FREQUENCY: Q   CIRCULATION: 300

AFFILIATION: American Real Estate and Urban Economics Association, School of Business, Indiana University, Bloomington, IN 47405

AUDIENCE: Academic/Professional

PERCENT OF UNSOLICITED ARTICLES/ISSUE: 100%   ISSN: 0092-914X

EDITORIAL POLICY: Focuses on "research and scholarly studies of current and emerging real estate issues. . . . Specifically, its purpose is to improve real estate analysis and related decisions and to develop further the theoretical framework and institutional arrangements within which these real estate decisions are made."

REVIEW INFORMATION

REFEREED: Yes (II-A)   ACCEPTANCE RATE: 31%

NUMBER OF REVIEWER(S)/MS., EXCLUDING IN-HOUSE EDITOR(S): 2

REVIEWER(S): Board and external   ARTICLES/AVG. ISSUE: 4

REVIEWING CRITERIA USED: BLIND REVIEW: Yes (External review only)

  MANUSCRIPT SUBMISSION AIDS: 2

  BIAS SAFEGUARDS: 3, 4, 5, 6, 9

AVERAGE REVIEW TIME: 2 mos.   PUBLICATION TIME LAG: 3 mos.

MANUSCRIPT RETURNED WITH COMMENTS: Yes

MANUSCRIPT INFORMATION

GUIDELINES PUBLISHED: No; not available

STYLE REQUIREMENTS PUBLISHED: Each issue

STYLE MANUAL USED: In-house

PREFERRED TOPICS: Real estate, finance, economics, housing, valuation, investment

QUERY LETTER: No   SIMULTANEOUS SUBMISSION: No

ABSTRACT WITH MANUSCRIPT: Yes   COVER LETTER: No

NUMBER OF MANUSCRIPT COPIES: 3   MANUSCRIPT LENGTH: 14 pp.

SUBMISSION FEE: No   PAGE CHARGES: No

MANUSCRIPT ACKNOWLEDGED: Yes   EARLY PUBLICATION OPTION: No

COPYRIGHT OWNER: Journal   REPRINTS: Purchase required

AUTHOR COMPENSATION: None

MANUSCRIPT ADDRESS: Editors, AREUEA Journal, The University of Georgia, College of Business Administration, Athens, GA 30602

Atlantic Economic Journal

FIRST PUBLISHED: 1973   FREQUENCY: Q   CIRCULATION: 1,500
AFFILIATION: Atlantic Economic Society. Address same as journal's.

AUDIENCE: Academic/Professional; Business/Industrial
PERCENT OF UNSOLICITED ARTICLES/ISSUE: 81-100%   ISSN: 0192-4254
EDITORIAL POLICY: Papers in all areas of economics are considered,
  both theoretical and applied.

REVIEW INFORMATION

REFEREED: No   ACCEPTANCE RATE: 15%
NUMBER OF REVIEWER(S)/MS., EXCLUDING IN-HOUSE EDITOR(S): 1
REVIEWER(S): Board   ARTICLES/AVG. ISSUE: 10
REVIEWING CRITERIA USED: BLIND REVIEW: No
  MANUSCRIPT SUBMISSION AIDS: 0
  BIAS SAFEGUARDS: 9
AVERAGE REVIEW TIME: 6 mos.   PUBLICATION TIME LAG: 3 mos.
MANUSCRIPT RETURNED WITH COMMENTS: Yes, SASE required

MANUSCRIPT INFORMATION

GUIDELINES PUBLISHED: No; available on request
STYLE REQUIREMENTS PUBLISHED: No; available on request
STYLE MANUAL USED: In-house
PREFERRED TOPICS: No preferred field

QUERY LETTER: No   SIMULTANEOUS SUBMISSION: No
ABSTRACT WITH MANUSCRIPT: No   COVER LETTER: Yes
NUMBER OF MANUSCRIPT COPIES: 2   MANUSCRIPT LENGTH: 25 pp.

SUBMISSION FEE: $15.   PAGE CHARGES: $20. per page
                                     for nonmembers/nonsubscribers
MANUSCRIPT ACKNOWLEDGED: Yes   EARLY PUBLICATION OPTION: Yes
COPYRIGHT OWNER: Journal   REPRINTS: Optional purchase

AUTHOR COMPENSATION: 3 free journals
MANUSCRIPT ADDRESS: Dr. John M. Virgo, Managing Editor, Atlantic
  Economic Journal, Southern Illinois University-Edwardsville, Box
  1101, Edwardsville, IL 62026-1101

Aussenwirtschaft

FIRST PUBLISHED: 1946   FREQUENCY: Q   CIRCULATION: 2,000

AFFILIATION: University of St. Gallen. Address same as journal's.

AUDIENCE: Academic/Professional; Business/Industrial; Government

PERCENT OF UNSOLICITED ARTICLES/ISSUE: 61-80%   ISSN: 0004-8216

EDITORIAL POLICY: Aims to present the latest research into the theory
and practice of international economic relations. It endeavors
to maintain a balance between theory and practice.

REVIEW INFORMATION

REFEREED: Yes (II-B)   ACCEPTANCE RATE: 30%

NUMBER OF REVIEWER(S)/MS., EXCLUDING IN-HOUSE EDITOR(S): 6

REVIEWER(S): 5 board, 1 external   ARTICLES/AVG. ISSUE: 4-5

REVIEWING CRITERIA USED: BLIND REVIEW: No

  MANUSCRIPT SUBMISSION AIDS: 0

  BIAS SAFEGUARDS: 4, 5

AVERAGE REVIEW TIME: 2 mos.   PUBLICATION TIME LAG: 4-6 mos.

MANUSCRIPT RETURNED WITH COMMENTS: No

MANUSCRIPT INFORMATION

GUIDELINES PUBLISHED: No; available on request

STYLE REQUIREMENTS PUBLISHED: No; not available

STYLE MANUAL USED: In-house

PREFERRED TOPICS: International economic relations

QUERY LETTER: No   SIMULTANEOUS SUBMISSION: No

ABSTRACT WITH MANUSCRIPT: 100 wds.   COVER LETTER: No

NUMBER OF MANUSCRIPT COPIES: 2   MANUSCRIPT LENGTH: 20 pp.

SUBMISSION FEE: No   PAGE CHARGES: No

MANUSCRIPT ACKNOWLEDGED: Yes   EARLY PUBLICATION OPTION: No

COPYRIGHT OWNER: Journal   REPRINTS: Optional purchase

AUTHOR COMPENSATION: Fee, 3 free journals and 20 free reprints

MANUSCRIPT ADDRESS: Prof. Dr. Hans Bachmann, Editor, Aussenwirtschaft,
Schweizeriches Instit für Aussenwirtschaft, Dufourst. 48, CH-9000
St. Gallen, Switzerland

Australian Bulletin of Labour

FIRST PUBLISHED: 1974　　　　FREQUENCY: Q　　　　CIRCULATION: 920

AFFILIATION: Flinders University, National Institute of Labour Studies, Inc. Address same as journal's.

AUDIENCE: Academic/Professional; Business/Industrial; Government

PERCENT OF UNSOLICITED ARTICLES/ISSUE: 41-60%　　　ISSN: 0311-6336

EDITORIAL POLICY: To publish articles of academic quality, but also of general interest to labour market practitioners. Topicality and policy relevance are additional criteria used by the editors.

REVIEW INFORMATION

REFEREED: No　　　　　　　　　　　　ACCEPTANCE RATE: 40%

NUMBER OF REVIEWER(S)/MS., EXCLUDING IN-HOUSE EDITOR(S): 0

REVIEWER(S): 6 in-house editors　　　ARTICLES/AVG. ISSUE: 4

REVIEWING CRITERIA USED:　　　　　　BLIND REVIEW: No

　MANUSCRIPT SUBMISSION AIDS: 2

　BIAS SAFEGUARDS: 4, 9

AVERAGE REVIEW TIME: 3 wks.　　　PUBLICATION TIME LAG: 3 mos.

MANUSCRIPT RETURNED WITH COMMENTS: No

MANUSCRIPT INFORMATION

GUIDELINES PUBLISHED: No; not available

STYLE REQUIREMENTS PUBLISHED: Each issue

STYLE MANUAL USED: Australia; Harvard

PREFERRED TOPICS: Labour economics, industrial relations (employee-employer relations)

QUERY LETTER: No　　　　　　　SIMULTANEOUS SUBMISSION: Yes

ABSTRACT WITH MANUSCRIPT: No　　COVER LETTER: Yes

NUMBER OF MANUSCRIPT COPIES: 2　MANUSCRIPT LENGTH: N.R.

SUBMISSION FEE: No　　　　　　　PAGE CHARGES: No

MANUSCRIPT ACKNOWLEDGED: Yes　　EARLY PUBLICATION OPTION: Yes

COPYRIGHT OWNER: Journal　　　　REPRINTS: Optional purchase

AUTHOR COMPENSATION: None

MANUSCRIPT ADDRESS: Editors, Australian Bulletin of Labour, National Institute of Labour Studies, Inc., Flinders University of South Australia, Bedford Park, S.A. 5042, Australia

Australian Economic History Review

FIRST PUBLISHED: 1962   FREQUENCY: S-A   CIRCULATION: 500

AFFILIATION: Economic History Society of Australia and New Zealand. Address same as journal's.

AUDIENCE: Academic/Professional

PERCENT OF UNSOLICITED ARTICLES/ISSUE: 90%   ISSN: 0004-8992

EDITORIAL POLICY: To provide an outlet for research in Australian and New Zealand economic and social history. (Papers in other fields are also considered.) To promote the discipline of economic history.

REVIEW INFORMATION

REFEREED: Yes (I-B)   ACCEPTANCE RATE: 65%

NUMBER OF REVIEWER(S)/MS., EXCLUDING IN-HOUSE EDITOR(S): 2

REVIEWER(S): External   ARTICLES/AVG. ISSUE: 4

REVIEWING CRITERIA USED: BLIND REVIEW: No

  MANUSCRIPT SUBMISSION AIDS: 0

  BIAS SAFEGUARDS: 4, 5, 6, 7, 9

AVERAGE REVIEW TIME: 2 mos.   PUBLICATION TIME LAG: 12 mos.

MANUSCRIPT RETURNED WITH COMMENTS: Yes

MANUSCRIPT INFORMATION

GUIDELINES PUBLISHED: No; not available

STYLE REQUIREMENTS PUBLISHED: No; not available

STYLE MANUAL USED: In-house

PREFERRED TOPICS: Australian and New Zealand economic/social history

QUERY LETTER: No   SIMULTANEOUS SUBMISSION: No

ABSTRACT WITH MANUSCRIPT: No   COVER LETTER: No

NUMBER OF MANUSCRIPT COPIES: 2   MANUSCRIPT LENGTH: 8,000 wds. max.

SUBMISSION FEE: No   PAGE CHARGES: No

MANUSCRIPT ACKNOWLEDGED: Yes   EARLY PUBLICATION OPTION: No

COPYRIGHT OWNER: Publisher   REPRINTS: Optional purchase

AUTHOR COMPENSATION: 12 free reprints/tear sheets

MANUSCRIPT ADDRESS: A. E. Dingle, Editor, Australian Economic History Review, Department of Economic History, Monash University, Clayton, Victoria 3168, Australia

The Australian Economic Review

FIRST PUBLISHED: 1968   FREQUENCY: Q   CIRCULATION: 1,900

AFFILIATION: University of Melbourne, Institute of Applied Economic and Social Research. Address same as journal's.

AUDIENCE: Academic/Professional; Business/Industrial; Government

PERCENT OF UNSOLICITED ARTICLES/ISSUE: 41–60%   ISSN: 0004-9018

EDITORIAL POLICY: "Contains contributed articles on applied economic and social issues. The second and fourth issues include assessments by members of the Institute staff of the short-term prospects for the Australian economy. The Institute invites submissions of articles particularly on topics of interest to an Australian audience."

REVIEW INFORMATION

REFEREED: Yes (II-B)   ACCEPTANCE RATE: 50%

NUMBER OF REVIEWER(S)/MS., EXCLUDING IN-HOUSE EDITOR(S): 2

REVIEWER(S): Board and external   ARTICLES/AVG. ISSUE: 4

REVIEWING CRITERIA USED: BLIND REVIEW: No

  MANUSCRIPT SUBMISSION AIDS: 0

  BIAS SAFEGUARDS: 4, 5, 6, 9, 10

AVERAGE REVIEW TIME: 2 mos.   PUBLICATION TIME LAG: 3 mos.

MANUSCRIPT RETURNED WITH COMMENTS: No

MANUSCRIPT INFORMATION

GUIDELINES PUBLISHED: No; available on request

STYLE REQUIREMENTS PUBLISHED: No; available on request

STYLE MANUAL USED: Australia

PREFERRED TOPICS: Applied economics and social research with special reference to Australia

QUERY LETTER: No   SIMULTANEOUS SUBMISSION: No

ABSTRACT WITH MANUSCRIPT: 100–150 wds.   COVER LETTER: Yes

NUMBER OF MANUSCRIPT COPIES: 4   MANUSCRIPT LENGTH: No limit

SUBMISSION FEE: No   PAGE CHARGES: No

MANUSCRIPT ACKNOWLEDGED: Yes   EARLY PUBLICATION OPTION: Yes

COPYRIGHT OWNER: University of Melbourne REPRINTS: Not available

AUTHOR COMPENSATION: 2 free journals and 12 free reprints/tear sheets

MANUSCRIPT ADDRESS: Nellie Lentini, Assistant Editor, The Australian Economic Review, University of Melbourne, Institute of Applied Economic and Social Research, Parkville, Victoria 3052, Australia

The Australian Journal of Agricultural Economics

FIRST PUBLISHED: 1957   FREQUENCY: 6/Yr.   CIRCULATION: 1,400

AFFILIATION: Australian Agricultural Economics Society, Suite 302
  Clunies Ross House, 191 Royal Parade, Parkville, Vic. 3052, Australia

AUDIENCE: Academic/Professional; Government

PERCENT OF UNSOLICITED ARTICLES/ISSUE: 100%   ISSN: 0004-9395

EDITORIAL POLICY: Provide "an outlet for creative work in agricultural
  and applied economics. To this end, manuscripts should have relevance
  to the economics of agriculture or natural resources or to issues
  which have a direct impact on agriculture. Contributions whether
  applied or methodological are equally encouraged."

REVIEW INFORMATION

REFEREED: Yes (I-A)   ACCEPTANCE RATE: 25%

NUMBER OF REVIEWER(S)/MS., EXCLUDING IN-HOUSE EDITOR(S): 2

REVIEWER(S): External   ARTICLES/AVG. ISSUE: 5

REVIEWING CRITERIA USED: BLIND REVIEW: Yes (Board
  MANUSCRIPT SUBMISSION AIDS: 1, 2   and external review)

  BIAS SAFEGUARDS: 3, 5, 6, 7, 8, 9, 10

AVERAGE REVIEW TIME: 4 mos.   PUBLICATION TIME LAG: 4 mos.

MANUSCRIPT RETURNED WITH COMMENTS: Yes, SASE required

MANUSCRIPT INFORMATION

GUIDELINES PUBLISHED: Each issue

STYLE REQUIREMENTS PUBLISHED: Each issue

STYLE MANUAL USED: Australia

PREFERRED TOPICS: Applied economics in agriculture, resource issues,
  economic development; quantitative methods in agricultural economics

QUERY LETTER: No   SIMULTANEOUS SUBMISSION: No

ABSTRACT WITH MANUSCRIPT: 100 wds. COVER LETTER: Yes

NUMBER OF MANUSCRIPT COPIES: 6   MANUSCRIPT LENGTH: 30 pp.

SUBMISSION FEE: Aus.$70. for   PAGE CHARGES: No
  nonmembers/nonsubscribers

MANUSCRIPT ACKNOWLEDGED: Yes   EARLY PUBLICATION OPTION: No

COPYRIGHT OWNER: Journal   REPRINTS: Optional purchase

AUTHOR COMPENSATION: None

MANUSCRIPT ADDRESS: Dr. B. S. Fisher and Mrs. C. Tanner, Editors, The
  Australian Journal of Agricultural Economics, Department of
  Agricultural Economics, University of Sydney, N.S.W. 2006, Australia

Australian Tax Forum

FIRST PUBLISHED: 1984   FREQUENCY: Q   CIRCULATION: 815

AFFILIATION: Monash University, Centre of Policy Studies and the
   Centre for Commercial Law & Applied Legal Research. Address same
   as journal's.

AUDIENCE: Academic/Professional; Business/Industrial; Government

PERCENT OF UNSOLICITED ARTICLES/ISSUE: 11-20%   ISSN: 0812-695X

EDITORIAL POLICY: "An independent journal whose objective is to provide a forum for the discussion of issues in tax policy, law and
   reform. Its aim is to promote dialogue between those professions
   that contribute most to the development of the Australian tax system."

REVIEW INFORMATION

REFEREED: No   ACCEPTANCE RATE: 60%

NUMBER OF REVIEWER(S)/MS., EXCLUDING IN-HOUSE EDITOR(S): 1

REVIEWER(S): External   ARTICLES/AVG. ISSUE: 6

REVIEWING CRITERIA USED: BLIND REVIEW: No

   MANUSCRIPT SUBMISSION AIDS: 1

   BIAS SAFEGUARDS: 4, 5, 6, 9*

AVERAGE REVIEW TIME: 4 wks.   PUBLICATION TIME LAG: 3 mos.

MANUSCRIPT RETURNED WITH COMMENTS: Yes

MANUSCRIPT INFORMATION

GUIDELINES PUBLISHED: Each issue

STYLE REQUIREMENTS PUBLISHED: No; available on request

STYLE MANUAL USED: In-house

PREFERRED TOPICS: Tax policy

QUERY LETTER: No   SIMULTANEOUS SUBMISSION: Yes

ABSTRACT WITH MANUSCRIPT: No   COVER LETTER: Yes

NUMBER OF MANUSCRIPT COPIES: 1   MANUSCRIPT LENGTH: 10-50 pp.

SUBMISSION FEE: No   PAGE CHARGES: No

MANUSCRIPT ACKNOWLEDGED: Yes   EARLY PUBLICATION OPTION: Yes

COPYRIGHT OWNER: None claimed   REPRINTS: Optional purchase

AUTHOR COMPENSATION: 15 free reprints/tear sheets

MANUSCRIPT ADDRESS: Richard Krever, Executive Editor, Australian
   Tax Forum, Faculty of Law, Monash University, Clayton, Victoria
   3168, Australia

Banca Nazionale del Lavoro Quarterly Review

FIRST PUBLISHED: 1947   FREQUENCY: Q   CIRCULATION: 4,650
AFFILIATION: Banca Nazionale del Lavoro. Address same as journal's.

AUDIENCE: Academic/Professional; Business/Industrial; Government
PERCENT OF UNSOLICITED ARTICLES/ISSUE: 61-80%   ISSN: 0005-4607
EDITORIAL POLICY: The journal's policy is to publish articles that
  are original contributions in their specific fields, and which
  will interest and stimulate reflection among both academic and
  professional readers.

REVIEW INFORMATION

REFEREED: No   ACCEPTANCE RATE: 10%
NUMBER OF REVIEWER(S)/MS., EXCLUDING IN-HOUSE EDITOR(S): 1
REVIEWER(S): Board or external   ARTICLES/AVG. ISSUE: 5
REVIEWING CRITERIA USED: BLIND REVIEW: No
  MANUSCRIPT SUBMISSION AIDS: 0
  BIAS SAFEGUARDS: 4, 5, 6, 9*
AVERAGE REVIEW TIME: 4-6 wks.   PUBLICATION TIME LAG: 6 mos.
MANUSCRIPT RETURNED WITH COMMENTS: No

MANUSCRIPT INFORMATION

GUIDELINES PUBLISHED: No; not available
STYLE REQUIREMENTS PUBLISHED: No; not available
STYLE MANUAL USED: In-house
PREFERRED TOPICS: Monetary and financial problems and developments,
  international finance

QUERY LETTER: No   SIMULTANEOUS SUBMISSION: No
ABSTRACT WITH MANUSCRIPT: 100 wds. COVER LETTER: No
NUMBER OF MANUSCRIPT COPIES: 2   MANUSCRIPT LENGTH: 10-25 pp.

SUBMISSION FEE: No   PAGE CHARGES: No

MANUSCRIPT ACKNOWLEDGED: Yes, if req. EARLY PUBLICATION OPTION: No
COPYRIGHT OWNER: Publisher   REPRINTS: Not available

AUTHOR COMPENSATION: Fee, free subscription and reprints/tear sheets
MANUSCRIPT ADDRESS: Dr. Luigi Ceriani, Editor, Banca Nazionale del
  Lavoro Quarterly Review, Via V. Veneto 119, 00187 Roma, Italy

The Bangladesh Development Studies

FIRST PUBLISHED: 1973   FREQUENCY: Q   CIRCULATION: 1,000

AFFILIATION: Bangladesh Institute of Development Studies. Address same as journal's.

AUDIENCE: Academic/Professional; Government

PERCENT OF UNSOLICITED ARTICLES/ISSUE: 81-100%   ISSN: 0304-095X

EDITORIAL POLICY: To disseminate results of research/theoretical analysis related to problems of underdevelopment, with focus on Bangladesh or on problems pertinent to Bangladesh. Sociological, political and "political economy" approaches are welcome as well as more orthodox economic analysis.

REVIEW INFORMATION

REFEREED: No   ACCEPTANCE RATE: 40%

NUMBER OF REVIEWER(S)/MS., EXCLUDING IN-HOUSE EDITOR(S): 1

REVIEWER(S): External   ARTICLES/AVG. ISSUE: 4

REVIEWING CRITERIA USED: BLIND REVIEW: Yes, (Board and
  MANUSCRIPT SUBMISSION AIDS: 1, 2   external review)

  BIAS SAFEGUARDS: 3, 5, 6, 9

AVERAGE REVIEW TIME: 4 mos.   PUBLICATION TIME LAG: 6 mos.

MANUSCRIPT RETURNED WITH COMMENTS: No

MANUSCRIPT INFORMATION

GUIDELINES PUBLISHED: Vol. 9, No. 4 (1981); also on request

STYLE REQUIREMENTS PUBLISHED: Vol. 9, No. 4 (1981); also on request

STYLE MANUAL USED: In-house

PREFERRED TOPICS: Development theory and policy; rural development, industry, trade and exchange rate regimes, etc.; demography; "peasant studies"; economic history; sociology of development

QUERY LETTER: No   SIMULTANEOUS SUBMISSION: No

ABSTRACT WITH MANUSCRIPT: 100-150 wds. COVER LETTER: Yes

NUMBER OF MANUSCRIPT COPIES: 2   MANUSCRIPT LENGTH: 40 pp.

SUBMISSION FEE: No   PAGE CHARGES: No

MANUSCRIPT ACKNOWLEDGED: Yes, SASE req. EARLY PUBLICATION OPTION: No

COPYRIGHT OWNER: Journal   REPRINTS: Optional purchase

AUTHOR COMPENSATION: 10 free reprints/tear sheets

MANUSCRIPT ADDRESS: Abu Ahmed Abdullah, Executive Editor, The Bangladesh Development Studies, Adamjee Court, Motijheel Commercial Area, Dhaka-2, Bangladesh

British Journal of Industrial Relations

FIRST PUBLISHED: 1963   FREQUENCY: 3/Yr.   CIRCULATION: 2,000

AFFILIATION: London School of Economics and Political Science.
Address same as journal's.

AUDIENCE: Academic/Professional; Business/Industrial; Government

PERCENT OF UNSOLICITED ARTICLES/ISSUE: 81-100%   ISSN: 0007-1080

EDITORIAL POLICY: "A journal of research and analysis covering every
aspect of industrial relations in Britain and overseas."

REVIEW INFORMATION

REFEREED: Yes (II-A)   ACCEPTANCE RATE: 20%

NUMBER OF REVIEWER(S)/MS., EXCLUDING IN-HOUSE EDITOR(S): 2

REVIEWER(S): Board and external   ARTICLES/AVG. ISSUE: 6

REVIEWING CRITERIA USED: BLIND REVIEW: Yes (External
  MANUSCRIPT SUBMISSION AIDS: 0   review only)
  BIAS SAFEGUARDS: 3, 4, 5, 6, 9

AVERAGE REVIEW TIME: 12 wks.   PUBLICATION TIME LAG: 9 mos.

MANUSCRIPT RETURNED WITH COMMENTS: Yes

MANUSCRIPT INFORMATION

GUIDELINES PUBLISHED: No; available on request

STYLE REQUIREMENTS PUBLISHED: No; available on request

STYLE MANUAL USED: In-house

PREFERRED TOPICS: Industrial relations interpreted broadly

QUERY LETTER: No   SIMULTANEOUS SUBMISSION: No

ABSTRACT WITH MANUSCRIPT: 50 wds.   COVER LETTER: Yes

NUMBER OF MANUSCRIPT COPIES: 2   MANUSCRIPT LENGTH: 6,000 wds.

SUBMISSION FEE: No   PAGE CHARGES: No

MANUSCRIPT ACKNOWLEDGED: Yes   EARLY PUBLICATION OPTION: Yes

COPYRIGHT OWNER: Journal   REPRINTS: Optional purchase

AUTHOR COMPENSATION: 1 free journal

MANUSCRIPT ADDRESS: B.C. Roberts, Editor, British Journal of
  Industrial Relations, London School of Economics and Political
  Science, Houghton Street, Aldwych, London WC2A 2AE, U.K.

British Review of Economic Issues

FIRST PUBLISHED: 1977   FREQUENCY: S-A   CIRCULATION: 200

AFFILIATION: Association of Polytechnic Teachers in Economics. Address same as journal's.

AUDIENCE: Academic/Professional; Government

PERCENT OF UNSOLICITED ARTICLES/ISSUE: 95%   ISSN: 0141-4739

EDITORIAL POLICY: "Will consider papers falling into one or more of the following categories: 1) Papers dealing with aspects of economic theory; 2) Papers dealing with issues in applied economics; 3) Papers surveying and evaluating textbooks; 4) Papers surveying or providing an exposition of latest developments in particular subject areas; 5) Papers dealing with presentational methods."

REVIEW INFORMATION

REFEREED: Yes (I-B)   ACCEPTANCE RATE: 40%

NUMBER OF REVIEWER(S)/MS., EXCLUDING IN-HOUSE EDITOR(S): 2

REVIEWER(S): External   ARTICLES/AVG. ISSUE: 4-5

REVIEWING CRITERIA USED: BLIND REVIEW: No

  MANUSCRIPT SUBMISSION AIDS: 1, 2

  BIAS SAFEGUARDS: 5, 6, 7, 9

AVERAGE REVIEW TIME: 3 mos.   PUBLICATION TIME LAG: 6 mos.

MANUSCRIPT RETURNED WITH COMMENTS: No

MANUSCRIPT INFORMATION

GUIDELINES PUBLISHED: Each issue

STYLE REQUIREMENTS PUBLISHED: Each issue

STYLE MANUAL USED: In-house

PREFERRED TOPICS: Economic theory, applied economics

QUERY LETTER: No   SIMULTANEOUS SUBMISSION: No

ABSTRACT WITH MANUSCRIPT: No   COVER LETTER: No

NUMBER OF MANUSCRIPT COPIES: 3   MANUSCRIPT LENGTH: 20-25 pp.

SUBMISSION FEE: No   PAGE CHARGES: No

MANUSCRIPT ACKNOWLEDGED: Yes   EARLY PUBLICATION OPTION: No

COPYRIGHT OWNER: Journal   REPRINTS: Not available

AUTHOR COMPENSATION: 1 free journal

MANUSCRIPT ADDRESS: Dr. P. Arestis, Editor, British Review of Economic Issues, Economics Division, Thames Polytechnic, Wellington Street, London, SE18 6PF, U.K.

Bulletin of Economic Research

FIRST PUBLISHED: 1949   FREQUENCY: 3/Yr.   CIRCULATION: 600

AFFILIATION: Universities of Hull, Leeds, Sheffield, York and
  Bradford

AUDIENCE: Academic/Professional; Government

PERCENT OF UNSOLICITED ARTICLES/ISSUE: 61-80%   ISSN: 0044-0590

EDITORIAL POLICY: To publish the best unsolicited articles received;
  an invited survey article in each issue; and to encourage submission
  of short notes for rapid editor-only refereeing.

REVIEW INFORMATION

REFEREED: Yes (I-B)   ACCEPTANCE RATE: 40%

NUMBER OF REVIEWER(S)/MS., EXCLUDING IN-HOUSE EDITOR(S): 2

REVIEWER(S): External   ARTICLES/AVG. ISSUE: 6

REVIEWING CRITERIA USED: BLIND REVIEW: No

  MANUSCRIPT SUBMISSION AIDS: 2

  BIAS SAFEGUARDS: 4, 5, 6, 7, 9

AVERAGE REVIEW TIME: 2 mos.   PUBLICATION TIME LAG: 4 mos.

MANUSCRIPT RETURNED WITH COMMENTS: No

MANUSCRIPT INFORMATION

GUIDELINES PUBLISHED: No; not available

STYLE REQUIREMENTS PUBLISHED: Each issue

STYLE MANUAL USED: In-house

PREFERRED TOPICS: All aspects of economics, both theoretical and
  applied

QUERY LETTER: No   SIMULTANEOUS SUBMISSION: Yes

ABSTRACT WITH MANUSCRIPT: No   COVER LETTER: Yes

NUMBER OF MANUSCRIPT COPIES: 3   MANUSCRIPT LENGTH: 30 pp. max.

SUBMISSION FEE: No   PAGE CHARGES: No

MANUSCRIPT ACKNOWLEDGED: Yes   EARLY PUBLICATION OPTION: Yes

COPYRIGHT OWNER: Joint with publisher   REPRINTS: Optional purchase

AUTHOR COMPENSATION: 15 free reprints

MANUSCRIPT ADDRESS: Dr. Peter J. Lambert, Joint Editor, Bulletin of
  Economic Research, Department of Economics and Related Studies,
  University of York, Heslington, York, YO1 5DD, U.K.

Bulletin of Indonesian Economic Studies

FIRST PUBLISHED: 1965   FREQUENCY: 3/Yr.   CIRCULATION: 1,500

AFFILIATION: Australian National University, Research School of Pacific Studies, Department of Economics. Address same as journal's.

AUDIENCE: Academic/Professional; Business/Industrial; Government

PERCENT OF UNSOLICITED ARTICLES/ISSUE: 61-80%   ISSN: 0007-4918

EDITORIAL POLICY: Publishes applied studies of economic conditions in Indonesia, including a regular "Survey of Recent Developments." Considers manuscripts submitted in English or in Indonesian.

REVIEW INFORMATION

REFEREED: Yes (II-B)   ACCEPTANCE RATE: 50%

NUMBER OF REVIEWER(S)/MS., EXCLUDING IN-HOUSE EDITOR(S): 2

REVIEWER(S): Board and external   ARTICLES/AVG. ISSUE: 5

REVIEWING CRITERIA USED: BLIND REVIEW: No

  MANUSCRIPT SUBMISSION AIDS: 0

  BIAS SAFEGUARDS: 4, 5, 6, 9*

AVERAGE REVIEW TIME: 3 mos.   PUBLICATION TIME LAG: 8 mos.

MANUSCRIPT RETURNED WITH COMMENTS: No

MANUSCRIPT INFORMATION

GUIDELINES PUBLISHED: No; not available

STYLE REQUIREMENTS PUBLISHED: No; available on request

STYLE MANUAL USED: Australia

PREFERRED TOPICS: Applied studies of Indonesian economic development

QUERY LETTER: No   SIMULTANEOUS SUBMISSION: No

ABSTRACT WITH MANUSCRIPT: 100 wds.   COVER LETTER: Yes

NUMBER OF MANUSCRIPT COPIES: 2   MANUSCRIPT LENGTH: 8,000 wds.

SUBMISSION FEE: No   PAGE CHARGES: No

MANUSCRIPT ACKNOWLEDGED: Yes   EARLY PUBLICATION OPTION: No

COPYRIGHT OWNER: Journal   REPRINTS: Not available

AUTHOR COMPENSATION: 1 free journal and 25 free reprints/tear sheets

MANUSCRIPT ADDRESS: Dr. Anne Booth, Editor, Bulletin of Indonesian Economic Studies, Research School of Pacific Studies, Australian National University, G.P.O. Box 4, Canberra, A.C.T. 2601, Australia

Business Economics

FIRST PUBLISHED: 1965   FREQUENCY: Q   CIRCULATION: 4,695

AFFILIATION: National Association of Business Economists, 28349
  Chagrin Blvd., Suite 201, Cleveland, OH 44122-4589

AUDIENCE: Business/Industrial; Government; Academic/Professional

PERCENT OF UNSOLICITED ARTICLES/ISSUE: 21-40%   ISSN: 0007-666X

EDITORIAL POLICY: Publishes articles of interest to practicing business
  economists: economic policy, economic forecasting techniques,
  economic analysis, industry perspectives, financial markets.

REVIEW INFORMATION

REFEREED: Yes (II-A)   ACCEPTANCE RATE: 16%

NUMBER OF REVIEWER(S)/MS., EXCLUDING IN-HOUSE EDITOR(S): 2

REVIEWER(S): Board and/or external   ARTICLES/AVG. ISSUE: 12

REVIEWING CRITERIA USED: BLIND REVIEW: Yes (Board and
  MANUSCRIPT SUBMISSION AIDS: 1, 2   external review)
  BIAS SAFEGUARDS: 3, 5, 8, 9*

AVERAGE REVIEW TIME: 5 wks.   PUBLICATION TIME LAG: 4-6 mos.

MANUSCRIPT RETURNED WITH COMMENTS: No

MANUSCRIPT INFORMATION

GUIDELINES PUBLISHED: Each issue

STYLE REQUIREMENTS PUBLISHED: Each issue

STYLE MANUAL USED: Chicago

PREFERRED TOPICS: Economics, finance

QUERY LETTER: No   SIMULTANEOUS SUBMISSION: Yes

ABSTRACT WITH MANUSCRIPT: 150 wds.   COVER LETTER: Yes

NUMBER OF MANUSCRIPT COPIES: 3   MANUSCRIPT LENGTH: 16 pp. max.

SUBMISSION FEE: No   PAGE CHARGES: No

MANUSCRIPT ACKNOWLEDGED: Yes   EARLY PUBLICATION OPTION: No

COPYRIGHT OWNER: Journal   REPRINTS: Optional purchase

AUTHOR COMPENSATION: None

MANUSCRIPT ADDRESS: Edmund A. Mennis, Editor, Business Economics,
  405 Via Chico, Suite 7, Palos Verdes Estates, CA 90274

Business History Review

FIRST PUBLISHED: 1926   FREQUENCY: Q   CIRCULATION: 1,900
AFFILIATION: Harvard Business School. Address same as journal's.

AUDIENCE: Academic/Professional
PERCENT OF UNSOLICITED ARTICLES/ISSUE: 90-95%   ISSN: 0007-6805
EDITORIAL POLICY: To publish articles which make a scholarly
  contribution to the field of business history--either original
  research or synthesis of previous research.

REVIEW INFORMATION

REFEREED: Yes (II-A)   ACCEPTANCE RATE: 15-20%
NUMBER OF REVIEWER(S)/MS., EXCLUDING IN-HOUSE EDITOR(S): 2
REVIEWER(S): Board and/or external   ARTICLES/AVG. ISSUE: 4
REVIEWING CRITERIA USED: BLIND REVIEW: Yes (All except
  MANUSCRIPT SUBMISSION AIDS: 2   final selection)
  BIAS SAFEGUARDS: 3, 5, 6, 9
AVERAGE REVIEW TIME: 3 mos.   PUBLICATION TIME LAG: 6 mos.
MANUSCRIPT RETURNED WITH COMMENTS: No

MANUSCRIPT INFORMATION

GUIDELINES PUBLISHED: No; available on request
STYLE REQUIREMENTS PUBLISHED: Spring 1984 issue
STYLE MANUAL USED: In-house; Chicago
PREFERRED TOPICS: Business history of all periods and countries

QUERY LETTER: No   SIMULTANEOUS SUBMISSION: No
ABSTRACT WITH MANUSCRIPT: 100 wds. COVER LETTER: Yes
NUMBER OF MANUSCRIPT COPIES: 3   MANUSCRIPT LENGTH: 50 pp.

SUBMISSION FEE: No   PAGE CHARGES: No

MANUSCRIPT ACKNOWLEDGED: Yes   EARLY PUBLICATION OPTION: No
COPYRIGHT OWNER: Joint with President REPRINTS: Optional purchase
  and Fellows of Harvard College
AUTHOR COMPENSATION: 1 free journal and 25 free reprints/tear sheets
MANUSCRIPT ADDRESS: Patricia L. Denault, Coordinating Editor, Teele
  317, Harvard Business School, Soldiers Field, Boston, MA 02163

Cambridge Journal of Economics

FIRST PUBLISHED: 1977   FREQUENCY: Q   CIRCULATION: 1,550

AFFILIATION: Cambridge Political Economy Society Limited. Address same as journal's.

AUDIENCE: Academic/Professional; Business/Industrial; Government

PERCENT OF UNSOLICITED ARTICLES/ISSUE: 81-100%   ISSN: 0309-166X

EDITORIAL POLICY: To provide a focus for theoretical and applied work, with strong emphasis on realism of analysis, the provision and use of empirical evidence, and the formulation of economic policies.

REVIEW INFORMATION

REFEREED: Yes (I-B)   ACCEPTANCE RATE: 20%

NUMBER OF REVIEWER(S)/MS., EXCLUDING IN-HOUSE EDITOR(S): 2

REVIEWER(S): External   ARTICLES/AVG. ISSUE: 6

REVIEWING CRITERIA USED: BLIND REVIEW: No

  MANUSCRIPT SUBMISSION AIDS: 1, 2

  BIAS SAFEGUARDS: 5, 6, 7, 8, 9*

AVERAGE REVIEW TIME: 3-4 mos.   PUBLICATION TIME LAG: 3 mos.

MANUSCRIPT RETURNED WITH COMMENTS: No

MANUSCRIPT INFORMATION

GUIDELINES PUBLISHED: Each issue

STYLE REQUIREMENTS PUBLISHED: Each issue

STYLE MANUAL USED: In-house

PREFERRED TOPICS: Unemployment, inflation, the organization of production, the distribution of social product, class conflict, uneven development and instability in the world economy

QUERY LETTER: No   SIMULTANEOUS SUBMISSION: No

ABSTRACT WITH MANUSCRIPT: No   COVER LETTER: Yes

NUMBER OF MANUSCRIPT COPIES: 3   MANUSCRIPT LENGTH: 7,500 wds. max.

SUBMISSION FEE: No   PAGE CHARGES: No

MANUSCRIPT ACKNOWLEDGED: Yes   EARLY PUBLICATION OPTION: No

COPYRIGHT OWNER: Author and publisher   REPRINTS: Optional purchase

AUTHOR COMPENSATION: 20 free reprints/tear sheets

MANUSCRIPT ADDRESS: Ms. Ann Newton, Managing Editor, Cambridge Journal of Economics, Faculty of Economics and Politics, Sidgwick Avenue, Cambridge, CB3 9DD, U.K.

Canadian Journal of Agricultural Economics /
Revue Canadienne d'Économie Rurale

FIRST PUBLISHED: 1952   FREQUENCY: 3/Yr.   CIRCULATION: 600

AFFILIATION: Canadian Agricultural Economics and Farm Management Society,
   Suite 907, 151 Slater St., Ottawa, Ontario, Canada K1P 5H4

AUDIENCE: Academic/Professional; Business/Industrial; Government

PERCENT OF UNSOLICITED ARTICLES/ISSUE: 41-60%   ISSN: 0008-3976

EDITORIAL POLICY: To reflect topical and research interests and
   findings of the profession.

REVIEW INFORMATION

REFEREED: Yes (II-A)   ACCEPTANCE RATE: 45%

NUMBER OF REVIEWER(S)/MS., EXCLUDING IN-HOUSE EDITOR(S): 3

REVIEWER(S): Board and/or external   ARTICLES/AVG. ISSUE: 9

REVIEWING CRITERIA USED: BLIND REVIEW: Yes (External
   MANUSCRIPT SUBMISSION AIDS: 1, 2   review only)

   BIAS SAFEGUARDS: 3, 5, 6, 8, 9*, 10

AVERAGE REVIEW TIME: 4 mos.   PUBLICATION TIME LAG: 2 mos.

MANUSCRIPT RETURNED WITH COMMENTS: Yes, SASE required

MANUSCRIPT INFORMATION

GUIDELINES PUBLISHED: Each issue; also available on request

STYLE REQUIREMENTS PUBLISHED: Each issue; also available on request

STYLE MANUAL USED: Chicago

PREFERRED TOPICS: Marketing, production economics, farm management,
   agricultural policy, etc.

QUERY LETTER: Yes   SIMULTANEOUS SUBMISSION: No

ABSTRACT WITH MANUSCRIPT: 100 wds.   COVER LETTER: Yes

NUMBER OF MANUSCRIPT COPIES: 3   MANUSCRIPT LENGTH: 12-20 pp.

SUBMISSION FEE: No   PAGE CHARGES: Can. $25. per
   page

MANUSCRIPT ACKNOWLEDGED: Yes   EARLY PUBLICATION OPTION: No

COPYRIGHT OWNER: Journal   REPRINTS: Optional purchase

AUTHOR COMPENSATION: None

MANUSCRIPT ADDRESS: Dr. Norman J. Beaton, Editor, Canadian Journal of
   Agricultural Economics, Department of Agricultural Economics,
   University of Manitoba, Winnipeg, Manitoba, Canada R3T 2N2

The Canadian Journal of Economics / La Revue Canadienne d'Économique

FIRST PUBLISHED: 1968   FREQUENCY: Irreg.   CIRCULATION: 3,000

AFFILIATION: Canadian Economics Association, Department of Economics, McGill University, Montreal, Quebec, Canada H3A 2T5

AUDIENCE: Academic/Professional

PERCENT OF UNSOLICITED ARTICLES/ISSUE: 95%   ISSN: 0008-4085

EDITORIAL POLICY: "Interested in publishing papers that are significant contributions to knowledge in all areas of economics, with the exception of extremely narrow papers addressed to small specialist audiences." Text also in French.

REVIEW INFORMATION

REFEREED: Yes (I-B)   ACCEPTANCE RATE: 20%

NUMBER OF REVIEWER(S)/MS., EXCLUDING IN-HOUSE EDITOR(S): 2

REVIEWER(S): External   ARTICLES/AVG. ISSUE: 12

REVIEWING CRITERIA USED: BLIND REVIEW: No

  MANUSCRIPT SUBMISSION AIDS: 1

  BIAS SAFEGUARDS: 5, 7, 9

AVERAGE REVIEW TIME: 2 mos.   PUBLICATION TIME LAG: 9 mos.

MANUSCRIPT RETURNED WITH COMMENTS: No

MANUSCRIPT INFORMATION

GUIDELINES PUBLISHED: Each issue

STYLE REQUIREMENTS PUBLISHED: No; available on request

STYLE MANUAL USED: In-house

PREFERRED TOPICS: All areas of economics

QUERY LETTER: No   SIMULTANEOUS SUBMISSION: No

ABSTRACT WITH MANUSCRIPT: 100 wds.   COVER LETTER: Yes

NUMBER OF MANUSCRIPT COPIES: 3   MANUSCRIPT LENGTH: Not specified

SUBMISSION FEE: Can.$34. for non-   PAGE CHARGES: No
  members/nonsubscribers

MANUSCRIPT ACKNOWLEDGED: Yes   EARLY PUBLICATION OPTION: No

COPYRIGHT OWNER: Journal   REPRINTS: Not available

AUTHOR COMPENSATION: None

MANUSCRIPT ADDRESS: Prof. Michael Parkin, Managing Editor, The Canadian Journal of Economics, SSC, University of Western Ontario, London, Ontario, Canada N6A 5C2

Canadian Public Policy / Analyse de Politiques

FIRST PUBLISHED: 1975   FREQUENCY: Q   CIRCULATION: 2,000

AFFILIATION: CEA, CPSA, CALT, CSAA, CAG, CASSW, IPAC, ASAC, CABE

AUDIENCE: Academic/Professional; Business/Industrial; Government

PERCENT OF UNSOLICITED ARTICLES/ISSUE: 61-80%   ISSN: 0317-0861

EDITORIAL POLICY: The journal seeks and publishes articles from
a variety of disciplines. The articles should analyze, rather
than describe, Canadian public policy.

REVIEW INFORMATION

REFEREED: Yes (I-A)   ACCEPTANCE RATE: 50%

NUMBER OF REVIEWER(S)/MS., EXCLUDING IN-HOUSE EDITOR(S): 3

REVIEWER(S): External   ARTICLES/AVG. ISSUE: 10

REVIEWING CRITERIA USED: BLIND REVIEW: Yes (Board
  MANUSCRIPT SUBMISSION AIDS: 0   and external review)
  BIAS SAFEGUARDS: 3, 5, 6, 7, 9

AVERAGE REVIEW TIME: 10 wks.   PUBLICATION TIME LAG: 22 wks.

MANUSCRIPT RETURNED WITH COMMENTS: Yes

MANUSCRIPT INFORMATION

GUIDELINES PUBLISHED: No; available on request

STYLE REQUIREMENTS PUBLISHED: No; available on request

STYLE MANUAL USED: In-house

PREFERRED TOPICS: Emphasis is on policy analysis: micro-economic,
  macro-economic, political, administrative, federal/provincial,
  sociological, anthropological, legal-constitutional

QUERY LETTER: No   SIMULTANEOUS SUBMISSION: No

ABSTRACT WITH MANUSCRIPT: 100 wds.   COVER LETTER: Yes

NUMBER OF MANUSCRIPT COPIES: 5   MANUSCRIPT LENGTH: 5,000 wds.
                                       max.

SUBMISSION FEE: No   PAGE CHARGES: No

MANUSCRIPT ACKNOWLEDGED: Yes   EARLY PUBLICATION OPTION: No

COPYRIGHT OWNER: Journal   REPRINTS: Optional purchase

AUTHOR COMPENSATION: None

MANUSCRIPT ADDRESS: Prof. Kenneth Norrie, Editor, Canadian Public
  Policy/ Analyse de Politiques, Department of Economics, University
  of Alberta, Edmonton, Alberta, Canada T6G 2H4

The Cato Journal

FIRST PUBLISHED: 1981   FREQUENCY: 3/Yr.   CIRCULATION: 3,500
AFFILIATION: Cato Institute. Address same as journal's.

AUDIENCE: Academic/Professional; Business/Industrial; Government
PERCENT OF UNSOLICITED ARTICLES/ISSUE: 11-20%   ISSN: 0273-3072
EDITORIAL POLICY: Accepts only those articles that are well-researched
   analyses of important public-policy issues and that have clarity of
   thought and empirical support for basic hypotheses. Prefers to avoid
   the jargon of the technician and the highly mathematical presenta-
   tions of most economic journals. The journal is also interdisciplinary
   and accepts articles on broad philosophical issues as well as specific
   policy questions.   REVIEW INFORMATION

REFEREED: No   ACCEPTANCE RATE: 25%
NUMBER OF REVIEWER(S)/MS., EXCLUDING IN-HOUSE EDITOR(S): 1
REVIEWER(S): Board or external   ARTICLES/AVG. ISSUE: 14
REVIEWING CRITERIA USED: BLIND REVIEW: Yes (Board review
   MANUSCRIPT SUBMISSION AIDS: 1   only)
   BIAS SAFEGUARDS: 3, 4, 5, 6, 9*
AVERAGE REVIEW TIME: 2-3 mos.   PUBLICATION TIME LAG: 3-6 mos.
MANUSCRIPT RETURNED WITH COMMENTS: Yes, if requested; SASE required

MANUSCRIPT INFORMATION

GUIDELINES PUBLISHED: Each issue (brief); also on request (detailed)
STYLE REQUIREMENTS PUBLISHED: No; available on request
STYLE MANUAL USED: Chicago
PREFERRED TOPICS: Economics, especially public policy

QUERY LETTER: No   SIMULTANEOUS SUBMISSION: No
ABSTRACT WITH MANUSCRIPT: No   COVER LETTER: Yes
NUMBER OF MANUSCRIPT COPIES: 3   MANUSCRIPT LENGTH: 15-30 pp.

SUBMISSION FEE: No   PAGE CHARGES: No

MANUSCRIPT ACKNOWLEDGED: Yes, SASE pref. EARLY PUBLICATION OPTION: Yes
COPYRIGHT OWNER: Journal   REPRINTS: Optional purchase

AUTHOR COMPENSATION: 1 free journal and 25 free reprints/tear sheets
MANUSCRIPT ADDRESS: Dr. James A. Dorn, Editor, The Cato Journal,
   Cato Institute, 224 Second Street, SE, Washington, D.C. 20003

CEPAL Review / Revista de la CEPAL

FIRST PUBLISHED: 1976   FREQUENCY: 3/Yr.   CIRCULATION: 5,000

AFFILIATION: U.N. Economic Commission for Latin America and the
  Caribbean. Address same as journal's.

AUDIENCE: Academic/Professional; Government

PERCENT OF UNSOLICITED ARTICLES/ISSUE: 81-100%   ISSN: 0251-2920

EDITORIAL POLICY: Dedicated to the publication and dissemination of
  economic and sociological articles for readers in the Latin American
  region. Authors must be staff members of the United Nations or its
  agencies and related bodies. Contributions of consultants, experts,
  and retired or ex-staff members can also be submitted for consider-
  ation.

REVIEW INFORMATION

REFEREED: No   ACCEPTANCE RATE: 100%

NUMBER OF REVIEWER(S)/MS., EXCLUDING IN-HOUSE EDITOR(S): 0

REVIEWER(S): Editor   ARTICLES/AVG. ISSUE: 10

REVIEWING CRITERIA USED: BLIND REVIEW: No

  MANUSCRIPT SUBMISSION AIDS: 0

  BIAS SAFEGUARDS: 0

AVERAGE REVIEW TIME: 1 mo.   PUBLICATION TIME LAG: 2-3 mos.

MANUSCRIPT RETURNED WITH COMMENTS: Yes

MANUSCRIPT INFORMATION

GUIDELINES PUBLISHED: No; not available

STYLE REQUIREMENTS PUBLISHED: No; available on request

STYLE MANUAL USED: In-house; U.N.

PREFERRED TOPICS: Socio-economic development

QUERY LETTER: No   SIMULTANEOUS SUBMISSION: No

ABSTRACT WITH MANUSCRIPT: No   COVER LETTER: Yes

NUMBER OF MANUSCRIPT COPIES: 2   MANUSCRIPT LENGTH: N.R.

SUBMISSION FEE: No   PAGE CHARGES: No

MANUSCRIPT ACKNOWLEDGED: Yes   EARLY PUBLICATION OPTION: No

COPYRIGHT OWNER: Journal   REPRINTS: Not available

AUTHOR COMPENSATION: 2 free journals and 50 free reprints/tear sheets

MANUSCRIPT ADDRESS: Adolfo Gurrieri, Technical Secretary, Revista de
  la Cepal/Cepal Review, Edificio Naciones Unida, Ave. Dag Hammarskjold,
  Casilla 179-D, Santiago, Chile

Challenge

FIRST PUBLISHED: 1952   FREQUENCY: Bi-M   CIRCULATION: 5,000
AFFILIATION: None

AUDIENCE: Academic/Professional; Business/Industrial; Government
PERCENT OF UNSOLICITED ARTICLES/ISSUE: 61-80%   ISSN: 0577-5132
EDITORIAL POLICY: Freedom for diversity in all analyses and view-
   points on economics, current events, and economic policy.

REVIEW INFORMATION

REFEREED: No   ACCEPTANCE RATE: 10%
NUMBER OF REVIEWER(S)/MS., EXCLUDING IN-HOUSE EDITOR(S): 0
REVIEWER(S): Editor   ARTICLES/AVG. ISSUE: 5-7
REVIEWING CRITERIA USED: BLIND REVIEW: No
   MANUSCRIPT SUBMISSION AIDS: 0
   BIAS SAFEGUARDS: 9*
AVERAGE REVIEW TIME: 1-3 mos.   PUBLICATION TIME LAG: 1-3 mos.
MANUSCRIPT RETURNED WITH COMMENTS: No

MANUSCRIPT INFORMATION

GUIDELINES PUBLISHED: No; available on request
STYLE REQUIREMENTS PUBLISHED: No; available on request
STYLE MANUAL USED: Chicago
PREFERRED TOPICS: Economics, current events, economic policy

QUERY LETTER: Yes   SIMULTANEOUS SUBMISSION: Yes
ABSTRACT WITH MANUSCRIPT: No   COVER LETTER: Yes
NUMBER OF MANUSCRIPT COPIES: 2   MANUSCRIPT LENGTH: 15-18 pp.

SUBMISSION FEE: No   PAGE CHARGES: No

MANUSCRIPT ACKNOWLEDGED: Yes   EARLY PUBLICATION OPTION: No
COPYRIGHT OWNER: Publisher   REPRINTS: Optional purchase

AUTHOR COMPENSATION: 5 free journals
MANUSCRIPT ADDRESS: Richard D. Bartel, Manuscript Editor, Challenge,
   80 Business Park Drive, Armonk, NY   10504

Comparative Economic Studies

FIRST PUBLISHED: 1975   FREQUENCY: 4/Yr.   CIRCULATION: 650

AFFILIATION: Association for Comparative Economic Studies, Department of
  Economics, University of Notre Dame, Notre Dame, IN 46556

AUDIENCE: Academic/Professional; Business/Industrial; Government

PERCENT OF UNSOLICITED ARTICLES/ISSUE: 100%   ISSN: 0360-5930

EDITORIAL POLICY: Publishes manuscripts on planning, growth and
  development either explicitly comparative or dealing with a single
  country. General emphasis toward problems of centrally planned
  and developing socialist countries.

REVIEW INFORMATION

REFEREED: No   ACCEPTANCE RATE: 30%

NUMBER OF REVIEWER(S)/MS., EXCLUDING IN-HOUSE EDITOR(S): 1

REVIEWER(S): External   ARTICLES/AVG. ISSUE: 6

REVIEWING CRITERIA USED: BLIND REVIEW: Yes (External
  MANUSCRIPT SUBMISSION AIDS: 0   review only)
  BIAS SAFEGUARDS: 3, 5, 9

AVERAGE REVIEW TIME: 6 wks.   PUBLICATION TIME LAG: 3 mos.

MANUSCRIPT RETURNED WITH COMMENTS: No

MANUSCRIPT INFORMATION

GUIDELINES PUBLISHED: No; not available

STYLE REQUIREMENTS PUBLISHED: No; not available

STYLE MANUAL USED: Chicago

PREFERRED TOPICS: Comparative economics

QUERY LETTER: No   SIMULTANEOUS SUBMISSION: No

ABSTRACT WITH MANUSCRIPT: No   COVER LETTER: Yes

NUMBER OF MANUSCRIPT COPIES: 3   MANUSCRIPT LENGTH: 30 pp.

SUBMISSION FEE: No   PAGE CHARGES: No

MANUSCRIPT ACKNOWLEDGED: Yes   EARLY PUBLICATION OPTION: No

COPYRIGHT OWNER: Journal   REPRINTS: Optional purchase

AUTHOR COMPENSATION: 25 free reprints/tear sheets

MANUSCRIPT ADDRESS: Josef C. Brada, Editor, Comparative Economic
  Studies, Department of Economics, Arizona State University,
  Tempe, AZ 85287

Conflict Management and Peace Science

FIRST PUBLISHED: 1973   FREQUENCY: S-A   CIRCULATION: 800

AFFILIATION: Peace Science Society (International), School of
  Management, State University of New York, Binghamton, NY 13901

AUDIENCE: Academic/Professional

PERCENT OF UNSOLICITED ARTICLES/ISSUE: 61-80%   ISSN: 0738-8942

EDITORIAL POLICY: To foster exchange of ideas and promote studies
  focusing on peace analysis and utilizing tools, methods and
  theoretical frameworks specifically designed for peace science.
  Economic methods and aspects are heavily emphasized.

REVIEW INFORMATION

REFEREED: Yes (I-A)   ACCEPTANCE RATE: 25%

NUMBER OF REVIEWER(S)/MS., EXCLUDING IN-HOUSE EDITOR(S): 3

REVIEWER(S): 1 board, 2 external   ARTICLES/AVG. ISSUE: 5

REVIEWING CRITERIA USED: BLIND REVIEW: Yes (Entire
  MANUSCRIPT SUBMISSION AIDS: 0   review)
  BIAS SAFEGUARDS: 3, 5, 6, 7, 9

AVERAGE REVIEW TIME: 3 mos.   PUBLICATION TIME LAG: 9 mos.

MANUSCRIPT RETURNED WITH COMMENTS: Yes, SASE required

MANUSCRIPT INFORMATION

GUIDELINES PUBLISHED: No; available on request

STYLE REQUIREMENTS PUBLISHED: No; available on request

STYLE MANUAL USED: Chicago

PREFERRED TOPICS: Peace science: economic and applied mathematical
  (O.R.) methods

QUERY LETTER: No   SIMULTANEOUS SUBMISSION: Yes

ABSTRACT WITH MANUSCRIPT: No   COVER LETTER: Yes

NUMBER OF MANUSCRIPT COPIES: 2   MANUSCRIPT LENGTH: 10-30 pp.

SUBMISSION FEE: $10.   PAGE CHARGES: No

MANUSCRIPT ACKNOWLEDGED: Yes   EARLY PUBLICATION OPTION: Yes

COPYRIGHT OWNER: Journal   REPRINTS: Optional purchase

AUTHOR COMPENSATION: None

MANUSCRIPT ADDRESS: Walter Isard, Editor, Conflict Management and
  Peace Science, 476 Uris Hall, Department of Economics, Cornell
  University, Ithaca, NY 14853

Contemporary Policy Issues

FIRST PUBLISHED: 1982   FREQUENCY: Q   CIRCULATION: 3,500

AFFILIATION: California State University, Long Beach, and Western
  Economic Association International. Address same as journal's.

AUDIENCE: Academic/Professional; Business/Industrial; Government

PERCENT OF UNSOLICITED ARTICLES/ISSUE: 0-10%   ISSN: 0735-0007

EDITORIAL POLICY: To focus economic research and analysis on contemporary policy issues of vital concern to business, government, and
  other decision-makers.

REVIEW INFORMATION

REFEREED: Yes (I-B)   ACCEPTANCE RATE: 12%

NUMBER OF REVIEWER(S)/MS., EXCLUDING IN-HOUSE EDITOR(S): 2

REVIEWER(S): External   ARTICLES/AVG. ISSUE: 10

REVIEWING CRITERIA USED: BLIND REVIEW: No

  MANUSCRIPT SUBMISSION AIDS: 0

  BIAS SAFEGUARDS: 4, 5, 6, 7, 9*

AVERAGE REVIEW TIME: 4 mos.   PUBLICATION TIME LAG: 12 mos.

MANUSCRIPT RETURNED WITH COMMENTS: No

MANUSCRIPT INFORMATION

GUIDELINES PUBLISHED: No; available on request

STYLE REQUIREMENTS PUBLISHED: No; available on request

STYLE MANUAL USED: In-house

PREFERRED TOPICS: All economic fields considered

QUERY LETTER: No   SIMULTANEOUS SUBMISSION: No

ABSTRACT WITH MANUSCRIPT: Yes   COVER LETTER: Yes

NUMBER OF MANUSCRIPT COPIES: 3   MANUSCRIPT LENGTH: 25 pp.

SUBMISSION FEE: No   PAGE CHARGES: No

MANUSCRIPT ACKNOWLEDGED: Yes   EARLY PUBLICATION OPTION: No

COPYRIGHT OWNER: Journal   REPRINTS: Optional purchase

AUTHOR COMPENSATION: None

MANUSCRIPT ADDRESS: Eldon J. Dvorak, Editor, Contemporary Policy
  Issues, 7400 Center Avenue, Huntington Beach, CA 92647

Czechoslovak Economic Digest

FIRST PUBLISHED: 1970   FREQUENCY: Irreg.   CIRCULATION: 550

AFFILIATION: Press Agency Orbis, Central Editorial Office. Address
same as journal's.

AUDIENCE: Academic/Professional; Government

PERCENT OF UNSOLICITED ARTICLES/ISSUE: 81-100%   ISSN: 0045-9461

EDITORIAL POLICY: Deals with the Czechoslovak economy--social,
political, and economic philosophy. Editions in English, French,
and German.

REVIEW INFORMATION

REFEREED: No   ACCEPTANCE RATE: N.R.

NUMBER OF REVIEWER(S)/MS., EXCLUDING IN-HOUSE EDITOR(S): 0

REVIEWER(S): Editor   ARTICLES/AVG. ISSUE: 5-6

REVIEWING CRITERIA USED: BLIND REVIEW: No

  MANUSCRIPT SUBMISSION AIDS: 0

  BIAS SAFEGUARDS: 4

AVERAGE REVIEW TIME: N.R.   PUBLICATION TIME LAG: 6-8 wks.

MANUSCRIPT RETURNED WITH COMMENTS: No

MANUSCRIPT INFORMATION

GUIDELINES PUBLISHED: No; not available

STYLE REQUIREMENTS PUBLISHED: No; not available

STYLE MANUAL USED: In-house

PREFERRED TOPICS: Macroeconomics

QUERY LETTER: No   SIMULTANEOUS SUBMISSION: No

ABSTRACT WITH MANUSCRIPT: No   COVER LETTER: No

NUMBER OF MANUSCRIPT COPIES: N.R. MANUSCRIPT LENGTH: N.R.

SUBMISSION FEE: No   PAGE CHARGES: No

MANUSCRIPT ACKNOWLEDGED: No   EARLY PUBLICATION OPTION: Yes

COPYRIGHT OWNER: Journal   REPRINTS: Optional purchase

AUTHOR COMPENSATION: Fee

MANUSCRIPT ADDRESS: Dr. Vít Suchý, Editor, Czechoslovak Economic
Digest, Orbis Press Agency Feature Service, 120 41 Prague 2,
Vinohradská 46, Czechoslovakia

Demography

FIRST PUBLISHED: 1964   FREQUENCY: Q   CIRCULATION: 4,000

AFFILIATION: Population Association of America, Box 14182, Benjamin
  Franklin Station, Washington, D.C. 20044

AUDIENCE: Academic/Professional

PERCENT OF UNSOLICITED ARTICLES/ISSUE: 100%   ISSN: 0070-3370

EDITORIAL POLICY: We welcome articles of general interest to scholars
  of population phenomena. We encourage contributions from persons
  in all social science disciplines and in other disciplines, such
  as biology, whose work is related to the study of human populations.

REVIEW INFORMATION

REFEREED: Yes (I-A)   ACCEPTANCE RATE: 12%

NUMBER OF REVIEWER(S)/MS., EXCLUDING IN-HOUSE EDITOR(S): 3

REVIEWER(S): External   ARTICLES/AVG. ISSUE: 10

REVIEWING CRITERIA USED: BLIND REVIEW: Yes (External
  MANUSCRIPT SUBMISSION AIDS: 1, 2   review only)
  BIAS SAFEGUARDS: 3, 4, 5, 6, 7, 9

AVERAGE REVIEW TIME: 4 mos.   PUBLICATION TIME LAG: 5-6 mos.

MANUSCRIPT RETURNED WITH COMMENTS: No

MANUSCRIPT INFORMATION

GUIDELINES PUBLISHED: Each issue

STYLE REQUIREMENTS PUBLISHED: Each issue

STYLE MANUAL USED: Chicago

PREFERRED TOPICS: Population phenomena, either technical or nontechnical

QUERY LETTER: No   SIMULTANEOUS SUBMISSION: No

ABSTRACT WITH MANUSCRIPT: 100 wds.   COVER LETTER: Yes

NUMBER OF MANUSCRIPT COPIES: 4   MANUSCRIPT LENGTH: 25 pp. max.

SUBMISSION FEE: No   PAGE CHARGES: $20. per page
                                        requested, not required

MANUSCRIPT ACKNOWLEDGED: Yes   EARLY PUBLICATION OPTION: No

COPYRIGHT OWNER: Publisher   REPRINTS: Optional purchase

AUTHOR COMPENSATION: 100 free reprints if page charges are honored

MANUSCRIPT ADDRESS: Gordon F. De Jong, Editor, Demography, Population
  Issues Research Center, Department of Sociology, Pennsylvania State
  University, University Park, PA 16802

Eastern Economic Journal

FIRST PUBLISHED: 1974   FREQUENCY: Q   CIRCULATION: 1,200

AFFILIATION: Eastern Economic Association, Department of Economics,
  University of Connecticut U-63, Storrs, CT   06268

AUDIENCE: Academic/Professional

PERCENT OF UNSOLICITED ARTICLES/ISSUE: 81-100%   ISSN: 0094-5056

EDITORIAL POLICY: "Committed to free and open intellectual inquiry
  from diverse philosophical perspectives in all areas of theoretical
  and applied research related to economics."

REVIEW INFORMATION

REFEREED: Yes (I-A)   ACCEPTANCE RATE: 40%

NUMBER OF REVIEWER(S)/MS., EXCLUDING IN-HOUSE EDITOR(S): 3

REVIEWER(S): 1 board, 2 external   ARTICLES/AVG. ISSUE: 8

REVIEWING CRITERIA USED: BLIND REVIEW: Yes (All except
  MANUSCRIPT SUBMISSION AIDS: 0   final selection)
  BIAS SAFEGUARDS: 3, 5, 7, 9

AVERAGE REVIEW TIME: 4 mos.   PUBLICATION TIME LAG: 6 mos.

MANUSCRIPT RETURNED WITH COMMENTS: Yes

MANUSCRIPT INFORMATION

GUIDELINES PUBLISHED: No; available on request

STYLE REQUIREMENTS PUBLISHED: No; available on request

STYLE MANUAL USED: In-house

PREFERRED TOPICS: Economics

QUERY LETTER: No   SIMULTANEOUS SUBMISSION: No

ABSTRACT WITH MANUSCRIPT: No   COVER LETTER: Yes

NUMBER OF MANUSCRIPT COPIES: 3   MANUSCRIPT LENGTH: 30 pp. max.

SUBMISSION FEE: $15. for members/sub-   PAGE CHARGES: No
  scribers; $20. for others

MANUSCRIPT ACKNOWLEDGED: Yes   EARLY PUBLICATION OPTION: No

COPYRIGHT OWNER: Journal   REPRINTS: Optional purchase

AUTHOR COMPENSATION: None

MANUSCRIPT ADDRESS: Ingrid H. Rima, Editor, Eastern Economic Journal,
  Department of Economics, Temple University, Philadelphia, PA 19122

Econometric Reviews

FIRST PUBLISHED: 1982   FREQUENCY: S-A   CIRCULATION: N.R.

AFFILIATION: None

AUDIENCE: Academic/Professional

PERCENT OF UNSOLICITED ARTICLES/ISSUE: 21-40%   ISSN: 0747-4938

EDITORIAL POLICY: "Provides a regular forum for reviews of topical
  areas in econometrics followed by critical discussion. It is not
  concerned with marginal extensions of the existing frontiers of
  econometric knowledge, but rather with views from the frontiers
  as to how and why we arrived there and where we may most profitably
  direct future efforts."

REVIEW INFORMATION

REFEREED: Yes (III-B)   ACCEPTANCE RATE: 25%

NUMBER OF REVIEWER(S)/MS., EXCLUDING IN-HOUSE EDITOR(S): 3

REVIEWER(S): Board   ARTICLES/AVG. ISSUE: 2

REVIEWING CRITERIA USED: BLIND REVIEW: No

  MANUSCRIPT SUBMISSION AIDS: 1, 2

  BIAS SAFEGUARDS: 9

AVERAGE REVIEW TIME: 10 wks.   PUBLICATION TIME LAG: 3 mos.

MANUSCRIPT RETURNED WITH COMMENTS: Yes

MANUSCRIPT INFORMATION

GUIDELINES PUBLISHED: Vol. 1, No. 1 (1982)

STYLE REQUIREMENTS PUBLISHED: Vol. 1, No. 1 (1982)

STYLE MANUAL USED: In-house

PREFERRED TOPICS: Econometrics

QUERY LETTER: No   SIMULTANEOUS SUBMISSION: No

ABSTRACT WITH MANUSCRIPT: Yes   COVER LETTER: Yes

NUMBER OF MANUSCRIPT COPIES: 4   MANUSCRIPT LENGTH: 50 pp.

SUBMISSION FEE: No   PAGE CHARGES: No

MANUSCRIPT ACKNOWLEDGED: Yes   EARLY PUBLICATION OPTION: No

COPYRIGHT OWNER: Publisher   REPRINTS: Optional purchase

AUTHOR COMPENSATION: 10 free reprints

MANUSCRIPT ADDRESS: Dale J. Poirer, Editor, Econometric Reviews,
  Department of Economics, University of Toronto, 150 St. George
  Street, Toronto, Canada M5S 1A1

Econometrica

FIRST PUBLISHED: 1933   **FREQUENCY:** B-M   **CIRCULATION:** 6,000

AFFILIATION: Econometric Society, Department of Economics, Northwestern University, Evanston, IL 60201

AUDIENCE: Academic/Professional

PERCENT OF UNSOLICITED ARTICLES/ISSUE: 95-100%   **ISSN:** 0012-9682

EDITORIAL POLICY: Papers should be relevant to the scope of the society; i.e., they should advance application of mathematics and statistics to economics. They should be original, well-crafted and should contain new and correct theoretical or applied results.

REVIEW INFORMATION

REFEREED: Yes (II-B)   **ACCEPTANCE RATE:** 8%

NUMBER OF REVIEWER(S)/MS., EXCLUDING IN-HOUSE EDITOR(S): 2

REVIEWER(S): Board and external   **ARTICLES/AVG. ISSUE:** 12

REVIEWING CRITERIA USED: **BLIND REVIEW:** No

  MANUSCRIPT SUBMISSION AIDS: 1, 2

  BIAS SAFEGUARDS: 5, 6, 9

AVERAGE REVIEW TIME: 3 mos.   **PUBLICATION TIME LAG:** 9 mos.

MANUSCRIPT RETURNED WITH COMMENTS: No

MANUSCRIPT INFORMATION

GUIDELINES PUBLISHED: ⎫ Each issue (brief); July 1980
STYLE REQUIREMENTS PUBLISHED: ⎬ (detailed); also available on request

STYLE MANUAL USED: In-house

PREFERRED TOPICS: Mathematical economics and econometrics

QUERY LETTER: No   **SIMULTANEOUS SUBMISSION:** No

ABSTRACT WITH MANUSCRIPT: Yes   **COVER LETTER:** Yes

NUMBER OF MANUSCRIPT COPIES: 4   **MANUSCRIPT LENGTH:** Not specified

SUBMISSION FEE: No   **PAGE CHARGES:** No

MANUSCRIPT ACKNOWLEDGED: Yes   **EARLY PUBLICATION OPTION:** No

COPYRIGHT OWNER: Econometric Society   **REPRINTS:** Optional purchase

AUTHOR COMPENSATION: None

MANUSCRIPT ADDRESS: Professor Angus Deaton, Editor, Econometrica, 311 Woodrow Wilson School of Public and International Affairs, Princeton University, Princeton, NJ 08544

Economia Internazionale

FIRST PUBLISHED: 1948   FREQUENCY: Q   CIRCULATION: 1,000

AFFILIATION: Camera di Commercio, Industria, Artigianato e Agricoltura, Instituto di Economia Internazionale. Address same as journal's.

AUDIENCE: Academic/Professional

PERCENT OF UNSOLICITED ARTICLES/ISSUE: 61-80%   ISSN: 0012-981X

EDITORIAL POLICY: To promote the study of international economics with a view to contributing to its advancement.

REVIEW INFORMATION

REFEREED: No   ACCEPTANCE RATE: 30%

NUMBER OF REVIEWER(S)/MS., EXCLUDING IN-HOUSE EDITOR(S): 1

REVIEWER(S): Board   ARTICLES/AVG. ISSUE: 6-8

REVIEWING CRITERIA USED: BLIND REVIEW: No

  MANUSCRIPT SUBMISSION AIDS: 1

  BIAS SAFEGUARDS: 0

AVERAGE REVIEW TIME: 1-2 mos.   PUBLICATION TIME LAG: 2 mos.

MANUSCRIPT RETURNED WITH COMMENTS: No

MANUSCRIPT INFORMATION

GUIDELINES PUBLISHED: Each issue

STYLE REQUIREMENTS PUBLISHED: No; not available

STYLE MANUAL USED: In-house

PREFERRED TOPICS: International economics

QUERY LETTER: No   SIMULTANEOUS SUBMISSION: Yes

ABSTRACT WITH MANUSCRIPT: 100 wds.   COVER LETTER: No

NUMBER OF MANUSCRIPT COPIES: 2   MANUSCRIPT LENGTH: 20 pp.

SUBMISSION FEE: No   PAGE CHARGES: No

MANUSCRIPT ACKNOWLEDGED: Yes   EARLY PUBLICATION OPTION: No

COPYRIGHT OWNER: None claimed   REPRINTS: Optional purchase

AUTHOR COMPENSATION: Free subscription

MANUSCRIPT ADDRESS: Prof. Orlando D'Alauro, Editor, Economia Internazionale, Instituto di Economia Internazionale, Via Garibaldi, 4, 16124 Genova, Italy

Economic Analysis and Workers' Management

FIRST PUBLISHED: 1967   FREQUENCY: Q   CIRCULATION: 1,000

AFFILIATION: International Association for the Economics of Self-Management. Address same as journal's.

AUDIENCE: Academic/Professional; Business/Industrial; Government

PERCENT OF UNSOLICITED ARTICLES/ISSUE: 81-100%   ISSN: 0013-3213

EDITORIAL POLICY: Economic analysis and economic theory in particular with respect to workers' management.

REVIEW INFORMATION

REFEREED: No   ACCEPTANCE RATE: 30%

NUMBER OF REVIEWER(S)/MS., EXCLUDING IN-HOUSE EDITOR(S): 1

REVIEWER(S): External   ARTICLES/AVG. ISSUE: 6-10

REVIEWING CRITERIA USED: BLIND REVIEW: (Board
  MANUSCRIPT SUBMISSION AIDS: 2   and external review)

  BIAS SAFEGUARDS: 3, 4, 5, 6, 9

AVERAGE REVIEW TIME: 2 mos.   PUBLICATION TIME LAG: 3 mos.

MANUSCRIPT RETURNED WITH COMMENTS: Yes

MANUSCRIPT INFORMATION

GUIDELINES PUBLISHED: No; available on request

STYLE REQUIREMENTS PUBLISHED: Each issue

STYLE MANUAL USED: In-house

PREFERRED TOPICS: Workers' management, economic theory and analysis

QUERY LETTER: No   SIMULTANEOUS SUBMISSION: Yes

ABSTRACT WITH MANUSCRIPT: No   COVER LETTER: No

NUMBER OF MANUSCRIPT COPIES: 3   MANUSCRIPT LENGTH: 10-40 pp.

SUBMISSION FEE: No   PAGE CHARGES: No

MANUSCRIPT ACKNOWLEDGED: Yes   EARLY PUBLICATION OPTION: No

COPYRIGHT OWNER: Journal   REPRINTS: Optional purchase

AUTHOR COMPENSATION: 1 free journal and 30 free reprints/tear sheets

MANUSCRIPT ADDRESS: Dr. Branko Horvat, Editor, Economic Analysis and Workers' Management, Zmaj Jovina 12, P.O. Box 11, 11000 Beograd, Yugoslavia

The Economic and Social Review

FIRST PUBLISHED: 1969   FREQUENCY: Q   CIRCULATION: 500
AFFILIATION: Economic and Social Studies. Address same as journal's.

AUDIENCE: Academic/Professional
PERCENT OF UNSOLICITED ARTICLES/ISSUE: 81-100%   ISSN: 0012-9984
EDITORIAL POLICY: Publication of papers of general significance,
  or of specific Irish interest, in any of the social sciences.

REVIEW INFORMATION

REFEREED: Yes (I-A)   ACCEPTANCE RATE: 60%
NUMBER OF REVIEWER(S)/MS., EXCLUDING IN-HOUSE EDITOR(S): 2
REVIEWER(S): External   ARTICLES/AVG. ISSUE: 5
REVIEWING CRITERIA USED: BLIND REVIEW: Yes (External
  MANUSCRIPT SUBMISSION AIDS: 1, 2   review only)
  BIAS SAFEGUARDS: 3, 4, 5, 7, 9*
AVERAGE REVIEW TIME: 3 mos.   PUBLICATION TIME LAG: 6 mos.
MANUSCRIPT RETURNED WITH COMMENTS: No

MANUSCRIPT INFORMATION

GUIDELINES PUBLISHED: Each issue
STYLE REQUIREMENTS PUBLISHED: Each issue
STYLE MANUAL USED: In-house
PREFERRED TOPICS: Very wide--unifying theme is usually Irish interest

QUERY LETTER: No   SIMULTANEOUS SUBMISSION: No
ABSTRACT WITH MANUSCRIPT: 100 wds. COVER LETTER: Yes
NUMBER OF MANUSCRIPT COPIES: 3   MANUSCRIPT LENGTH: 9,000 wds.
                                     max.
SUBMISSION FEE: No   PAGE CHARGES: No

MANUSCRIPT ACKNOWLEDGED: Yes   EARLY PUBLICATION OPTION: No
COPYRIGHT OWNER: None claimed   REPRINTS: Optional purchase

AUTHOR COMPENSATION: 30 free reprints/tear sheets
MANUSCRIPT ADDRESS: Prof. Denis Conniffe, Editor, The Economic and
  Social Review, The Economic and Social Research Institute, 4
  Burlington Road, Dublin 4, Ireland

Economic Development and Cultural Change

FIRST PUBLISHED: 1952   FREQUENCY: Q   CIRCULATION: 4,000

AFFILIATION: None

AUDIENCE: Academic/Professional; Business/Industrial; Government

PERCENT OF UNSOLICITED ARTICLES/ISSUE: 100%   ISSN: 0013-0079

EDITORIAL POLICY: "Publishes articles by scholars from both the
  developing and the industrialized nations. Each issue of EDCC is
  international as well as interdisciplinary, offering a broad
  perspective on the most important developments. The only criteria
  imposed on EDCC's contributors are those of original and substantive scholarship of high quality."

REVIEW INFORMATION

REFEREED: Yes (I-B)   ACCEPTANCE RATE: 20%

NUMBER OF REVIEWER(S)/MS., EXCLUDING IN-HOUSE EDITOR(S): 2

REVIEWER(S): External   ARTICLES/AVG. ISSUE: 9

REVIEWING CRITERIA USED: BLIND REVIEW: No

  MANUSCRIPT SUBMISSION AIDS: 0

  BIAS SAFEGUARDS: 5, 7, 9*

AVERAGE REVIEW TIME: 4 mos.   PUBLICATION TIME LAG: 12 mos.

MANUSCRIPT RETURNED WITH COMMENTS: No

MANUSCRIPT INFORMATION

GUIDELINES PUBLISHED: No; available on request

STYLE REQUIREMENTS PUBLISHED: No; available on request

STYLE MANUAL USED: Chicago

PREFERRED TOPICS: Development economics, anthropology, population
  studies, political science, demography, etc.

QUERY LETTER: No   SIMULTANEOUS SUBMISSION: No

ABSTRACT WITH MANUSCRIPT: No   COVER LETTER: Yes

NUMBER OF MANUSCRIPT COPIES: 4   MANUSCRIPT LENGTH: 50 pp. max.

SUBMISSION FEE: No   PAGE CHARGES: No

MANUSCRIPT ACKNOWLEDGED: Yes   EARLY PUBLICATION OPTION: No

COPYRIGHT OWNER: Publisher   REPRINTS: Optional purchase

AUTHOR COMPENSATION: 10 free journals

MANUSCRIPT ADDRESS: Prof. D. Gale Johnson, Editor, Economic Development
  and Cultural Change, University of Chicago, 1130 East 59th Street,
  Chicago, IL 60637

Economic Geography

FIRST PUBLISHED: 1925   FREQUENCY: Q   CIRCULATION: 3,500

AFFILIATION: Clark University. Address same as journal's.

AUDIENCE: Academic/Professional

PERCENT OF UNSOLICITED ARTICLES/ISSUE: 95%   ISSN: 0013-0095

EDITORIAL POLICY: Publishes "articles in the fields of economic geography
and urban geography. The journal is published by Clark University
for the benefit of geographers, economists, urbanists, generalists
in education and the professions, as well as all those interested
in the intelligent utilization of the world's resources."

REVIEW INFORMATION

REFEREED: Yes (I-A)   ACCEPTANCE RATE: 50%

NUMBER OF REVIEWER(S)/MS., EXCLUDING IN-HOUSE EDITOR(S): 3

REVIEWER(S): External   ARTICLES/AVG. ISSUE: 4-5

REVIEWING CRITERIA USED: BLIND REVIEW: Yes (External
  MANUSCRIPT SUBMISSION AIDS: 2   review only)
  BIAS SAFEGUARDS: 3, 5, 6, 7, 9

AVERAGE REVIEW TIME: 3 mos.   PUBLICATION TIME LAG: 4 mos.

MANUSCRIPT RETURNED WITH COMMENTS: Yes

MANUSCRIPT INFORMATION

GUIDELINES PUBLISHED: No; not available

STYLE REQUIREMENTS PUBLISHED: Each issue

STYLE MANUAL USED: Chicago

PREFERRED TOPICS: Geography, economics, regional science

QUERY LETTER: No   SIMULTANEOUS SUBMISSION: No

ABSTRACT WITH MANUSCRIPT: 100 wds. COVER LETTER: Yes

NUMBER OF MANUSCRIPT COPIES: 3   MANUSCRIPT LENGTH: 30 pp.

SUBMISSION FEE: No   PAGE CHARGES: No

MANUSCRIPT ACKNOWLEDGED: Yes   EARLY PUBLICATION OPTION: No

COPYRIGHT OWNER: Journal   REPRINTS: Purchase required

AUTHOR COMPENSATION: None

MANUSCRIPT ADDRESS: Dr. Gerald J. Karaska, Editor, Economic Geography,
  Clark University, Worcester, MA 01610

The Economic History Review

FIRST PUBLISHED: 1927   FREQUENCY: Q   CIRCULATION: 4,000
AFFILIATION: Economic History Society. Address same as journal's.

AUDIENCE: Academic/Professional
PERCENT OF UNSOLICITED ARTICLES/ISSUE: 61-80%   ISSN: 0013-0117
EDITORIAL POLICY: To advance the study of all aspects of economic
  and social history, the history of economic thought, and related
  disciplines.

REVIEW INFORMATION

REFEREED: Yes (I-B)   ACCEPTANCE RATE: 7.5%
NUMBER OF REVIEWER(S)/MS., EXCLUDING IN-HOUSE EDITOR(S): 2
REVIEWER(S): External   ARTICLES/AVG. ISSUE: 6
REVIEWING CRITERIA USED: BLIND REVIEW: No
  MANUSCRIPT SUBMISSION AIDS: 1
  BIAS SAFEGUARDS: 4, 5, 6, 7, 9*, 10
AVERAGE REVIEW TIME: 3-4 mos.   PUBLICATION TIME LAG: 7-8 mos.
MANUSCRIPT RETURNED WITH COMMENTS: Yes, SASE required

MANUSCRIPT INFORMATION

GUIDELINES PUBLISHED: Each issue
STYLE REQUIREMENTS PUBLISHED: No; available on request
STYLE MANUAL USED: In-house
PREFERRED TOPICS: Economic and social history, history of economic
  thought

QUERY LETTER: No   SIMULTANEOUS SUBMISSION: No
ABSTRACT WITH MANUSCRIPT: 100 wds. COVER LETTER: Yes
NUMBER OF MANUSCRIPT COPIES: 2   MANUSCRIPT LENGTH: 8,000 wds.

SUBMISSION FEE: No   PAGE CHARGES: No

MANUSCRIPT ACKNOWLEDGED: Yes   EARLY PUBLICATION OPTION: Yes
COPYRIGHT OWNER: Journal   REPRINTS: Optional purchase

AUTHOR COMPENSATION: None
MANUSCRIPT ADDRESS: The Editors, The Economic History Review, School
  of Economic and Social Studies, University of East Anglia, Norwich,
  NR4 7TJ, U.K.

Economic Inquiry

FIRST PUBLISHED: 1962   FREQUENCY: Q   CIRCULATION: 2,000

AFFILIATION: Western Economic Association International, 7400 Center Ave.
  Huntington Beach, CA 92647

AUDIENCE: Academic/Professional

PERCENT OF UNSOLICITED ARTICLES/ISSUE: 90%   ISSN: 0095-2583

EDITORIAL POLICY: Publishes mainstream economic research in all
  areas. The research should not be narrowly directed, but should
  appeal to the general reader. The level of technique desired is
  that possessed by the average but active academic researcher.

REVIEW INFORMATION

REFEREED: Yes (I-B)   ACCEPTANCE RATE: 16%

NUMBER OF REVIEWER(S)/MS., EXCLUDING IN-HOUSE EDITOR(S): 2

REVIEWER(S): External   ARTICLES/AVG. ISSUE: 14

REVIEWING CRITERIA USED: BLIND REVIEW: No

  MANUSCRIPT SUBMISSION AIDS: 0

  BIAS SAFEGUARDS: 4, 5, 6, 7, 9

AVERAGE REVIEW TIME: 3 mos.   PUBLICATION TIME LAG: 9 mos.

MANUSCRIPT RETURNED WITH COMMENTS: Yes, SASE required

MANUSCRIPT INFORMATION

GUIDELINES PUBLISHED: No; not available

STYLE REQUIREMENTS PUBLISHED: No; available on request

STYLE MANUAL USED: In-house

PREFERRED TOPICS: All areas of economics

QUERY LETTER: No   SIMULTANEOUS SUBMISSION: No

ABSTRACT WITH MANUSCRIPT: 75 wds.   COVER LETTER: No

NUMBER OF MANUSCRIPT COPIES: 3   MANUSCRIPT LENGTH: 45 pp. max.

SUBMISSION FEE: $35. for members/   PAGE CHARGES: No
  subscribers; $80. for others

MANUSCRIPT ACKNOWLEDGED: Yes   EARLY PUBLICATION OPTION: No

COPYRIGHT OWNER: Western Economic   REPRINTS: Optional purchase
  Association

AUTHOR COMPENSATION: None

MANUSCRIPT ADDRESS: Thomas E. Borcherding, Managing Editor, Economic
  Inquiry, The Claremont Graduate School, Claremont, CA 91711

The Economic Journal

FIRST PUBLISHED: 1891   FREQUENCY: Q   CIRCULATION: 6,000
AFFILIATION: Royal Economic Society. Address same as journal's.

AUDIENCE: Academic/Professional; Business/Industrial; Government
PERCENT OF UNSOLICITED ARTICLES/ISSUE: 100%   ISSN: 0013-0133
EDITORIAL POLICY: A general economics journal covering the whole field
   of economics. It encourages communication between specialists in
   different areas of economics.

REVIEW INFORMATION

REFEREED: Yes (I-B)   ACCEPTANCE RATE: 15%
NUMBER OF REVIEWER(S)/MS., EXCLUDING IN-HOUSE EDITOR(S): 2
REVIEWER(S): External   ARTICLES/AVG. ISSUE: 10-12
REVIEWING CRITERIA USED: BLIND REVIEW: No
   MANUSCRIPT SUBMISSION AIDS: 1, 2
   BIAS SAFEGUARDS: 5, 7, 8, 9
AVERAGE REVIEW TIME: 9.5 wks.   PUBLICATION TIME LAG: 6 mos.
MANUSCRIPT RETURNED WITH COMMENTS: No, unless requested

MANUSCRIPT INFORMATION

GUIDELINES PUBLISHED: Each issue
STYLE REQUIREMENTS PUBLISHED: Each issue
STYLE MANUAL USED: In-house
PREFERRED TOPICS: All areas of economics

QUERY LETTER: No   SIMULTANEOUS SUBMISSION: No
ABSTRACT WITH MANUSCRIPT: No   COVER LETTER: No
NUMBER OF MANUSCRIPT COPIES: 3   MANUSCRIPT LENGTH: No limit

SUBMISSION FEE: $25. or 1 year sub-   PAGE CHARGES: No
   scription for nonmembers/nonsubscrib.
MANUSCRIPT ACKNOWLEDGED: Yes   EARLY PUBLICATION OPTION: No
COPYRIGHT OWNER: Journal   REPRINTS: Optional purchase

AUTHOR COMPENSATION: 50 free reprints/tear sheets
MANUSCRIPT ADDRESS: The Editor, Professor John D. Hey, The Economic
   Journal, University of York, Heslington, York   YO1 5DD, UK

Economic Notes

FIRST PUBLISHED: 1972   FREQUENCY: 3/Yr.   CIRCULATION: 2,000
AFFILIATION: Monte dei Paschi di Siena. Address same as journal's.

AUDIENCE: Academic/Professional; Business/Industrial; Government; Banks
PERCENT OF UNSOLICITED ARTICLES/ISSUE: 90%   ISSN: 0391-5026
EDITORIAL POLICY: Journal of international economics, monetary and
  economic theory, history of economic thought.

REVIEW INFORMATION

REFEREED: No   ACCEPTANCE RATE: 60%
NUMBER OF REVIEWER(S)/MS., EXCLUDING IN-HOUSE EDITOR(S): 1
REVIEWER(S): Board   ARTICLES/AVG. ISSUE: 9
REVIEWING CRITERIA USED: BLIND REVIEW: No
  MANUSCRIPT SUBMISSION AIDS: 0
  BIAS SAFEGUARDS: 5, 6, 9*
AVERAGE REVIEW TIME: 6 wks.   PUBLICATION TIME LAG: 2 mos.
MANUSCRIPT RETURNED WITH COMMENTS: No

MANUSCRIPT INFORMATION

GUIDELINES PUBLISHED: No; not available
STYLE REQUIREMENTS PUBLISHED: No; not available
STYLE MANUAL USED: In-house
PREFERRED TOPICS: Economic theory, history of economic thought,
  monetary theory, international economics

QUERY LETTER: No   SIMULTANEOUS SUBMISSION: No
ABSTRACT WITH MANUSCRIPT: 100 wds.   COVER LETTER: Yes
NUMBER OF MANUSCRIPT COPIES: 3   MANUSCRIPT LENGTH: 35 pp.

SUBMISSION FEE: No   PAGE CHARGES: No

MANUSCRIPT ACKNOWLEDGED: Yes   EARLY PUBLICATION OPTION: Yes
COPYRIGHT OWNER: Publisher   REPRINTS: Optional purchase

AUTHOR COMPENSATION: Fee and 50 free reprints/tear sheets
MANUSCRIPT ADDRESS: Dr. Lorenzo Maccari, Editor, Economic Notes,
  Monte dei Paschi di Siena, Piazza Salimbeni 3, 53100 Siena, Italy

The Economic Record

FIRST PUBLISHED: 1927   FREQUENCY: Q   CIRCULATION: 3,500
AFFILIATION: Economic Society of Australia. Address same as journal's.

AUDIENCE: Academic/Professional; Business/Industrial; Government
PERCENT OF UNSOLICITED ARTICLES/ISSUE: 90%   ISSN: 0013-0249
EDITORIAL POLICY: Theoretical and applied studies assessed by peer
  reviewers as making a significant contribution to the body of
  economic knowledge.

REVIEW INFORMATION

REFEREED: Yes (I-B)   ACCEPTANCE RATE: 30%
NUMBER OF REVIEWER(S)/MS., EXCLUDING IN-HOUSE EDITOR(S): 2
REVIEWER(S): External   ARTICLES/AVG. ISSUE: 8
REVIEWING CRITERIA USED: BLIND REVIEW: No
  MANUSCRIPT SUBMISSION AIDS: 2
  BIAS SAFEGUARDS: 5, 7, 9
AVERAGE REVIEW TIME: 3 mos.   PUBLICATION TIME LAG: 5 mos.
MANUSCRIPT RETURNED WITH COMMENTS: Yes

MANUSCRIPT INFORMATION

GUIDELINES PUBLISHED: No; available on request
STYLE REQUIREMENTS PUBLISHED: Each issue
STYLE MANUAL USED: N.R.
PREFERRED TOPICS: Economics

QUERY LETTER: No   SIMULTANEOUS SUBMISSION: No
ABSTRACT WITH MANUSCRIPT: 70 wds.   COVER LETTER: No
NUMBER OF MANUSCRIPT COPIES: 3   MANUSCRIPT LENGTH: N.R.

SUBMISSION FEE: Aus.$25. for non-   PAGE CHARGES: No
  members / nonsubscribers
MANUSCRIPT ACKNOWLEDGED: Yes   EARLY PUBLICATION OPTION: No
COPYRIGHT OWNER: Joint   REPRINTS: Optional purchase

AUTHOR COMPENSATION: None
MANUSCRIPT ADDRESS: Prof. J. W. Freebairn, Editor, The Economic Record
  Monash University, Clayton, Victoria 3168, Australia

The Economic Studies Quarterly / Kikan Riron-Keizaigaku

FIRST PUBLISHED: 1950   FREQUENCY: Q   CIRCULATION: 2,800

AFFILIATION: Japan Association of Economics and Econometrics. Address same as journal's.

AUDIENCE: Academic/Professional

PERCENT OF UNSOLICITED ARTICLES/ISSUE: 90%   ISSN: 0557-109X

EDITORIAL POLICY: The journal is open to all researchers in any field of economics. The fields covered include economic theory, econometrics, mathematical economics, monetary and fiscal theory, international economics, etc., but emphasis is laid on quantitative analysis and Japanese economic studies.

REVIEW INFORMATION

REFEREED: No   ACCEPTANCE RATE: 30%

NUMBER OF REVIEWER(S)/MS., EXCLUDING IN-HOUSE EDITOR(S): 1

·REVIEWER(S): External   ARTICLES/AVG. ISSUE: 11

REVIEWING CRITERIA USED: BLIND REVIEW: Yes (External review only)

  MANUSCRIPT SUBMISSION AIDS: 1, 2

  BIAS SAFEGUARDS: 3, 5, 6, 9

AVERAGE REVIEW TIME: 4 mos.   PUBLICATION TIME LAG: 6 mos.

MANUSCRIPT RETURNED WITH COMMENTS: Yes

MANUSCRIPT INFORMATION

GUIDELINES PUBLISHED: Each issue

STYLE REQUIREMENTS PUBLISHED: First issue of each volume

STYLE MANUAL USED: In-house

PREFERRED TOPICS: Economic theory, econometrics

QUERY LETTER: No   SIMULTANEOUS SUBMISSION: No

ABSTRACT WITH MANUSCRIPT: 100 wds.   COVER LETTER: No

NUMBER OF MANUSCRIPT COPIES: 3   MANUSCRIPT LENGTH: 10-15 pp.

SUBMISSION FEE: No   PAGE CHARGES: No

MANUSCRIPT ACKNOWLEDGED: Yes   EARLY PUBLICATION OPTION: No

COPYRIGHT OWNER: Author   REPRINTS: Purchase required

AUTHOR COMPENSATION: None

MANUSCRIPT ADDRESS: The Editors, The Economic Studies Quarterly, The Japan Association of Economics and Econometrics, c/o The Institute of Statistical Research, 1-18-16 Shimbashi, Minato, Tokyo, Japan 105

Economica

FIRST PUBLISHED: 1921   FREQUENCY: Q   CIRCULATION: 2,850

AFFILIATION: London School of Economics and Political Science.
  Address same as journal's.

AUDIENCE: Academic/Professional; Business/Industrial; Government

PERCENT OF UNSOLICITED ARTICLES/ISSUE: 100%   ISSN: 0013-0427

EDITORIAL POLICY: "Devoted to Economics, Economic History, Statistics,
  and closely related problems."

REVIEW INFORMATION

REFEREED: Yes (I-B)   ACCEPTANCE RATE: 16%

NUMBER OF REVIEWER(S)/MS., EXCLUDING IN-HOUSE EDITOR(S): 2

REVIEWER(S): External   ARTICLES/AVG. ISSUE: 8

REVIEWING CRITERIA USED: BLIND REVIEW: No

  MANUSCRIPT SUBMISSION AIDS: 1

  BIAS SAFEGUARDS: 4, 5, 6, 7, 9

AVERAGE REVIEW TIME: 2 mos.   PUBLICATION TIME LAG: 9 mos.

MANUSCRIPT RETURNED WITH COMMENTS: No

MANUSCRIPT INFORMATION

GUIDELINES PUBLISHED: Each issue

STYLE REQUIREMENTS PUBLISHED: No; available on request

STYLE MANUAL USED: In-house

PREFERRED TOPICS: Economics

QUERY LETTER: No   SIMULTANEOUS SUBMISSION: No

ABSTRACT WITH MANUSCRIPT: 100 wds.   COVER LETTER: Yes

NUMBER OF MANUSCRIPT COPIES: 3   MANUSCRIPT LENGTH: 30 pp.

SUBMISSION FEE: Year's subscription   PAGE CHARGES: No
  for nonsubscriber contributors

MANUSCRIPT ACKNOWLEDGED: Yes   EARLY PUBLICATION OPTION: No

COPYRIGHT OWNER: Journal   REPRINTS: Optional purchase

AUTHOR COMPENSATION: None

MANUSCRIPT ADDRESS: J. J. Thomas, Managing Editor, Economica,
  Economica Publishing Office, London School of Economics and
  Political Science, Houghton Street, London WC2A 2AE, U.K.

Economics of Education Review

FIRST PUBLISHED: 1981   FREQUENCY: Q   CIRCULATION: 400
AFFILIATION: None

AUDIENCE: Academic/Professional
PERCENT OF UNSOLICITED ARTICLES/ISSUE: 95%   ISSN: 0272-7757

EDITORIAL POLICY: To provide a forum for exchange of ideas and research
   findings in all facets of the economics of education; to encourage
   the development of sound theoretical, empirical and policy research,
   demonstrating the role of economic analysis in the solution or
   improved understanding of educational problems and issues.

REVIEW INFORMATION

REFEREED: Yes (II-A)   ACCEPTANCE RATE: 40%
NUMBER OF REVIEWER(S)/MS., EXCLUDING IN-HOUSE EDITOR(S): 2
REVIEWER(S): Board and/or external   ARTICLES/AVG. ISSUE: 8
REVIEWING CRITERIA USED: BLIND REVIEW: Yes (Board
   MANUSCRIPT SUBMISSION AIDS: 1, 2   review only)
   BIAS SAFEGUARDS: 3, 4, 5, 6, 9
AVERAGE REVIEW TIME: 3 mos.   PUBLICATION TIME LAG: 12 mos.
MANUSCRIPT RETURNED WITH COMMENTS: Yes, if requested; SASE required

MANUSCRIPT INFORMATION

GUIDELINES PUBLISHED: Each issue; also available on request
STYLE REQUIREMENTS PUBLISHED: Each issue; also available on request
STYLE MANUAL USED: In-house
PREFERRED TOPICS: Economics of education, education finance

QUERY LETTER: No   SIMULTANEOUS SUBMISSION: No
ABSTRACT WITH MANUSCRIPT: 100 wds.   COVER LETTER: Yes
NUMBER OF MANUSCRIPT COPIES: 4   MANUSCRIPT LENGTH: 20 pp.

SUBMISSION FEE: No   PAGE CHARGES: Requested;
                                      not required
MANUSCRIPT ACKNOWLEDGED: Yes   EARLY PUBLICATION OPTION: Yes
COPYRIGHT OWNER: Publisher   REPRINTS: Optional purchase

AUTHOR COMPENSATION: None

MANUSCRIPT ADDRESS: Elchanan Cohn, Editor-in-Chief, Economics of
   Education Review, Department of Economics, University of South
   Carolina, Columbia, SC 29208

Economics of Planning

FIRST PUBLISHED: 1960   FREQUENCY: 3/Yr.   CIRCULATION: 800

AFFILIATION: University of Birmingham, Centre for Russian and East European Studies. Address same as journal's.

AUDIENCE: Academic/Professional; Government

PERCENT OF UNSOLICITED ARTICLES/ISSUE: 61-80%   ISSN: 0013-0451

EDITORIAL POLICY: The journal is concerned with all aspects of economic planning, including theory of planning, planning techniques and applications, both East and West, and practical experiences of planned economies

REVIEW INFORMATION

REFEREED: Yes (I-B)   ACCEPTANCE RATE: 50%

NUMBER OF REVIEWER(S)/MS., EXCLUDING IN-HOUSE EDITOR(S): 2

REVIEWER(S): External   ARTICLES/AVG. ISSUE: 4

REVIEWING CRITERIA USED: BLIND REVIEW: No

  MANUSCRIPT SUBMISSION AIDS: 0

  BIAS SAFEGUARDS: 4, 5, 6, 7, 8, 9*

AVERAGE REVIEW TIME: 3 mos.   PUBLICATION TIME LAG: 6 mos.

MANUSCRIPT RETURNED WITH COMMENTS: No

MANUSCRIPT INFORMATION

GUIDELINES PUBLISHED: No; not available

STYLE REQUIREMENTS PUBLISHED: No; available on request

STYLE MANUAL USED: MLA

PREFERRED TOPICS: Theory and practice of economic planning, economics of planned economies

QUERY LETTER: No   SIMULTANEOUS SUBMISSION: No

ABSTRACT WITH MANUSCRIPT: No   COVER LETTER: Yes

NUMBER OF MANUSCRIPT COPIES: 4   MANUSCRIPT LENGTH: 60 pp. max.

SUBMISSION FEE: No   PAGE CHARGES: No

MANUSCRIPT ACKNOWLEDGED: Yes   EARLY PUBLICATION OPTION: No

COPYRIGHT OWNER: N.R.   REPRINTS: Not available

AUTHOR COMPENSATION: None

MANUSCRIPT ADDRESS: Dr. Julian Cooper, Editor, Economics of Planning, Centre for Russian and East European Studies, P.O. Box 363, The University of Birmingham, Birmingham, B15 2TT, U.K.

De Economist

FIRST PUBLISHED: 1852   FREQUENCY: Q   CIRCULATION: 1,000
AFFILIATION: None

AUDIENCE: Academic/Professional; Government
PERCENT OF UNSOLICITED ARTICLES/ISSUE: 90%   ISSN: 0013-063X
EDITORIAL POLICY: A learned journal which aims to publish articles
  in the field of general economics.

REVIEW INFORMATION

REFEREED: Yes (III-B)   ACCEPTANCE RATE: 60%
NUMBER OF REVIEWER(S)/MS., EXCLUDING IN-HOUSE EDITOR(S): 2
REVIEWER(S): Board   ARTICLES/AVG. ISSUE: 6
REVIEWING CRITERIA USED: BLIND REVIEW: No
  MANUSCRIPT SUBMISSION AIDS: 2
  BIAS SAFEGUARDS: 5, 9
AVERAGE REVIEW TIME: 6 wks.   PUBLICATION TIME LAG: 4 mos.
MANUSCRIPT RETURNED WITH COMMENTS: Yes

MANUSCRIPT INFORMATION

GUIDELINES PUBLISHED: No; not available
STYLE REQUIREMENTS PUBLISHED: Each issue
STYLE MANUAL USED: In-house
PREFERRED TOPICS: General economics: macro-economics, micro-economics,
  international economics

QUERY LETTER: No   SIMULTANEOUS SUBMISSION: Yes
ABSTRACT WITH MANUSCRIPT: 100 wds. COVER LETTER: Yes
NUMBER OF MANUSCRIPT COPIES: 2   MANUSCRIPT LENGTH: 15-22 pp.

SUBMISSION FEE: No   PAGE CHARGES: No

MANUSCRIPT ACKNOWLEDGED: Yes   EARLY PUBLICATION OPTION: Yes
COPYRIGHT OWNER: Journal   REPRINTS: Optional purchase

AUTHOR COMPENSATION: 1 free journal and 25 free reprints/tear sheets
MANUSCRIPT ADDRESS: Prof. S. K. Kuipers, Managing Editor, De Economist,
  Department of Economics, University of Groningen, W.S.N.-gebouw,
  P.O. Box 800, 9700 AV Groningen, The Netherlands

Empirical Economics

FIRST PUBLISHED: 1976   FREQUENCY: Q   CIRCULATION: 400

AFFILIATION: Institute for Advanced Studies. Address same as journal's.

AUDIENCE: Academic/Professional; Business/Industrial

PERCENT OF UNSOLICITED ARTICLES/ISSUE: 81-100%   ISSN: 0377-7332

EDITORIAL POLICY: "Publishes contributions in the field of empirical
economic research using advanced statistical methods and tackling
the economic problems of our time. Preference will be given to
contributions in the field of economic policy and control." Includes "studies about all industrialized countries with special
emphasis to the European economies."

REVIEW INFORMATION

REFEREED: Yes (II-A)   ACCEPTANCE RATE: 25%

NUMBER OF REVIEWER(S)/MS., EXCLUDING IN-HOUSE EDITOR(S): 2

REVIEWER(S): Board and external   ARTICLES/AVG. ISSUE: 5

REVIEWING CRITERIA USED: BLIND REVIEW: Yes (Entire
  MANUSCRIPT SUBMISSION AIDS: 1, 2   review)

  BIAS SAFEGUARDS: 3, 5, 6, 9

AVERAGE REVIEW TIME: 4 mos.   PUBLICATION TIME LAG: 4 mos.

MANUSCRIPT RETURNED WITH COMMENTS: No

MANUSCRIPT INFORMATION

GUIDELINES PUBLISHED: Each issue

STYLE REQUIREMENTS PUBLISHED: Each issue

STYLE MANUAL USED: In-house

PREFERRED TOPICS: Economic policy and control, international comparisons

QUERY LETTER: No   SIMULTANEOUS SUBMISSION: No

ABSTRACT WITH MANUSCRIPT: 100 wds.   COVER LETTER: Yes

NUMBER OF MANUSCRIPT COPIES: 3   MANUSCRIPT LENGTH: N.R.

SUBMISSION FEE: No   PAGE CHARGES: No

MANUSCRIPT ACKNOWLEDGED: Yes   EARLY PUBLICATION OPTION: Yes

COPYRIGHT OWNER: Publisher   REPRINTS: Optional purchase

AUTHOR COMPENSATION: 1 free journal and 50 free reprints/tear sheets

MANUSCRIPT ADDRESS: Univ. Doz. Dr. Bernhard Böhm, Managing Editor,
  Empirical Economics, Institute for Advanced Studies, Stumpergasse
  56, A-1060 Vienna, Austria

The Energy Journal

FIRST PUBLISHED: 1980   FREQUENCY: Q   CIRCULATION: 2,000

AFFILIATION: International Association of Energy Economists, 1133
  15th St. N.W., #620, Washington, D.C. 20005

AUDIENCE: Academic/Professional; Business/Industrial; Government

PERCENT OF UNSOLICITED ARTICLES/ISSUE: 90%   ISSN: 0195-6574

EDITORIAL POLICY: "Devoted to the advancement and dissemination of
  knowledge concerning energy and related topics. Content and
  editorial board composition are international in scope. Although
  most articles published will emphasize the economic aspects of
  their subjects, coverage will be interdisciplinary."

REVIEW INFORMATION

REFEREED: Yes (II-B)   ACCEPTANCE RATE: 32%

NUMBER OF REVIEWER(S)/MS., EXCLUDING IN-HOUSE EDITOR(S): 2

REVIEWER(S): Board and/or external   ARTICLES/AVG. ISSUE: 12

REVIEWING CRITERIA USED: BLIND REVIEW: No

  MANUSCRIPT SUBMISSION AIDS: 0

  BIAS SAFEGUARDS: 4, 5, 9

AVERAGE REVIEW TIME: 10 wks.   PUBLICATION TIME LAG: 6 mos.

MANUSCRIPT RETURNED WITH COMMENTS: Yes

MANUSCRIPT INFORMATION

GUIDELINES PUBLISHED: No; available on request

STYLE REQUIREMENTS PUBLISHED: No; available on request

STYLE MANUAL USED: Chicago

PREFERRED TOPICS: Energy economics--research and policy

QUERY LETTER: No   SIMULTANEOUS SUBMISSION: No

ABSTRACT WITH MANUSCRIPT: No   COVER LETTER: Yes

NUMBER OF MANUSCRIPT COPIES: 3   MANUSCRIPT LENGTH: 25 pp.

SUBMISSION FEE: $25.   PAGE CHARGES: No

MANUSCRIPT ACKNOWLEDGED: Yes   EARLY PUBLICATION OPTION: No

COPYRIGHT OWNER: Publisher   REPRINTS: Optional purchase

AUTHOR COMPENSATION: None

MANUSCRIPT ADDRESS: Helmut J. Frank, Editor, The Energy Journal,
  Department of Economics, University of Arizona, Tucson, AZ 85721

European Economic Review

FIRST PUBLISHED: 1972   FREQUENCY: 6/Yr.   CIRCULATION: 2,200

AFFILIATION: European Finance Association, c/o EFMD, Rue Washington
40, B-1050 Brussels, Belguim

AUDIENCE: Academic/Professional

PERCENT OF UNSOLICITED ARTICLES/ISSUE: 90%   ISSN: 0014-2921

EDITORIAL POLICY: General economics journal, publishing research
results.

REVIEW INFORMATION

REFEREED: Yes (II-B)   ACCEPTANCE RATE: 25%

NUMBER OF REVIEWER(S)/MS., EXCLUDING IN-HOUSE EDITOR(S): 2

REVIEWER(S): Board and external   ARTICLES/AVG. ISSUE: 12

REVIEWING CRITERIA USED: BLIND REVIEW: No

  MANUSCRIPT SUBMISSION AIDS: 1, 2

  BIAS SAFEGUARDS: 5, 6, 9

AVERAGE REVIEW TIME: 20 wks.   PUBLICATION TIME LAG: 10 wks.

MANUSCRIPT RETURNED WITH COMMENTS: Yes

MANUSCRIPT INFORMATION

GUIDELINES PUBLISHED: Each issue

STYLE REQUIREMENTS PUBLISHED: Each issue

STYLE MANUAL USED: In-house

PREFERRED TOPICS: All areas of economics

QUERY LETTER: No   SIMULTANEOUS SUBMISSION: No

ABSTRACT WITH MANUSCRIPT: 100 wds.   COVER LETTER: No

NUMBER OF MANUSCRIPT COPIES: 2   MANUSCRIPT LENGTH: 10,000 wds.
                                   max.

SUBMISSION FEE: $25. for nonmembers/   PAGE CHARGES: No
  nonsubscribers

MANUSCRIPT ACKNOWLEDGED: No   EARLY PUBLICATION OPTION: No

COPYRIGHT OWNER: Publisher   REPRINTS: Optional purchase

AUTHOR COMPENSATION: None

MANUSCRIPT ADDRESS: Prof. Jean Waelbroeck, Editor, European Economic
Review, 12 Avenue de l'Oree, B-1050 Brussels, Belgium

European Review of Agricultural Economics

FIRST PUBLISHED: 1973   FREQUENCY: Q   CIRCULATION: 700
AFFILIATION: None

AUDIENCE: Academic/Professional
PERCENT OF UNSOLICITED ARTICLES/ISSUE: 61-80%   ISSN: 0165-1587
EDITORIAL POLICY: Serves as a forum for discussions about developments of theoretical and applied agricultural economics research
   in Europe and other parts of the world.

REVIEW INFORMATION

REFEREED: Yes (II-A)   ACCEPTANCE RATE: 50%
NUMBER OF REVIEWER(S)/MS., EXCLUDING IN-HOUSE EDITOR(S): 2
REVIEWER(S): Board and external   ARTICLES/AVG. ISSUE: 7
REVIEWING CRITERIA USED: BLIND REVIEW: Yes (Board
   MANUSCRIPT SUBMISSION AIDS: 1, 2   and external review)
   BIAS SAFEGUARDS: 3, 5, 6, 8, 9*
AVERAGE REVIEW TIME: 3 mos.   PUBLICATION TIME LAG: 5 mos.
MANUSCRIPT RETURNED WITH COMMENTS: Yes

MANUSCRIPT INFORMATION

GUIDELINES PUBLISHED: Each issue
STYLE REQUIREMENTS PUBLISHED: Each issue
STYLE MANUAL USED: In-house
PREFERRED TOPICS: Agricultural economics, agricultural marketing,
   policy, rural development

QUERY LETTER: No   SIMULTANEOUS SUBMISSION: No
ABSTRACT WITH MANUSCRIPT: 100 wds.   COVER LETTER: Yes
NUMBER OF MANUSCRIPT COPIES: 4   MANUSCRIPT LENGTH: 20 pp.

SUBMISSION FEE: No   PAGE CHARGES: No

MANUSCRIPT ACKNOWLEDGED: Yes   EARLY PUBLICATION OPTION: No
COPYRIGHT OWNER: Publisher   REPRINTS: Optional purchase

AUTHOR COMPENSATION: 1 free journal and 25 free reprints/tear sheets
MANUSCRIPT ADDRESS: Dr. Kees Burger, Editor, European Review of
   Agricultural Economics, Economic and Social Institute, Free
   University, P.O. Box 7161, 1007 MC Amsterdam, Netherlands

Explorations in Economic History

FIRST PUBLISHED: 1963   FREQUENCY: Q   CIRCULATION: 1,000
AFFILIATION: None

AUDIENCE: Academic/Professional
PERCENT OF UNSOLICITED ARTICLES/ISSUE: 81-100%   ISSN: 0014-4983
EDITORIAL POLICY: "Publishes research papers of scholarly merit on a
wide range of topics in economic history. The focus is wide,
encompassing all aspects of economic change, all historical times,
and all geographical places. . . . Preference is given to the use
of quantitative methods and explicit theoretical analysis, but all
approaches to historical inquiry are welcome."

REVIEW INFORMATION

REFEREED: Yes (II-A)   ACCEPTANCE RATE: 20%
NUMBER OF REVIEWER(S)/MS., EXCLUDING IN-HOUSE EDITOR(S): 2
REVIEWER(S): Board and external   ARTICLES/AVG. ISSUE: 6
REVIEWING CRITERIA USED: BLIND REVIEW: Yes (Board
  MANUSCRIPT SUBMISSION AIDS: 1, 2   and external review)
  BIAS SAFEGUARDS: 3, 5, 9
AVERAGE REVIEW TIME: 2.5 mos.   PUBLICATION TIME LAG: 4 mos.
MANUSCRIPT RETURNED WITH COMMENTS: Yes, SASE required

MANUSCRIPT INFORMATION

GUIDELINES PUBLISHED: Each issue
STYLE REQUIREMENTS PUBLISHED: Each issue
STYLE MANUAL USED: In-house
PREFERRED TOPICS: Economic history

QUERY LETTER: No   SIMULTANEOUS SUBMISSION: No
ABSTRACT WITH MANUSCRIPT: 100 wds.   COVER LETTER: Yes
NUMBER OF MANUSCRIPT COPIES: 3   MANUSCRIPT LENGTH: Not specified

SUBMISSION FEE: No   PAGE CHARGES: No

MANUSCRIPT ACKNOWLEDGED: Yes   EARLY PUBLICATION OPTION: No
COPYRIGHT OWNER: Publisher   REPRINTS: Optional purchase

AUTHOR COMPENSATION: None
MANUSCRIPT ADDRESS: Prof. Larry Neal, Editor, Explorations in Economic
History, 328 David Kinley Hall, University of Illinois, 1407 West
Gregory Drive, Urbana, IL 61801

The Financial Review

FIRST PUBLISHED: 1973   FREQUENCY: Q   CIRCULATION: 1,300

AFFILIATION: Eastern Finance Association, c/o Dr. Lon M. Carnes, Jr., School of Business, Georgia Southern College, Statesboro, GA 30460

AUDIENCE: Academic/Professional

PERCENT OF UNSOLICITED ARTICLES/ISSUE: 81-100%   ISSN: 0732-8516

EDITORIAL POLICY: To publish original research in finance as broadly defined to include financial economics, financial markets, corporate finance, speculative markets, investments, international finance, and money and banking.

REVIEW INFORMATION

REFEREED: Yes (II-A)   ACCEPTANCE RATE: 15%

NUMBER OF REVIEWER(S)/MS., EXCLUDING IN-HOUSE EDITOR(S): 2

REVIEWER(S): Board and external   ARTICLES/AVG. ISSUE: 15

REVIEWING CRITERIA USED: BLIND REVIEW: Yes (Preliminary
  MANUSCRIPT SUBMISSION AIDS: 2   screening only)
  BIAS SAFEGUARDS: 3, 5, 8, 9

AVERAGE REVIEW TIME: 6 wks.   PUBLICATION TIME LAG: 6 mos.

MANUSCRIPT RETURNED WITH COMMENTS: Yes, SASE required

MANUSCRIPT INFORMATION

GUIDELINES PUBLISHED: No; not available

STYLE REQUIREMENTS PUBLISHED: Each issue

STYLE MANUAL USED: Chicago

PREFERRED TOPICS: Financial economics, financial markets, corporate finance, speculative markets, investments, international finance, money and banking

QUERY LETTER: No   SIMULTANEOUS SUBMISSION: No

ABSTRACT WITH MANUSCRIPT: 100 wds.   COVER LETTER: Yes

NUMBER OF MANUSCRIPT COPIES: 3   MANUSCRIPT LENGTH: 20-30 pp.

SUBMISSION FEE: $15. for members/   PAGE CHARGES: No
subscribers; $25. for others

MANUSCRIPT ACKNOWLEDGED: Yes   EARLY PUBLICATION OPTION: No

COPYRIGHT OWNER: Journal   REPRINTS: Optional purchase

AUTHOR COMPENSATION: None

MANUSCRIPT ADDRESS: Professors Cheng F. Lee and Joseph E. Finnerty, Editors, The Financial Review, College of Commerce and Bus. Adm., University of Illinois, 1206 S. Sixth Street, Champaign, IL 61820

Fiscal Studies

FIRST PUBLISHED: 1979   FREQUENCY: Q   CIRCULATION: 1,400

AFFILIATION: Institute for Fiscal Studies. Address same as journal's.

AUDIENCE: Academic/Professional; Business/Industrial; Government

PERCENT OF UNSOLICITED ARTICLES/ISSUE: 11-20%   ISSN: 0143-5671

EDITORIAL POLICY: Concerned with the whole range of ways in which
  government action affects the private sector of the economy.
  Provides a forum for material which is accessible to a wider audience
  than that of academic journals in economics, and that is more topical
  than the publication schedules of such journals can accommodate, but
  which is nevertheless thoughtful and original.

REVIEW INFORMATION

REFEREED: No   ACCEPTANCE RATE: Not available

NUMBER OF REVIEWER(S)/MS., EXCLUDING IN-HOUSE EDITOR(S): 1

REVIEWER(S): External   ARTICLES/AVG. ISSUE: 6

REVIEWING CRITERIA USED: BLIND REVIEW: No

  MANUSCRIPT SUBMISSION AIDS: 1

  BIAS SAFEGUARDS: 5, 9

AVERAGE REVIEW TIME: 6 wks.   PUBLICATION TIME LAG: 6 wks.

MANUSCRIPT RETURNED WITH COMMENTS: On request; SASE required

MANUSCRIPT INFORMATION

GUIDELINES PUBLISHED: Each issue

STYLE REQUIREMENTS PUBLISHED: No; available with SASE

STYLE MANUAL USED: In-house

PREFERRED TOPICS: Fiscal policy; regulation and competition

QUERY LETTER: Yes   SIMULTANEOUS SUBMISSION: N.R.

ABSTRACT WITH MANUSCRIPT: No   COVER LETTER: Yes

NUMBER OF MANUSCRIPT COPIES: 3   MANUSCRIPT LENGTH: N.R.

SUBMISSION FEE: No   PAGE CHARGES: No

MANUSCRIPT ACKNOWLEDGED: Yes   EARLY PUBLICATION OPTION: Yes

COPYRIGHT OWNER: Journal   REPRINTS: Not available

AUTHOR COMPENSATION: None

MANUSCRIPT ADDRESS: Michael Keen, Editor, Fiscal Studies, Institute
  for Fiscal Studies, 180/182 Tottenham Court Road, London, WIP
  9LE, U.K.

Food Research Institute Studies

FIRST PUBLISHED: 1960   FREQUENCY: Irreg.   CIRCULATION: 1,000

AFFILIATION: Stanford University, Food Research Institute. Address same as journal's.

AUDIENCE: Academic/Professional

PERCENT OF UNSOLICITED ARTICLES/ISSUE: 21-40%   ISSN: 0193-9025

EDITORIAL POLICY: "Devoted to studies of agricultural economics, trade, and development. Research on commodity futures markets, international trade in basic agricultural commodities, the world grain economies, determinants of population growth, the food and agricultural economies of tropical Africa, Latin America, and southeastern Asia, agricultural productivity and policy in the U.S."

REVIEW INFORMATION

REFEREED: No   ACCEPTANCE RATE: 40%

NUMBER OF REVIEWER(S)/MS., EXCLUDING IN-HOUSE EDITOR(S): 1

REVIEWER(S): External   ARTICLES/AVG. ISSUE: 4-5

REVIEWING CRITERIA USED: BLIND REVIEW: No

  MANUSCRIPT SUBMISSION AIDS: 0

  BIAS SAFEGUARDS: 5, 6, 9*

AVERAGE REVIEW TIME: 1.5 mos.   PUBLICATION TIME LAG: 3-4 mos.

MANUSCRIPT RETURNED WITH COMMENTS: Sometimes

MANUSCRIPT INFORMATION

GUIDELINES PUBLISHED: No; available on request

STYLE REQUIREMENTS PUBLISHED: No; available on request

STYLE MANUAL USED: In-house

PREFERRED TOPICS: Agricultural economics, agricultural development and economic growth, international trade, development finance, demography, nutrition and development

QUERY LETTER: No   SIMULTANEOUS SUBMISSION: No

ABSTRACT WITH MANUSCRIPT: No   COVER LETTER: Yes

NUMBER OF MANUSCRIPT COPIES: 2   MANUSCRIPT LENGTH: N.R.

SUBMISSION FEE: No   PAGE CHARGES: No

MANUSCRIPT ACKNOWLEDGED: Yes   EARLY PUBLICATION OPTION: No

COPYRIGHT OWNER: Journal   REPRINTS: Optional purchase

AUTHOR COMPENSATION: 1 free journal and 50 free reprints/tear sheets

MANUSCRIPT ADDRESS: Walter P. Falcon, Editor, Food Research Institute Studies, Stanford University, Stanford, CA 94305

Giornale degli Economisti e Annali di Economia

FIRST PUBLISHED: 1875   FREQUENCY: B-M   CIRCULATION: 1,000

AFFILIATION: Università Commerciale Luigi Bocconi. Address same as journal's.

AUDIENCE: Academic/Professional

PERCENT OF UNSOLICITED ARTICLES/ISSUE: 61-80%   ISSN: 0017-0097

EDITORIAL POLICY: Publishes articles of economic theory and, less frequently, of applied economics without any predetermined restriction on the subject or area.

REVIEW INFORMATION

REFEREED: Yes (I-A)   ACCEPTANCE RATE: 20%

NUMBER OF REVIEWER(S)/MS., EXCLUDING IN-HOUSE EDITOR(S): 2

REVIEWER(S): External   ARTICLES/AVG. ISSUE: 5

REVIEWING CRITERIA USED: BLIND REVIEW: Yes (Final
  MANUSCRIPT SUBMISSION AIDS: 2   selection only)
  BIAS SAFEGUARDS: 3, 5, 7, 9*

AVERAGE REVIEW TIME: 2 mos.   PUBLICATION TIME LAG: 3 mos.

MANUSCRIPT RETURNED WITH COMMENTS: No

MANUSCRIPT INFORMATION

GUIDELINES PUBLISHED: No; not available

STYLE REQUIREMENTS PUBLISHED: Each issue

STYLE MANUAL USED: In-house

PREFERRED TOPICS: Economic theory

QUERY LETTER: No   SIMULTANEOUS SUBMISSION: No

ABSTRACT WITH MANUSCRIPT: 240 wds. max. COVER LETTER: No

NUMBER OF MANUSCRIPT COPIES: 2   MANUSCRIPT LENGTH: 20 pp. max.

SUBMISSION FEE: No   PAGE CHARGES: No

MANUSCRIPT ACKNOWLEDGED: Yes   EARLY PUBLICATION OPTION: No

COPYRIGHT OWNER: Journal   REPRINTS: Optional purchase

AUTHOR COMPENSATION: 100 free reprints/tear sheets

MANUSCRIPT ADDRESS: Mario Monti, Direttore, Giornale degli Economisti e Annali di Economia, Via Sarfatti 25, 20136 Milano, Italy

Growth and Change

FIRST PUBLISHED: 1970   FREQUENCY: Q   CIRCULATION: 1,051

AFFILIATION: University of Kentucky, College of Business and Economics, Center for Business and Economic Research. Address same as journal's.

AUDIENCE: Academic/Professional

PERCENT OF UNSOLICITED ARTICLES/ISSUE: 91-100%   ISSN: 0017-4815

EDITORIAL POLICY: Publishes "reports of empirical research which began from some innovation of theory or methodology and test a hypothesis in such a way as to contribute something new to existing knowledge." Seeks "contributions from economics, geography, public finance, urban and regional planning, agricultural economics, public policy, and related fields, either within one discipline or cross-disciplinary."

REVIEW INFORMATION

REFEREED: Yes (I-A)   ACCEPTANCE RATE: 18%

NUMBER OF REVIEWER(S)/MS., EXCLUDING IN-HOUSE EDITOR(S): 3

REVIEWER(S): External   ARTICLES/AVG. ISSUE: 7-8

REVIEWING CRITERIA USED: BLIND REVIEW: Yes (Board

MANUSCRIPT SUBMISSION AIDS: 1   and external review)

BIAS SAFEGUARDS: 3, 4, 5, 6, 7, 9

AVERAGE REVIEW TIME: 2-4 mos.   PUBLICATION TIME LAG: 2-4 mos.

MANUSCRIPT RETURNED WITH COMMENTS: Yes, if requested; SASE required

MANUSCRIPT INFORMATION

GUIDELINES PUBLISHED: Each issue (brief); on request (detailed)

STYLE REQUIREMENTS PUBLISHED: No; available on request

STYLE MANUAL USED: In-house; Chicago

PREFERRED TOPICS: Economics, geography, business administration, regional science, and other disciplines with emphasis on economic issues

QUERY LETTER: No   SIMULTANEOUS SUBMISSION: No

ABSTRACT WITH MANUSCRIPT: No   COVER LETTER: Yes

NUMBER OF MANUSCRIPT COPIES: 4   MANUSCRIPT LENGTH: 3,500 wds. max.

SUBMISSION FEE: No   PAGE CHARGES: No

MANUSCRIPT ACKNOWLEDGED: Yes   EARLY PUBLICATION OPTION: Yes

COPYRIGHT OWNER: Journal   REPRINTS: Optional purchase

AUTHOR COMPENSATION: None

MANUSCRIPT ADDRESS: Editor, Growth and Change, 301 Mathews Building, Center for Business and Economic Research, University of Kentucky, Lexington, KY 40506-0047

History of Political Economy

FIRST PUBLISHED: 1969   FREQUENCY: Q   CIRCULATION: 1,500

AFFILIATION: History of Economics Society, Department of Economics,
  University of Tennessee, Knoxville, TN 37996-0550

AUDIENCE: Academic/Professional

PERCENT OF UNSOLICITED ARTICLES/ISSUE: 95%   ISSN: 0018-2702

EDITORIAL POLICY: Deals with development of economic analysis and its
  relation to incellectual and social issues.

REVIEW INFORMATION

REFEREED: Yes (II-B)   ACCEPTANCE RATE: 25%

NUMBER OF REVIEWER(S)/MS., EXCLUDING IN-HOUSE EDITOR(S): 2

REVIEWER(S): Board and external   ARTICLES/AVG. ISSUE: 8

REVIEWING CRITERIA USED: BLIND REVIEW: No

  MANUSCRIPT SUBMISSION AIDS: 2

  BIAS SAFEGUARDS: 5, 6, 9

AVERAGE REVIEW TIME: 2 mos.   PUBLICATION TIME LAG: 12 mos.

MANUSCRIPT RETURNED WITH COMMENTS: No

MANUSCRIPT INFORMATION

GUIDELINES PUBLISHED: No; available on request

STYLE REQUIREMENTS PUBLISHED: Each issue

STYLE MANUAL USED: Chicago

PREFERRED TOPICS: History of economic thought

QUERY LETTER: No   SIMULTANEOUS SUBMISSION: No

ABSTRACT WITH MANUSCRIPT: No   COVER LETTER: Yes

NUMBER OF MANUSCRIPT COPIES: 2   MANUSCRIPT LENGTH: 20 pp.

SUBMISSION FEE: No   PAGE CHARGES: No

MANUSCRIPT ACKNOWLEDGED: Yes   EARLY PUBLICATION OPTION: No

COPYRIGHT OWNER: Publisher   REPRINTS: Optional purchase

AUTHOR COMPENSATION: 35 free reprints/tear sheets

MANUSCRIPT ADDRESS: Crauford D.W. Goodwin, Editor, History of
  Political Economy, Department of Economics, Duke University,
  Durham, NC 27706

Housing Finance Review

FIRST PUBLISHED: 1982   FREQUENCY: Q   CIRCULATION: 1,500

AFFILIATION: University of Pennsylvania, Wharton Real Estate
Center. Address same as journal's.

AUDIENCE: Academic/Professional; Business/Industrial

PERCENT OF UNSOLICITED ARTICLES/ISSUE: 81-100%   ISSN: 0276-4415

EDITORIAL POLICY: Presents the results of research in housing finance
and provides a forum for a continuing dialogue on policy issues
related to housing finance. All aspects of housing finance are
considered.

REVIEW INFORMATION

REFEREED: Yes (III-B)   ACCEPTANCE RATE: 40%

NUMBER OF REVIEWER(S)/MS., EXCLUDING IN-HOUSE EDITOR(S): 2

REVIEWER(S): Board   ARTICLES/AVG. ISSUE: 6

REVIEWING CRITERIA USED: BLIND REVIEW: No

  MANUSCRIPT SUBMISSION AIDS: 1, 2

  BIAS SAFEGUARDS: 5, 9

AVERAGE REVIEW TIME: 4 wks.   PUBLICATION TIME LAG: 3 mos.

MANUSCRIPT RETURNED WITH COMMENTS: Yes

MANUSCRIPT INFORMATION

GUIDELINES PUBLISHED: Each issue

STYLE REQUIREMENTS PUBLISHED: Each issue

STYLE MANUAL USED: Chicago

PREFERRED TOPICS: Housing finance

QUERY LETTER: No   SIMULTANEOUS SUBMISSION: No

ABSTRACT WITH MANUSCRIPT: 100 wds.   COVER LETTER: No

NUMBER OF MANUSCRIPT COPIES: 3   MANUSCRIPT LENGTH: 30 pp.

SUBMISSION FEE: No   PAGE CHARGES: No

MANUSCRIPT ACKNOWLEDGED: Yes   EARLY PUBLICATION OPTION: No

COPYRIGHT OWNER: Journal   REPRINTS: Optional purchase

AUTHOR COMPENSATION: None

MANUSCRIPT ADDRESS: Prof. Jack M. Guttentag, Editor, Housing Finance
Review, University of Pennsylvania, Wharton Real Estate Center,
3611 Locust Walk/CA, Philadelphia, PA 19104

The Indian Economic Journal

FIRST PUBLISHED: 1953   FREQUENCY: Q   CIRCULATION: 2,500

AFFILIATION: Indian Economic Association, Delhi School of Economics, Delhi 110009, India

AUDIENCE: Academic/Professional

PERCENT OF UNSOLICITED ARTICLES/ISSUE: 75%   ISSN: 0019-4662

EDITORIAL POLICY: "The Indian Economic Journal is devoted to a scientific discussion of theoretical and applied economics with special reference to India. It is thus a forum for professional economists and others working in the same field and is intended to help correct economic thinking specially with reference to Indian economic problems."

REVIEW INFORMATION

REFEREED: No   ACCEPTANCE RATE: 20%

NUMBER OF REVIEWER(S)/MS., EXCLUDING IN-HOUSE EDITOR(S): 1

REVIEWER(S): Board   ARTICLES/AVG. ISSUE: 7-10

REVIEWING CRITERIA USED: BLIND REVIEW: No

  MANUSCRIPT SUBMISSION AIDS: 0

  BIAS SAFEGUARDS: 4

AVERAGE REVIEW TIME: 16 mos.   PUBLICATION TIME LAG: 16 mos.

MANUSCRIPT RETURNED WITH COMMENTS: No

MANUSCRIPT INFORMATION

GUIDELINES PUBLISHED: No; not available

STYLE REQUIREMENTS PUBLISHED: No; not available

STYLE MANUAL USED: In-house

PREFERRED TOPICS: Theory of money, growth, planning, industry, transport, international economics, institutional economics, etc.

QUERY LETTER: No   SIMULTANEOUS SUBMISSION: No

ABSTRACT WITH MANUSCRIPT: 100-120 wds.   COVER LETTER: Yes

NUMBER OF MANUSCRIPT COPIES: 3   MANUSCRIPT LENGTH: 6,000 wds. max.

SUBMISSION FEE: No   PAGE CHARGES: No

MANUSCRIPT ACKNOWLEDGED: Yes   EARLY PUBLICATION OPTION: No

COPYRIGHT OWNER: Journal   REPRINTS: Not available

AUTHOR COMPENSATION: None

MANUSCRIPT ADDRESS: The Editor, The Indian Economic Journal, Department of Economics, University of Bombay, Vidyanagari P.O., Bombay-400 098

The Indian Economic Review

FIRST PUBLISHED: 1966   FREQUENCY: S-A   CIRCULATION: 800

AFFILIATION: University of Delhi, Delhi School of Economics. Address same as journal's.

AUDIENCE: Academic/Professional

PERCENT OF UNSOLICITED ARTICLES/ISSUE: 90%   ISSN: 0019-4670

EDITORIAL POLICY: "Publishes papers on theoretical and applied economics including econometrics, though it concentrates on subjects relating to the Indian Economy. Surveys of research in the area of economic development, special detailed reviews of official reports on the Indian economy and review articles are frequently published."

REVIEW INFORMATION

REFEREED: No   ACCEPTANCE RATE: 20%

NUMBER OF REVIEWER(S)/MS., EXCLUDING IN-HOUSE EDITOR(S): 1

REVIEWER(S): External   ARTICLES/AVG. ISSUE: 6

REVIEWING CRITERIA USED: BLIND REVIEW: No

  MANUSCRIPT SUBMISSION AIDS: 1, 2

  BIAS SAFEGUARDS: 4, 5, 6, 9

AVERAGE REVIEW TIME: 6 mos.   PUBLICATION TIME LAG: 10 mos.

MANUSCRIPT RETURNED WITH COMMENTS: Yes

MANUSCRIPT INFORMATION

GUIDELINES PUBLISHED: Each issue

STYLE REQUIREMENTS PUBLISHED: Each issue

STYLE MANUAL USED: In-house

PREFERRED TOPICS: Developing economies, applied economic issues

QUERY LETTER: No   SIMULTANEOUS SUBMISSION: No

ABSTRACT WITH MANUSCRIPT: No   COVER LETTER: No

NUMBER OF MANUSCRIPT COPIES: 2   MANUSCRIPT LENGTH: 25 pp.

SUBMISSION FEE: No   PAGE CHARGES: No

MANUSCRIPT ACKNOWLEDGED: Yes   EARLY PUBLICATION OPTION: No

COPYRIGHT OWNER: Joint   REPRINTS: Not available

AUTHOR COMPENSATION: One-year subscription and 25 free reprints

MANUSCRIPT ADDRESS: V. Pandit, Managing Editor, The Indian Economic Review, Delhi School of Economics, University of Delhi, Delhi 1-10007, India

Industrial and Labor Relations Review

FIRST PUBLISHED: 1947   FREQUENCY: Q   CIRCULATION: 4,166

AFFILIATION: Cornell University, New York State School of Industrial and Labor Relations. Address same as journal's.

AUDIENCE: Academic/Professional

PERCENT OF UNSOLICITED ARTICLES/ISSUE: 100%   ISSN: 0019-7939

EDITORIAL POLICY: To publish articles reporting results of original research in all aspects of industrial and labor relations.

REVIEW INFORMATION

REFEREED: Yes (I-A)   ACCEPTANCE RATE: 20%

NUMBER OF REVIEWER(S)/MS., EXCLUDING IN-HOUSE EDITOR(S): 2

REVIEWER(S): External   ARTICLES/AVG. ISSUE: 8-9

REVIEWING CRITERIA USED: BLIND REVIEW: Yes (Board
  MANUSCRIPT SUBMISSION AIDS: 1   and external review)
  BIAS SAFEGUARDS: 3, 5, 7, 9

AVERAGE REVIEW TIME: 3 mos.   PUBLICATION TIME LAG: 12 mos.

MANUSCRIPT RETURNED WITH COMMENTS: Yes, SASE required

MANUSCRIPT INFORMATION

GUIDELINES PUBLISHED: Each issue

STYLE REQUIREMENTS PUBLISHED: No; available on request

STYLE MANUAL USED: In-house; Chicago

PREFERRED TOPICS: Industrial and labor relations

QUERY LETTER: No   SIMULTANEOUS SUBMISSION: No

ABSTRACT WITH MANUSCRIPT: 125 wds.   COVER LETTER: Yes

NUMBER OF MANUSCRIPT COPIES: 3   MANUSCRIPT LENGTH: 25 pp.

SUBMISSION FEE: No   PAGE CHARGES: No

MANUSCRIPT ACKNOWLEDGED: Yes   EARLY PUBLICATION OPTION: No

COPYRIGHT OWNER: Journal   REPRINTS: Optional purchase

AUTHOR COMPENSATION: One-year subscription and 5 free journals

MANUSCRIPT ADDRESS: Editor, Industrial and Labor Relations Review, Room 201a Research Building, Cornell University, Ithaca, NY 14851-0952

Industrial Relations

FIRST PUBLISHED: 1961   FREQUENCY: 3/Yr.   CIRCULATION: 2,500

AFFILIATION: University of California, Berkeley, Institute of
Industrial Relations. Address same as journal's.

AUDIENCE: Academic/Professional; Business/Industrial; Government

PERCENT OF UNSOLICITED ARTICLES/ISSUE: 85%   ISSN: 0019-8676

EDITORIAL POLICY: Publishes articles on all aspects of the employment
relationship.

REVIEW INFORMATION

REFEREED: Yes (I-A)   ACCEPTANCE RATE: 15%

NUMBER OF REVIEWER(S)/MS., EXCLUDING IN-HOUSE EDITOR(S): 3

REVIEWER(S): 1 board, 2 external   ARTICLES/AVG. ISSUE: 10

REVIEWING CRITERIA USED: BLIND REVIEW: Yes (Board
  MANUSCRIPT SUBMISSION AIDS: 1, 2   and external review)

  BIAS SAFEGUARDS: 3, 4, 5, 6, 7, 9*, 10

AVERAGE REVIEW TIME: 2 mos.   PUBLICATION TIME LAG: 6 mos.

MANUSCRIPT RETURNED WITH COMMENTS: No

MANUSCRIPT INFORMATION

GUIDELINES PUBLISHED: Each issue

STYLE REQUIREMENTS PUBLISHED: Each issue; also available on request

STYLE MANUAL USED: In-house

PREFERRED TOPICS: Employment relationships

QUERY LETTER: No   SIMULTANEOUS SUBMISSION: No

ABSTRACT WITH MANUSCRIPT: No   COVER LETTER: Yes

NUMBER OF MANUSCRIPT COPIES: 3   MANUSCRIPT LENGTH: 20 pp.

SUBMISSION FEE: No   PAGE CHARGES: No

MANUSCRIPT ACKNOWLEDGED: Yes   EARLY PUBLICATION OPTION: No

COPYRIGHT OWNER: Journal   REPRINTS: Optional purchase

AUTHOR COMPENSATION: None

MANUSCRIPT ADDRESS: Managing Editor, Industrial Relations, Institute
of Industrial Relations, University of California, Berkeley, CA
94720

Information Economics and Policy

FIRST PUBLISHED: 1983   FREQUENCY: Q   CIRCULATION: 600
AFFILIATION: None

AUDIENCE: Academic/Professional
PERCENT OF UNSOLICITED ARTICLES/ISSUE: 90%   ISSN: 0167-6245
EDITORIAL POLICY: Theoretical and applied research on information
  economics that has applications to public policy.

REVIEW INFORMATION

REFEREED: Yes (II-B)   ACCEPTANCE RATE: 20%
NUMBER OF REVIEWER(S)/MS., EXCLUDING IN-HOUSE EDITOR(S): 2
REVIEWER(S): Board and external   ARTICLES/AVG. ISSUE: 3-4
REVIEWING CRITERIA USED: BLIND REVIEW: No
  MANUSCRIPT SUBMISSION AIDS: 1
  BIAS SAFEGUARDS: 5, 6, 9
AVERAGE REVIEW TIME: 3 mos.   PUBLICATION TIME LAG: 6 mos.
MANUSCRIPT RETURNED WITH COMMENTS: Yes

MANUSCRIPT INFORMATION

GUIDELINES PUBLISHED: Each issue; also available on request
STYLE REQUIREMENTS PUBLISHED: No; available on request
STYLE MANUAL USED: In-house
PREFERRED TOPICS: Economics of uncertainty, telecommunications
  economics, economic regulation

QUERY LETTER: No   SIMULTANEOUS SUBMISSION: No
ABSTRACT WITH MANUSCRIPT: 100 wds.   COVER LETTER: No
NUMBER OF MANUSCRIPT COPIES: 5   MANUSCRIPT LENGTH: No limit

SUBMISSION FEE: No   PAGE CHARGES: No

MANUSCRIPT ACKNOWLEDGED: Yes   EARLY PUBLICATION OPTION: No
COPYRIGHT OWNER: Publisher   REPRINTS: Not available

AUTHOR COMPENSATION: 1 free journal and 25 free reprints/tear sheets
MANUSCRIPT ADDRESS: Prof. Roger Noll, Editor-in-Chief, Information
  Economics and Policy, Department of Economics, Stanford University,
  Stanford, CA 94305

Inquiry

FIRST PUBLISHED: 1963   FREQUENCY: Q   CIRCULATION: 3,000

AFFILIATION: Blue Cross and Blue Shield Association. Address same as journal's.

AUDIENCE: Academic/Professional; Business/Industrial; Government

PERCENT OF UNSOLICITED ARTICLES/ISSUE: 61-80%   ISSN: 0046-9580

EDITORIAL POLICY: Publishes empirical research and policy papers on topics relating to the organization, provision, and financing of health care.

REVIEW INFORMATION

REFEREED: Yes (II-A)   ACCEPTANCE RATE: 50%

NUMBER OF REVIEWER(S)/MS., EXCLUDING IN-HOUSE EDITOR(S): 2

REVIEWER(S): Board and external   ARTICLES/AVG. ISSUE: 9-10

REVIEWING CRITERIA USED: BLIND REVIEW: Yes (Board

  MANUSCRIPT SUBMISSION AIDS: 1   review only)

  BIAS SAFEGUARDS: 3, 5, 8, 9*, 10

AVERAGE REVIEW TIME: 6 wks.   PUBLICATION TIME LAG: 4 mos.

MANUSCRIPT RETURNED WITH COMMENTS: No

MANUSCRIPT INFORMATION

GUIDELINES PUBLISHED: Each issue

STYLE REQUIREMENTS PUBLISHED: No; available on request

STYLE MANUAL USED: In-house; Chicago

PREFERRED TOPICS: Organization, provision, and financing of health care

QUERY LETTER: No   SIMULTANEOUS SUBMISSION: No

ABSTRACT WITH MANUSCRIPT: 120 wds.   COVER LETTER: Yes

NUMBER OF MANUSCRIPT COPIES: 3   MANUSCRIPT LENGTH: 30 pp. max.

SUBMISSION FEE: No   PAGE CHARGES: No

MANUSCRIPT ACKNOWLEDGED: Yes   EARLY PUBLICATION OPTION: No

COPYRIGHT OWNER: Blue Cross and Blue   REPRINTS: Optional purchase
  Shield Association

AUTHOR COMPENSATION: 10 free tear sheets

MANUSCRIPT ADDRESS: Roberta Gutman, Managing Editor, Inquiry, Blue Cross and Blue Shield Association, 676 North St. Clair Street, Chicago, IL 60611

International Economic Review

FIRST PUBLISHED: 1960   FREQUENCY: 3/Yr.   CIRCULATION: 2,000+

AFFILIATION: University of Pennsylvania, Department of Economics,
and Osaka University Institute of Social and Economic Research
Association, 6-1, Mihogaoka, Ibaraki, Osaka 567, Japan

AUDIENCE: Academic/Professional; Business/Industrial; Government

PERCENT OF UNSOLICITED ARTICLES/ISSUE: 100%   ISSN: 0020-6598

EDITORIAL POLICY: "Interested primarily in publishing articles on
quantitative economics and welcomes contributions of empirical
works, as well as those in mathematical economics and statistical
theory related to quantitative aspects of economics. . . . The
editors welcome also contributions to nonquantitative economics."

REVIEW INFORMATION

REFEREED: Yes (I-B)   ACCEPTANCE RATE: 20%

NUMBER OF REVIEWER(S)/MS., EXCLUDING IN-HOUSE EDITOR(S): 2

REVIEWER(S): External   ARTICLES/AVG. ISSUE: 15-18

REVIEWING CRITERIA USED: BLIND REVIEW: No

  MANUSCRIPT SUBMISSION AIDS: 1

  BIAS SAFEGUARDS: 4, 5, 6, 7, 9

AVERAGE REVIEW TIME: 3 mos.   PUBLICATION TIME LAG: 3-6 mos.

MANUSCRIPT RETURNED WITH COMMENTS: No

MANUSCRIPT INFORMATION

GUIDELINES PUBLISHED: Each issue

STYLE REQUIREMENTS PUBLISHED: No; available on request

STYLE MANUAL USED: Chicago

PREFERRED TOPICS: Quantitative economics

QUERY LETTER: No   SIMULTANEOUS SUBMISSION: No

ABSTRACT WITH MANUSCRIPT: Yes   COVER LETTER: Yes

NUMBER OF MANUSCRIPT COPIES: 3   MANUSCRIPT LENGTH: Not specified

SUBMISSION FEE: $35.   PAGE CHARGES: No

MANUSCRIPT ACKNOWLEDGED: Yes   EARLY PUBLICATION OPTION: No

COPYRIGHT OWNER: Journal and publisher REPRINTS: Optional purchase

AUTHOR COMPENSATION: None

MANUSCRIPT ADDRESS: Wilfred J. Ethier, Editor, International Economic
Review, Department of Economics, 3718 Locust Walk, University of
Pennsylvania, Philadelphia, PA 19104

International Journal of Industrial Organization

FIRST PUBLISHED: 1983   FREQUENCY: Q   CIRCULATION: 800

AFFILIATION: European Association for Research in Industrial Economics, c/o EIASM, Place Stephenie 20, B-1050 Bruxelles, Belguim.

AUDIENCE: Academic/Professional

PERCENT OF UNSOLICITED ARTICLES/ISSUE: 100%   ISSN: 0167-7187

EDITORIAL POLICY: "An international venture with strong roots in
Europe and Japan, but also with important connexions with the
U.S." Aims at a "full coverage of both theoretical and empirical
questions within the field of Industrial Organization, broadly
defined."

REVIEW INFORMATION

REFEREED: Yes (I-B)   ACCEPTANCE RATE: 33%

NUMBER OF REVIEWER(S)/MS., EXCLUDING IN-HOUSE EDITOR(S): 2

REVIEWER(S): External   ARTICLES/AVG. ISSUE: 8

REVIEWING CRITERIA USED: BLIND REVIEW: No

  MANUSCRIPT SUBMISSION AIDS: 1, 2

  BIAS SAFEGUARDS: 5, 6, 7, 9

AVERAGE REVIEW TIME: 2-3 mos.   PUBLICATION TIME LAG: 6 mos.

MANUSCRIPT RETURNED WITH COMMENTS: No

MANUSCRIPT INFORMATION

GUIDELINES PUBLISHED: Each issue

STYLE REQUIREMENTS PUBLISHED: Each issue

STYLE MANUAL USED: In-house

PREFERRED TOPICS: Industrial organization: "market structure and performance . . . internal organization of firms, all facets of technological change, productivity analysis," etc.

QUERY LETTER: No   SIMULTANEOUS SUBMISSION: No

ABSTRACT WITH MANUSCRIPT: 100 wds.   COVER LETTER: Yes

NUMBER OF MANUSCRIPT COPIES: 3   MANUSCRIPT LENGTH: No limit

SUBMISSION FEE: No   PAGE CHARGES: No

MANUSCRIPT ACKNOWLEDGED: Yes   EARLY PUBLICATION OPTION: No

COPYRIGHT OWNER: Publisher   REPRINTS: Optional purchase

AUTHOR COMPENSATION: None

MANUSCRIPT ADDRESS: Dr. P. L. Stoneman, Managing Editor, International
Journal of Industrial Organization, Department of Economics,
University of Warwick, Coventry, CV4 7AL, U.K.

International Journal of Social Economics

FIRST PUBLISHED: 1974   FREQUENCY: 7/Yr.   CIRCULATION: 500

AFFILIATION: International Institute of Social Economics, Enholmes
  Hall, Patrington, Hull, England HU12 OPR

AUDIENCE: Academic/Professional; Business/Industrial; Government

PERCENT OF UNSOLICITED ARTICLES/ISSUE: 61-80%   ISSN: 0306-8293

EDITORIAL POLICY: To provide reports of current developments in
  the field of social economics; to facilitate the interchange of
  information about social economics among practitioners on a world-
  wide basis.

REVIEW INFORMATION

REFEREED: Yes (III-B)   ACCEPTANCE RATE: 50%

NUMBER OF REVIEWER(S)/MS., EXCLUDING IN-HOUSE EDITOR(S): 2

REVIEWER(S): Board   ARTICLES/AVG. ISSUE: 6

REVIEWING CRITERIA USED: BLIND REVIEW: No

  MANUSCRIPT SUBMISSION AIDS: 1

  BIAS SAFEGUARDS: 4, 5, 6

AVERAGE REVIEW TIME: 2 wks.   PUBLICATION TIME LAG: 12-24 mos.

MANUSCRIPT RETURNED WITH COMMENTS: No

MANUSCRIPT INFORMATION

GUIDELINES PUBLISHED: Each issue (excl. special issues or monographs)

STYLE REQUIREMENTS PUBLISHED: No; available on request

STYLE MANUAL USED: MLA

PREFERRED TOPICS: Social economics

QUERY LETTER: No   SIMULTANEOUS SUBMISSION: No

ABSTRACT WITH MANUSCRIPT: 100 wds.   COVER LETTER: Yes

NUMBER OF MANUSCRIPT COPIES: 2   MANUSCRIPT LENGTH: 6,000 wds.

SUBMISSION FEE: No   PAGE CHARGES: No

MANUSCRIPT ACKNOWLEDGED: Yes, SASE req. EARLY PUBLICATION OPTION: No

COPYRIGHT OWNER: Publisher   REPRINTS: Optional purchase

AUTHOR COMPENSATION: None

MANUSCRIPT ADDRESS: Dr. John Conway O'Brien, Editor, International
  Journal of Social Economics, Applied Ethics Program, California
  State University, Fresno, CA 93740

International Labour Review

FIRST PUBLISHED: 1921   FREQUENCY: B-M   CIRCULATION: 9,800

AFFILIATION: International Labour Organisation. Address same as journal's.

AUDIENCE: Academic/Professional; Business/Industrial; Government

PERCENT OF UNSOLICITED ARTICLES/ISSUE: 0-10%   ISSN: 0020-7780

EDITORIAL POLICY: Publishes articles of more than parochial (ideally, broad international) interest on a wide range of "labour" issues extending through employment, promotion, training, occupational safety and health, industrial relations, social security, conditions of work, freedom of association, development economics, etc. Editions in English, French, and Spanish.

REVIEW INFORMATION

REFEREED: Yes (III-B)   ACCEPTANCE RATE: 9%

NUMBER OF REVIEWER(S)/MS., EXCLUDING IN-HOUSE EDITOR(S): 2

REVIEWER(S): ILO specialists   ARTICLES/AVG. ISSUE: 8

REVIEWING CRITERIA USED: BLIND REVIEW: No

  MANUSCRIPT SUBMISSION AIDS: 1, 2

  BIAS SAFEGUARDS: 0

AVERAGE REVIEW TIME: 5 wks.   PUBLICATION TIME LAG: 3 mos.

MANUSCRIPT RETURNED WITH COMMENTS: No

MANUSCRIPT INFORMATION

GUIDELINES PUBLISHED: Each issue

STYLE REQUIREMENTS PUBLISHED: Each issue

STYLE MANUAL USED: In-house

PREFERRED TOPICS: Wide range of "labour" issues

QUERY LETTER: No   SIMULTANEOUS SUBMISSION: No

ABSTRACT WITH MANUSCRIPT: 100 wds.   COVER LETTER: Yes

NUMBER OF MANUSCRIPT COPIES: 2   MANUSCRIPT LENGTH: 25 pp.

SUBMISSION FEE: No   PAGE CHARGES: No

MANUSCRIPT ACKNOWLEDGED: Yes   EARLY PUBLICATION OPTION: No

COPYRIGHT OWNER: Publisher   REPRINTS: Optional purchase

AUTHOR COMPENSATION: 2 free journals and 25 free reprints/tear sheets

MANUSCRIPT ADDRESS: The Chief Editor, International Labour Review, International Labour Office, CH-1211 Geneva 22, Switzerland

International Organization

FIRST PUBLISHED: 1947   FREQUENCY: Q   CIRCULATION: 2,900

AFFILIATION: World Peace Foundation, 22 Batterymarch St., Boston, MA 02109

AUDIENCE: Academic/Professional

PERCENT OF UNSOLICITED ARTICLES/ISSUE: 81-100%   ISSN: 0020-8183

EDITORIAL POLICY: Publishes manuscripts on all aspects of world politics and international political economy.

REVIEW INFORMATION

REFEREED: Yes (III-A)   ACCEPTANCE RATE: 16.4%

NUMBER OF REVIEWER(S)/MS., EXCLUDING IN-HOUSE EDITOR(S): 2

REVIEWER(S): Board   ARTICLES/AVG. ISSUE: 5-6

REVIEWING CRITERIA USED: BLIND REVIEW: Yes (Board and external review)

  MANUSCRIPT SUBMISSION AIDS: 1, 2

  BIAS SAFEGUARDS: 3, 5, 9, 10

AVERAGE REVIEW TIME: 6-8 wks.   PUBLICATION TIME LAG: Varies

MANUSCRIPT RETURNED WITH COMMENTS: No

MANUSCRIPT INFORMATION

GUIDELINES PUBLISHED: Each issue

STYLE REQUIREMENTS PUBLISHED: Each issue

STYLE MANUAL USED: Chicago

PREFERRED TOPICS: World politics, international political economy

QUERY LETTER: No   SIMULTANEOUS SUBMISSION: No

ABSTRACT WITH MANUSCRIPT: No   COVER LETTER: Yes

NUMBER OF MANUSCRIPT COPIES: 3   MANUSCRIPT LENGTH: 60 pp. max.

SUBMISSION FEE: No   PAGE CHARGES: No

MANUSCRIPT ACKNOWLEDGED: Yes   EARLY PUBLICATION OPTION: No

COPYRIGHT OWNER: Publisher   REPRINTS: Optional purchase

AUTHOR COMPENSATION: 25 free reprints/tear sheets

MANUSCRIPT ADDRESS: Editor, International Organization, Department of Political Science, Stanford University, Stanford, CA 94305

International Regional Science Review

FIRST PUBLISHED: 1965   FREQUENCY: 3/Yr.   CIRCULATION: 3,262

AFFILIATION: Regional Science Association, University of Illinois, 901
   South Mathews, Urbana, IL 61801, and West Virginia University,
   Regional Research Institute, Morgantown, WV 26506

AUDIENCE: Academic/Professional; Government

PERCENT OF UNSOLICITED ARTICLES/ISSUE: 95%   ISSN: 0160-0176

EDITORIAL POLICY: Seeks manuscripts that advance the fields of
   regional science, regional economics, economic geography, and
   related areas, whether they do so theoretically, conceptually,
   methodologically, empirically, or otherwise. Particularly seeks
   manuscripts dealing with planning and policy issues in which the
   spatial or regional dimension plays a central role.

REVIEW INFORMATION

REFEREED: Yes (I-A)   ACCEPTANCE RATE: 15%

NUMBER OF REVIEWER(S)/MS., EXCLUDING IN-HOUSE EDITOR(S): 3

REVIEWER(S): 1 board, 2 external   ARTICLES/AVG. ISSUE: 6

REVIEWING CRITERIA USED: BLIND REVIEW: Yes (Board
   MANUSCRIPT SUBMISSION AIDS: 1, 2   and external review)

   BIAS SAFEGUARDS: 3, 5, 6, 7, 9

AVERAGE REVIEW TIME: 10 wks.   PUBLICATION TIME LAG: 10 mos.

MANUSCRIPT RETURNED WITH COMMENTS: No

MANUSCRIPT INFORMATION

GUIDELINES PUBLISHED: Each issue

STYLE REQUIREMENTS PUBLISHED: Vol. 9, No. 1 (1984); also on request

STYLE MANUAL USED: In-house; Chicago

PREFERRED TOPICS: Regional economics, population economics, economic
   geography, regional labor economics, urban and regional policy,
   industrial location

QUERY LETTER: No   SIMULTANEOUS SUBMISSION: No

ABSTRACT WITH MANUSCRIPT: 100 wds.   COVER LETTER: Yes

NUMBER OF MANUSCRIPT COPIES: 4   MANUSCRIPT LENGTH: 15-80 pp.

SUBMISSION FEE: No   PAGE CHARGES: No

MANUSCRIPT ACKNOWLEDGED: Yes   EARLY PUBLICATION OPTION: Yes

COPYRIGHT OWNER: Journal   REPRINTS: Optional purchase

AUTHOR COMPENSATION: None

MANUSCRIPT ADDRESS: Andrew M. Isserman, Editor, International Regional
   Science Review, Regional Research Institute, West Virginia University,
   Morgantown, WV 26506

International Review of Law and Economics

FIRST PUBLISHED: 1981   FREQUENCY: S-A   CIRCULATION: 600
AFFILIATION: None

AUDIENCE: Academic/Professional; Government
PERCENT OF UNSOLICITED ARTICLES/ISSUE: 100%   ISSN: 0144-8188
EDITORIAL POLICY: Publishes articles at interface of law and
  economics. Catholic with respect to method. International in scope.

REVIEW INFORMATION

REFEREED: Yes (I-B)   ACCEPTANCE RATE: 30%
NUMBER OF REVIEWER(S)/MS., EXCLUDING IN-HOUSE EDITOR(S): 2
REVIEWER(S): External   ARTICLES/AVG. ISSUE: 8-10
REVIEWING CRITERIA USED: BLIND REVIEW: No
  MANUSCRIPT SUBMISSION AIDS: 1, 2
  BIAS SAFEGUARDS: 4, 5, 6, 7, 9
AVERAGE REVIEW TIME: 3 mos.   PUBLICATION TIME LAG: 6 mos.
MANUSCRIPT RETURNED WITH COMMENTS: Yes

MANUSCRIPT INFORMATION

GUIDELINES PUBLISHED: Each issue
STYLE REQUIREMENTS PUBLISHED: Each issue
STYLE MANUAL USED: In-house
PREFERRED TOPICS: Law and economics only

QUERY LETTER: No   SIMULTANEOUS SUBMISSION: No
ABSTRACT WITH MANUSCRIPT: No   COVER LETTER: Yes
NUMBER OF MANUSCRIPT COPIES: 2   MANUSCRIPT LENGTH: 10,000
                                        wds. max.
SUBMISSION FEE: No   PAGE CHARGES: No

MANUSCRIPT ACKNOWLEDGED: Yes   EARLY PUBLICATION OPTION: Yes
COPYRIGHT OWNER: Journal   REPRINTS: Optional purchase

AUTHOR COMPENSATION: None
MANUSCRIPT ADDRESS: Prof. C. K. Rowley, Editor, International
  Review of Law and Economics, Center for Study of Public Choice,
  George Mason University, Fairfax, VA 22030

Jahrbücher für Nationalökonomie und Statistik

FIRST PUBLISHED: 1863   FREQUENCY: Q   CIRCULATION: 1,000
AFFILIATION: None

AUDIENCE: Academic/Professional
PERCENT OF UNSOLICITED ARTICLES/ISSUE: 95-100%   ISSN: 0021-4027
EDITORIAL POLICY: Devoted to publications in the field of economic
  theory and statistical methodology; only high-level contributions
  that avoid over-mathematization are accepted. Moreover, sufficient
  novelty and originality are required.

REVIEW INFORMATION

REFEREED: No   ACCEPTANCE RATE: 75%
NUMBER OF REVIEWER(S)/MS., EXCLUDING IN-HOUSE EDITOR(S): 1
REVIEWER(S): External   ARTICLES/AVG. ISSUE: 5-6
REVIEWING CRITERIA USED: BLIND REVIEW: No
  MANUSCRIPT SUBMISSION AIDS: 1, 2
  BIAS SAFEGUARDS: 4, 5, 6, 9*
AVERAGE REVIEW TIME: 2 mos.   PUBLICATION TIME LAG: 6 mos.
MANUSCRIPT RETURNED WITH COMMENTS: Yes

MANUSCRIPT INFORMATION

GUIDELINES PUBLISHED: Each issue
STYLE REQUIREMENTS PUBLISHED: Each issue
STYLE MANUAL USED: In-house
PREFERRED TOPICS: Economic theory, statistics, econometrics

QUERY LETTER: No   SIMULTANEOUS SUBMISSION: No
ABSTRACT WITH MANUSCRIPT: 100 wds.   COVER LETTER: No
NUMBER OF MANUSCRIPT COPIES: 2   MANUSCRIPT LENGTH: 12-15 pp.

SUBMISSION FEE: No   PAGE CHARGES: No

MANUSCRIPT ACKNOWLEDGED: Yes   EARLY PUBLICATION OPTION: No
COPYRIGHT OWNER: Publisher   REPRINTS: Not available

AUTHOR COMPENSATION: None
MANUSCRIPT ADDRESS: Prof. Dr. Alfred E. Ott, Editor, Jahrbücher für
  Nationalökonomie und Statistik, Wirtschaftswissenschaftliches
  Seminar, Mohlstrasse 36, 7400 Tübingen, West Germany (B.R.D.)

Journal for Studies in Economics and Econometrics /
Tydskrif vir Studies in Ekonomie en Ekonometrie

FIRST PUBLISHED: 1977   FREQUENCY: Q   CIRCULATION: 500
AFFILIATION: None

AUDIENCE: Academic/Professional
PERCENT OF UNSOLICITED ARTICLES/ISSUE: 95%   ISSN: 0379-6205
EDITORIAL POLICY: "An international journal that publishes articles
  in the field of study of Economics (in the widest sense of the word).
  All contributions are welcome but are subject to an objective selection procedure to ensure that all published articles answer the
  criteria of scientific objectivity, importance, competence, repli-
  cability and intelligibility."

REVIEW INFORMATION

REFEREED: Yes (I-A)   ACCEPTANCE RATE: 30%
NUMBER OF REVIEWER(S)/MS., EXCLUDING IN-HOUSE EDITOR(S): 2
REVIEWER(S): External   ARTICLES/AVG. ISSUE: 4
REVIEWING CRITERIA USED: BLIND REVIEW: Yes (All except
  MANUSCRIPT SUBMISSION AIDS: 1, 2   final selection)
  BIAS SAFEGUARDS: 3, 4, 5, 6, 7, 8, 9
AVERAGE REVIEW TIME: 4 wks.   PUBLICATION TIME LAG: 2 wks.
MANUSCRIPT RETURNED WITH COMMENTS: Yes, SASE required

MANUSCRIPT INFORMATION

GUIDELINES PUBLISHED: Each issue
STYLE REQUIREMENTS PUBLISHED: Each issue
STYLE MANUAL USED: In-house
PREFERRED TOPICS: Economics

QUERY LETTER: No   SIMULTANEOUS SUBMISSION: Yes
ABSTRACT WITH MANUSCRIPT: 150 wds. COVER LETTER: Yes
NUMBER OF MANUSCRIPT COPIES: 4   MANUSCRIPT LENGTH: 25 pp.

SUBMISSION FEE: No   PAGE CHARGES: No

MANUSCRIPT ACKNOWLEDGED: Yes   EARLY PUBLICATION OPTION: No
COPYRIGHT OWNER: Publisher   REPRINTS: Optional purchase

AUTHOR COMPENSATION: None
MANUSCRIPT ADDRESS: O. D. J. Stuart, Editor, Journal for Studies in
  Economics and Econometrics, Bureau for Economic Research, Private
  Bag 5050, University of Stellenbosch 7600, South Africa

Journal of Accounting and Economics

FIRST PUBLISHED: 1979   FREQUENCY: 3/Yr.   CIRCULATION: 900

AFFILIATION: University of Rochester, Graduate School of Management. Address same as journal's.

AUDIENCE: Academic/Professional

PERCENT OF UNSOLICITED ARTICLES/ISSUE: 90%   ISSN: 0165-4101

EDITORIAL POLICY: Publishes articles on the application of economic theory to the explanation of accounting phenomena.

REVIEW INFORMATION

REFEREED: No   ACCEPTANCE RATE: 13%

NUMBER OF REVIEWER(S)/MS., EXCLUDING IN-HOUSE EDITOR(S): 1

REVIEWER(S): Board   ARTICLES/AVG. ISSUE: 4

REVIEWING CRITERIA USED: BLIND REVIEW: Yes (Board
  MANUSCRIPT SUBMISSION AIDS: 1, 2   review only)
  BIAS SAFEGUARDS: 3, 5, 9

AVERAGE REVIEW TIME: 5 wks.   PUBLICATION TIME LAG: 4 mos.

MANUSCRIPT RETURNED WITH COMMENTS: Yes

MANUSCRIPT INFORMATION

GUIDELINES PUBLISHED: Each issue

STYLE REQUIREMENTS PUBLISHED: Each issue

STYLE MANUAL USED: In-house

PREFERRED TOPICS: Accounting, economics, finance

QUERY LETTER: No   SIMULTANEOUS SUBMISSION: No

ABSTRACT WITH MANUSCRIPT: 100 wds.   COVER LETTER: Yes

NUMBER OF MANUSCRIPT COPIES: 3   MANUSCRIPT LENGTH: 20 printed
                                        pages

SUBMISSION FEE: $40. for subscribers; PAGE CHARGES: No
  $50. for nonsubscribers

MANUSCRIPT ACKNOWLEDGED: Yes   EARLY PUBLICATION OPTION: No

COPYRIGHT OWNER: Publisher   REPRINTS: Optional purchase

AUTHOR COMPENSATION: None

MANUSCRIPT ADDRESS: Prof. Ross L. Watts, Editor, Journal of Accounting and Economics, Graduate School of Management, University of Rochester, Rochester, NY 14627

Journal of Accounting Research

FIRST PUBLISHED: 1963   FREQUENCY: S-A   CIRCULATION: 3,000

AFFILIATION: University of Chicago, Graduate School of Business,
   Institute of Professional Accounting. Address same as journal's.

AUDIENCE: Academic/Professional; Business/Industrial

PERCENT OF UNSOLICITED ARTICLES/ISSUE: 100%   ISSN: 0021-8456

EDITORIAL POLICY: Reports "new developments in accounting occasioned

   by similarly new developments in management science--operations

   research, the behavioral sciences and other related accounting

   fields."

REVIEW INFORMATION

REFEREED: No   ACCEPTANCE RATE: 11-20%

NUMBER OF REVIEWER(S)/MS., EXCLUDING IN-HOUSE EDITOR(S): 1

REVIEWER(S): Board or external   ARTICLES/AVG. ISSUE: 15

REVIEWING CRITERIA USED: BLIND REVIEW: Yes (See journal
   MANUSCRIPT SUBMISSION AIDS: 1   guidelines)
   BIAS SAFEGUARDS: 3, 5, 9

AVERAGE REVIEW TIME: 3 mos.   PUBLICATION TIME LAG: 12 mos.

MANUSCRIPT RETURNED WITH COMMENTS: Yes

MANUSCRIPT INFORMATION

GUIDELINES PUBLISHED: Each issue (brief); also on request (detailed)

STYLE REQUIREMENTS PUBLISHED: No; available on request

STYLE MANUAL USED: In-house

PREFERRED TOPICS: Accounting

QUERY LETTER: No   SIMULTANEOUS SUBMISSION: No

ABSTRACT WITH MANUSCRIPT: No   COVER LETTER: Yes

NUMBER OF MANUSCRIPT COPIES: 3   MANUSCRIPT LENGTH: Varies

SUBMISSION FEE: $35.00   PAGE CHARGES: No

MANUSCRIPT ACKNOWLEDGED: No   EARLY PUBLICATION OPTION: N.R.

COPYRIGHT OWNER: Journal   REPRINTS: Optional purchase

AUTHOR COMPENSATION: None

MANUSCRIPT ADDRESS: Editor, Journal of Accounting Research, Graduate
   School of Business, University of Chicago, 1101 East 58th Street,
   Chicago, IL 60637

Journal of Banking and Finance

FIRST PUBLISHED: 1977   FREQUENCY: Q   CIRCULATION: 1,000

AFFILIATION: European Finance Association, c/o EFMD, Rue Washington 40,
 B-1050, Brussels, Belguim, and French Finance Association.

AUDIENCE: Academic/Professional

PERCENT OF UNSOLICITED ARTICLES/ISSUE: 100%   ISSN: 0378-4266

EDITORIAL POLICY: Aims "to provide an outlet for the increasing flow
 of scholarly research concerning financial institutions and the
 money and capital markets within which they function. The emphasis
 will primarily be on applied and policy oriented research."

REVIEW INFORMATION

REFEREED: Yes (II-A)   ACCEPTANCE RATE: 20%

NUMBER OF REVIEWER(S)/MS., EXCLUDING IN-HOUSE EDITOR(S): 2

REVIEWER(S): Board and external   ARTICLES/AVG. ISSUE: 8-10

REVIEWING CRITERIA USED: BLIND REVIEW: Yes (Board
  MANUSCRIPT SUBMISSION AIDS: 1, 2   and external review)

  BIAS SAFEGUARDS: 3, 5, 6, 9

AVERAGE REVIEW TIME: 2-3 mos.   PUBLICATION TIME LAG: 6-9 mos.

MANUSCRIPT RETURNED WITH COMMENTS: Yes

MANUSCRIPT INFORMATION

GUIDELINES PUBLISHED: Each issue

STYLE REQUIREMENTS PUBLISHED: Each issue

STYLE MANUAL USED: In-house

PREFERRED TOPICS: Banking and finance, especially international

QUERY LETTER: No   SIMULTANEOUS SUBMISSION: No

ABSTRACT WITH MANUSCRIPT: 100-150 wds. COVER LETTER: Yes

NUMBER OF MANUSCRIPT COPIES: 4   MANUSCRIPT LENGTH: 4-35 pp.

SUBMISSION FEE: $20. for members/   PAGE CHARGES: No
  subscribers; $45. for others

MANUSCRIPT ACKNOWLEDGED: Yes   EARLY PUBLICATION OPTION: No

COPYRIGHT OWNER: Publisher   REPRINTS: Optional purchase

AUTHOR COMPENSATION: None

MANUSCRIPT ADDRESS: Emilia Carulli, Assistant to Editor, Journal of
 Banking and Finance, A.B.I., Piazza del Gesu, 49, 00186 Roma, Italy

The Journal of Behavioral Economics

FIRST PUBLISHED: 1972   FREQUENCY: S-A   CIRCULATION: 450

AFFILIATION: Western Illinois University, College of Business, Center for Business and Economic Research. Address same as journal's.

AUDIENCE: Academic/Professional

PERCENT OF UNSOLICITED ARTICLES/ISSUE: 61-80%   ISSN: 0090-5720

EDITORIAL POLICY: "The two goals of The Journal are to (1) further knowledge of real economic phenomena by integrating psychological and sociological variables into economic analysis and (2) promote interdisciplinary research by academicians and practitioners dealing in economics, the behavioral sciences and public policy."

REVIEW INFORMATION

REFEREED: Yes (III-B)   ACCEPTANCE RATE: 30%

NUMBER OF REVIEWER(S)/MS., EXCLUDING IN-HOUSE EDITOR(S): 3

REVIEWER(S): Board   ARTICLES/AVG. ISSUE: 6

REVIEWING CRITERIA USED: BLIND REVIEW: No

  MANUSCRIPT SUBMISSION AIDS: 1, 2

  BIAS SAFEGUARDS: 4, 5, 6, 8, 9

AVERAGE REVIEW TIME: 3 mos.   PUBLICATION TIME LAG: 12 mos.

MANUSCRIPT RETURNED WITH COMMENTS: Occasionally

MANUSCRIPT INFORMATION

GUIDELINES PUBLISHED: Each issue; also available on request

STYLE REQUIREMENTS PUBLISHED: Each issue; also available on request

STYLE MANUAL USED: In-house

PREFERRED TOPICS: Economics, psychology, sociology, political science, marketing, management

QUERY LETTER: No   SIMULTANEOUS SUBMISSION: Yes

ABSTRACT WITH MANUSCRIPT: 2 pp.   COVER LETTER: Yes

NUMBER OF MANUSCRIPT COPIES: 3   MANUSCRIPT LENGTH: 10-30 pp.

SUBMISSION FEE: No   PAGE CHARGES: No

MANUSCRIPT ACKNOWLEDGED: Yes   EARLY PUBLICATION OPTION: No

COPYRIGHT OWNER: Publisher   REPRINTS: Optional purchase

AUTHOR COMPENSATION: 1 free journal and 5 free reprints

MANUSCRIPT ADDRESS: Dr. Richard E. Hattwick, Editor, The Journal of Behavioral Economics, Center for Business and Economic Research, Western Illinois University, Macomb, IL 61455

Journal of Business

FIRST PUBLISHED: 1928   FREQUENCY: Q   CIRCULATION: 5,000

AFFILIATION: University of Chicago, Graduate School of Business. Address same as journal's.

AUDIENCE: Academic/Professional

PERCENT OF UNSOLICITED ARTICLES/ISSUE: 81-100%   ISSN: 0021-9398

EDITORIAL POLICY: "Devoted to the publication of important new ideas and research findings in business administration. . . . Will publish only papers that make an original and substantive contribution to knowledge and that are prepared in a manner consistent with high standards of scholarship and evidence."

REVIEW INFORMATION

REFEREED: Yes (I-B)   ACCEPTANCE RATE: 40-50%

NUMBER OF REVIEWER(S)/MS., EXCLUDING IN-HOUSE EDITOR(S): 2

REVIEWER(S): External   ARTICLES/AVG. ISSUE: 6-8

REVIEWING CRITERIA USED: BLIND REVIEW: No

  MANUSCRIPT SUBMISSION AIDS: 0

  BIAS SAFEGUARDS: 5, 7, 9

AVERAGE REVIEW TIME: 3 mos.   PUBLICATION TIME LAG: 7 mos.

MANUSCRIPT RETURNED WITH COMMENTS: Yes

MANUSCRIPT INFORMATION

GUIDELINES PUBLISHED: No; available on request

STYLE REQUIREMENTS PUBLISHED: No; available on request

STYLE MANUAL USED: Chicago

PREFERRED TOPICS: "Entire range of disciplines and practices which together comprise business administration"

QUERY LETTER: No   SIMULTANEOUS SUBMISSION: No

ABSTRACT WITH MANUSCRIPT: 100 wds.   COVER LETTER: Yes

NUMBER OF MANUSCRIPT COPIES: 2   MANUSCRIPT LENGTH: No limit

SUBMISSION FEE: No   PAGE CHARGES: No

MANUSCRIPT ACKNOWLEDGED: Yes   EARLY PUBLICATION OPTION: No

COPYRIGHT OWNER: Publisher   REPRINTS: Optional purchase

AUTHOR COMPENSATION: 10 free journals

MANUSCRIPT ADDRESS: Editor, Journal of Business, Graduate School of Business, University of Chicago, 1101 East 58th Street, Chicago, IL 60637

Journal of Business and Economic Statistics

FIRST PUBLISHED: 1983   FREQUENCY: Q   CIRCULATION: 2,400

AFFILIATION: American Statistical Association, 806 15th St., N.W., Washington, D.C. 20005

AUDIENCE: Academic/Professional; Business/Industrial; Government

PERCENT OF UNSOLICITED ARTICLES/ISSUE: 81-100%   ISSN: 0735-0015

EDITORIAL POLICY: Publishes articles dealing with applied problems in business and economic statistics.

REVIEW INFORMATION

REFEREED: Yes (I-B)   ACCEPTANCE RATE: 25%

NUMBER OF REVIEWER(S)/MS., EXCLUDING IN-HOUSE EDITOR(S): 3

REVIEWER(S): 1 board, 2 external   ARTICLES/AVG. ISSUE: 10

REVIEWING CRITERIA USED: BLIND REVIEW: No

  MANUSCRIPT SUBMISSION AIDS: 1

  BIAS SAFEGUARDS: 4, 5, 7, 9

AVERAGE REVIEW TIME: 3 mos.   PUBLICATION TIME LAG: 5 mos.

MANUSCRIPT RETURNED WITH COMMENTS: No

MANUSCRIPT INFORMATION

GUIDELINES PUBLISHED: Each issue

STYLE REQUIREMENTS PUBLISHED: No; available on request

STYLE MANUAL USED: ASA

PREFERRED TOPICS: Business and economic statistics

QUERY LETTER: No   SIMULTANEOUS SUBMISSION: No

ABSTRACT WITH MANUSCRIPT: 200 wds.   COVER LETTER: Yes

NUMBER OF MANUSCRIPT COPIES: 4   MANUSCRIPT LENGTH: 30 pp.

SUBMISSION FEE: No   PAGE CHARGES: No

MANUSCRIPT ACKNOWLEDGED: Yes   EARLY PUBLICATION OPTION: No

COPYRIGHT OWNER: Journal   REPRINTS: Optional purchase

AUTHOR COMPENSATION: None

MANUSCRIPT ADDRESS: Prof. A. Ronald Gallant, Editor, Journal of Business and Economic Statistics, North Carolina State University, P.O. Box 8203, Raleigh, NC 27695-8203

Journal of Common Market Studies

FIRST PUBLISHED: 1962   FREQUENCY: Q   CIRCULATION: 1,500

AFFILIATION: University Association for Contemporary European Studies.
  Address same as journal's.

AUDIENCE: Academic/Professional; Government

PERCENT OF UNSOLICITED ARTICLES/ISSUE: 81-100%   ISSN: 0021-9886

EDITORIAL POLICY: The analysis of international integration and the
  experience of regional groupings throughout the world, with particular
  attention to the EEC. The journal seeks to maintain an interdisciplinary character. It particularly invites contributions that
  throw light on important current policy issues.

REVIEW INFORMATION

REFEREED: Yes (I-B)   ACCEPTANCE RATE: 40%

NUMBER OF REVIEWER(S)/MS., EXCLUDING IN-HOUSE EDITOR(S): 2

REVIEWER(S): External   ARTICLES/AVG. ISSUE: 4

REVIEWING CRITERIA USED: BLIND REVIEW: No

  MANUSCRIPT SUBMISSION AIDS: 1, 2

  BIAS SAFEGUARDS: 5, 7, 9*

AVERAGE REVIEW TIME: 6 wks.   PUBLICATION TIME LAG: 6-12 mos.

MANUSCRIPT RETURNED WITH COMMENTS: Occasionally

MANUSCRIPT INFORMATION

GUIDELINES PUBLISHED: Each issue

STYLE REQUIREMENTS PUBLISHED: Each issue

STYLE MANUAL USED: In-house

PREFERRED TOPICS: Economic integration, political economy

QUERY LETTER: No   SIMULTANEOUS SUBMISSION: No

ABSTRACT WITH MANUSCRIPT: 100 wds.   COVER LETTER: No

NUMBER OF MANUSCRIPT COPIES: 2   MANUSCRIPT LENGTH: 20 pp.

SUBMISSION FEE: No   PAGE CHARGES: No

MANUSCRIPT ACKNOWLEDGED: Yes   EARLY PUBLICATION OPTION: No

COPYRIGHT OWNER: Publisher   REPRINTS: Optional purchase

AUTHOR COMPENSATION: Free reprints/tear sheets

MANUSCRIPT ADDRESS: The Editor, Journal of Common Market Studies,
  UACES Secretariat, King's College London, The Strand, London,
  WC2R 2LS, U.K.

Journal of Comparative Economics

FIRST PUBLISHED: 1977   FREQUENCY: Q   CIRCULATION: 2,200

AFFILIATION: Association for Comparative Economic Studies, Department of Economics, University of Notre Dame, Notre Dame, IN 46556

AUDIENCE: Academic/Professional; Government

PERCENT OF UNSOLICITED ARTICLES/ISSUE: 95%   ISSN: 0147-5967

EDITORIAL POLICY: Devoted to the analysis and study of comtemporary, historical, and hypothetical economic systems. Such analyses may involve comparisons of the performance of different economic systems or subsystems, studies linking outcomes to the system characteristics in one economy, or investigations of the origin and evolution of one or more economic systems.

REVIEW INFORMATION

REFEREED: Yes (I-A)   ACCEPTANCE RATE: 18%

NUMBER OF REVIEWER(S)/MS., EXCLUDING IN-HOUSE EDITOR(S): 2

REVIEWER(S): External   ARTICLES/AVG. ISSUE: 6

REVIEWING CRITERIA USED: BLIND REVIEW: Yes (Board
  MANUSCRIPT SUBMISSION AIDS: 1, 2   and external review)
  BIAS SAFEGUARDS: 3, 5, 7, 9

AVERAGE REVIEW TIME: 8 wks.   PUBLICATION TIME LAG: 4 mos.

MANUSCRIPT RETURNED WITH COMMENTS: Yes, SASE required

MANUSCRIPT INFORMATION

GUIDELINES PUBLISHED: Each issue

STYLE REQUIREMENTS PUBLISHED: Each issue

STYLE MANUAL USED: In-house

PREFERRED TOPICS: Comparative economics

QUERY LETTER: No   SIMULTANEOUS SUBMISSION: No

ABSTRACT WITH MANUSCRIPT: 100 wds. COVER LETTER: Yes

NUMBER OF MANUSCRIPT COPIES: 3   MANUSCRIPT LENGTH: 30 pp.

SUBMISSION FEE: No   PAGE CHARGES: No

MANUSCRIPT ACKNOWLEDGED: Yes   EARLY PUBLICATION OPTION: No

COPYRIGHT OWNER: Publisher   REPRINTS: Optional purchase

AUTHOR COMPENSATION: 50 free reprints/tear sheets

MANUSCRIPT ADDRESS: Prof. J. C. Brada, Editor, Journal of Comparative Economics, Department of Economics, Arizona State University, Tempe, AZ 85287

Journal of Consumer Research

FIRST PUBLISHED: 1974   FREQUENCY: Q   CIRCULATION: 3,200

AFFILIATION: AAA, AAPOR, ACR, AEA, AHEA, AMA, APA, ASA, AStA, ICA, SPSP, TIMS

AUDIENCE: Academic/Professional; Business/Industrial

PERCENT OF UNSOLICITED ARTICLES/ISSUE: 100%   ISSN: 0093-5301

EDITORIAL POLICY: Publishes research on consumer behavior.

REVIEW INFORMATION

REFEREED: Yes (II-A)   ACCEPTANCE RATE: 20%

NUMBER OF REVIEWER(S)/MS., EXCLUDING IN-HOUSE EDITOR(S): 3

REVIEWER(S): 2 board, 1 external   ARTICLES/AVG. ISSUE: 14

REVIEWING CRITERIA USED: BLIND REVIEW: Yes (Board
  MANUSCRIPT SUBMISSION AIDS: 1, 2   and external review)
  BIAS SAFEGUARDS: 3, 4, 5, 6, 8, 9

AVERAGE REVIEW TIME: 10 wks.   PUBLICATION TIME LAG: 4 mos.

MANUSCRIPT RETURNED WITH COMMENTS: No

MANUSCRIPT INFORMATION

GUIDELINES PUBLISHED: ⎫   Each issue (brief); June 1985
STYLE REQUIREMENTS PUBLISHED: ⎬   (detailed); also available on request
STYLE MANUAL USED: Chicago   ⎭

PREFERRED TOPICS: Consumer behavior

QUERY LETTER: No   SIMULTANEOUS SUBMISSION: No

ABSTRACT WITH MANUSCRIPT: 100 wds.   COVER LETTER: Yes

NUMBER OF MANUSCRIPT COPIES: 5   MANUSCRIPT LENGTH: No limit

SUBMISSION FEE: No   PAGE CHARGES: No

MANUSCRIPT ACKNOWLEDGED: Yes   EARLY PUBLICATION OPTION: No

COPYRIGHT OWNER: Journal   REPRINTS: Optional purchase

AUTHOR COMPENSATION: None

MANUSCRIPT ADDRESS: Richard J. Lutz, Editor, Journal of Consumer Research, College of Business Administration, University of Florida, Gainesville, FL 32611

Journal of Cultural Economics

FIRST PUBLISHED: 1977   FREQUENCY: S-A   CIRCULATION: 600

AFFILIATION: Association for Cultural Economics. Address same as
   journal's.

AUDIENCE: Academic/Professional; Government

PERCENT OF UNSOLICITED ARTICLES/ISSUE: 95%   ISSN: 0885-2545

EDITORIAL POLICY: Aims to encourage the application of economics to
   arts and cultural research.

REVIEW INFORMATION

REFEREED: Yes (II-B)   ACCEPTANCE RATE: 50%

NUMBER OF REVIEWER(S)/MS., EXCLUDING IN-HOUSE EDITOR(S): 2

REVIEWER(S): Board and external   ARTICLES/AVG. ISSUE: 8

REVIEWING CRITERIA USED: BLIND REVIEW: No

   MANUSCRIPT SUBMISSION AIDS: 1

   BIAS SAFEGUARDS: 5, 8, 9

AVERAGE REVIEW TIME: 6 mos.   PUBLICATION TIME LAG: 6 mos.

MANUSCRIPT RETURNED WITH COMMENTS: Yes

MANUSCRIPT INFORMATION

GUIDELINES PUBLISHED: Each issue

STYLE REQUIREMENTS PUBLISHED: No; available on request

STYLE MANUAL USED: Chicago

PREFERRED TOPICS: Economics as applied to arts and cultural research

QUERY LETTER: No   SIMULTANEOUS SUBMISSION: Yes

ABSTRACT WITH MANUSCRIPT: No   COVER LETTER: Yes

NUMBER OF MANUSCRIPT COPIES: 3   MANUSCRIPT LENGTH: 15-25 pp.

SUBMISSION FEE: No   PAGE CHARGES: No

MANUSCRIPT ACKNOWLEDGED: Yes   EARLY PUBLICATION OPTION: No

COPYRIGHT OWNER: Journal   REPRINTS: Optional purchase

AUTHOR COMPENSATION: 2 free journals

MANUSCRIPT ADDRESS: William S. Hendon, Editor, Journal of Cultural
   Economics, Department of Urban Studies, University of Akron, Akron,
   OH 44325

The Journal of Developing Areas

FIRST PUBLISHED: 1966   FREQUENCY: Q   CIRCULATION: 1,530
AFFILIATION: Western Illinois University. Address same as journal's.

AUDIENCE: Academic/Professional; Government
PERCENT OF UNSOLICITED ARTICLES/ISSUE: 100%   ISSN: 0022-037X
EDITORIAL POLICY: "Intends to stimulate the descriptive, theoretical,
  and comparative study of regional development, past and present,
  with the object of promoting fuller understanding of the human
  relationship to the developmental process."

REVIEW INFORMATION

REFEREED: Yes (I-A)   ACCEPTANCE RATE: 9.4%
NUMBER OF REVIEWER(S)/MS., EXCLUDING IN-HOUSE EDITOR(S): 3
REVIEWER(S): External   ARTICLES/AVG. ISSUE: 5-6
REVIEWING CRITERIA USED: BLIND REVIEW: Yes (Board
  MANUSCRIPT SUBMISSION AIDS: 1, 2   and external review)
  BIAS SAFEGUARDS: 3, 5, 7, 9*
AVERAGE REVIEW TIME: 6 mos.   PUBLICATION TIME LAG: 9-12 mos.
MANUSCRIPT RETURNED WITH COMMENTS: No

MANUSCRIPT INFORMATION

GUIDELINES PUBLISHED: Each issue (brief); also on request (detailed)
STYLE REQUIREMENTS PUBLISHED: Each issue
STYLE MANUAL USED: Chicago
PREFERRED TOPICS: Social sciences with focus on Third World or
  development issues

QUERY LETTER: No   SIMULTANEOUS SUBMISSION: No
ABSTRACT WITH MANUSCRIPT: No   COVER LETTER: Yes
NUMBER OF MANUSCRIPT COPIES: 3   MANUSCRIPT LENGTH: 20-35 pp.
                                        preferred

SUBMISSION FEE: No   PAGE CHARGES: No

MANUSCRIPT ACKNOWLEDGED: Yes   EARLY PUBLICATION OPTION: No
COPYRIGHT OWNER: Western Illinois   REPRINTS: Optional purchase
  University
AUTHOR COMPENSATION: 5 free journals

MANUSCRIPT ADDRESS: Nicholas C. Pano, Editor, The Journal of Developing Areas, Western Illinois University, Macomb, IL 61455

Journal of Development Economics

FIRST PUBLISHED: 1974   FREQUENCY: Q   CIRCULATION: 1,100
AFFILIATION: None

AUDIENCE: Academic/Professional
PERCENT OF UNSOLICITED ARTICLES/ISSUE: 100%   ISSN: 0304-3878
EDITORIAL POLICY: To advance scholarly research in the area of
   development economics.

REVIEW INFORMATION

REFEREED: Yes (I-B)   ACCEPTANCE RATE: 25%
NUMBER OF REVIEWER(S)/MS., EXCLUDING IN-HOUSE EDITOR(S): 2
REVIEWER(S): External   ARTICLES/AVG. ISSUE: 9
REVIEWING CRITERIA USED: BLIND REVIEW: No
  MANUSCRIPT SUBMISSION AIDS: 2
  BIAS SAFEGUARDS: 5, 6, 7, 9
AVERAGE REVIEW TIME: 10 wks.   PUBLICATION TIME LAG: 6 mos.
MANUSCRIPT RETURNED WITH COMMENTS: Yes

MANUSCRIPT INFORMATION

GUIDELINES PUBLISHED: No; not available
STYLE REQUIREMENTS PUBLISHED: Each issue
STYLE MANUAL USED: In-house
PREFERRED TOPICS: Development economics

QUERY LETTER: No   SIMULTANEOUS SUBMISSION: No
ABSTRACT WITH MANUSCRIPT: 100 wds.   COVER LETTER: Yes
NUMBER OF MANUSCRIPT COPIES: 3   MANUSCRIPT LENGTH: No limit

SUBMISSION FEE: $60.   PAGE CHARGES: No

MANUSCRIPT ACKNOWLEDGED: Yes   EARLY PUBLICATION OPTION: No
COPYRIGHT OWNER: Journal   REPRINTS: Optional purchase

AUTHOR COMPENSATION: None

MANUSCRIPT ADDRESS: Prof. Pranab Bardhan, Editor, Journal of Development Economics, Department of Economics, University of California
  at Berkeley, Berkeley, CA 94720

The Journal of Development Studies

FIRST PUBLISHED: 1964   FREQUENCY: Q   CIRCULATION: 1,600
AFFILIATION: None

AUDIENCE: Academic/Professional

PERCENT OF UNSOLICITED ARTICLES/ISSUE: 81-100%   ISSN: 0022-0388

EDITORIAL POLICY: Since its foundation in 1964, JDS has established
  itself as a major international forum for the discussion of the
  fundamental issues of development. It has published many seminal
  articles, opened up many areas of debate, and broadened its scope
  to interpret the concept of development in its widest sense.

REVIEW INFORMATION

REFEREED: No   ACCEPTANCE RATE: 10%

NUMBER OF REVIEWER(S)/MS., EXCLUDING IN-HOUSE EDITOR(S): 1

REVIEWER(S): External   ARTICLES/AVG. ISSUE: 7-9

REVIEWING CRITERIA USED: BLIND REVIEW: No

  MANUSCRIPT SUBMISSION AIDS: 2

  BIAS SAFEGUARDS: 4, 5, 6, 8, 9*

AVERAGE REVIEW TIME: 3-6 mos.   PUBLICATION TIME LAG: N.R.

MANUSCRIPT RETURNED WITH COMMENTS: No

MANUSCRIPT INFORMATION

GUIDELINES PUBLISHED: No; available on request

STYLE REQUIREMENTS PUBLISHED: Each issue

STYLE MANUAL USED: In-house

PREFERRED TOPICS: Economics, history, sociology, politics and
  anthropology of the Third World, and international relations thereof

QUERY LETTER: No   SIMULTANEOUS SUBMISSION: No

ABSTRACT WITH MANUSCRIPT: 100 wds.   COVER LETTER: Yes

NUMBER OF MANUSCRIPT COPIES: 2   MANUSCRIPT LENGTH: 3,000-
                                       9,000 wds.

SUBMISSION FEE: No   PAGE CHARGES: No

MANUSCRIPT ACKNOWLEDGED: Yes   EARLY PUBLICATION OPTION: No

COPYRIGHT OWNER: Publisher   REPRINTS: Optional purchase

AUTHOR COMPENSATION: 25 free reprints/tear sheets

MANUSCRIPT ADDRESS: Administrative Editor, The Journal of Development Studies, Frank Cass and Co. Ltd., Gainsborough House, 11
  Gainsborough Road, London E11 1RS, U.K.

Journal of Econometrics

FIRST PUBLISHED: 1973   FREQUENCY: M   CIRCULATION: 1,400

AFFILIATION: None

AUDIENCE: Academic/Professional

PERCENT OF UNSOLICITED ARTICLES/ISSUE: 61-80%   ISSN: 0304-4076

EDITORIAL POLICY: "Designed to serve as an outlet for important new research in both theoretical and applied econometrics. Papers dealing with . . . the application of statistical inference to economic data as well as papers dealing with the application of econometric techniques to substantive areas of economics fall within the scope of the Journal."

REVIEW INFORMATION

REFEREED: Yes (I-B)   ACCEPTANCE RATE: 14%

NUMBER OF REVIEWER(S)/MS., EXCLUDING IN-HOUSE EDITOR(S): 3

REVIEWER(S): 1 board, 2 external   ARTICLES/AVG. ISSUE: 15-20

REVIEWING CRITERIA USED: BLIND REVIEW: No

  MANUSCRIPT SUBMISSION AIDS: 1, 2

  BIAS SAFEGUARDS: 4, 5, 6, 7, 9

AVERAGE REVIEW TIME: 4 mos.   PUBLICATION TIME LAG: 4 mos.

MANUSCRIPT RETURNED WITH COMMENTS: No

MANUSCRIPT INFORMATION

GUIDELINES PUBLISHED: Each issue

STYLE REQUIREMENTS PUBLISHED: Each issue

STYLE MANUAL USED: In-house

PREFERRED TOPICS: Theoretical and applied econometrics

QUERY LETTER: No   SIMULTANEOUS SUBMISSION: No

ABSTRACT WITH MANUSCRIPT: 100 wds.   COVER LETTER: Yes

NUMBER OF MANUSCRIPT COPIES: 4   MANUSCRIPT LENGTH: No limit

SUBMISSION FEE: $25.   PAGE CHARGES: No

MANUSCRIPT ACKNOWLEDGED: Yes   EARLY PUBLICATION OPTION: No

COPYRIGHT OWNER: Publisher   REPRINTS: Optional purchase

AUTHOR COMPENSATION: Free reprints/tear sheets

MANUSCRIPT ADDRESS: Prof. Dennis Aigner, Editor, Journal of Econometrics, Department of Economics, University of Southern California, University Park, Los Angeles, CA 90089-0035

Journal of Economic and Social Measurement

FIRST PUBLISHED: 1980   FREQUENCY: 4/Yr.   CIRCULATION: 300+
AFFILIATION: None

AUDIENCE: Academic/Professional; Government
PERCENT OF UNSOLICITED ARTICLES/ISSUE: 81-100%   ISSN: 0747-9662
EDITORIAL POLICY: Publishes articles that are concerned with the pro-
    cess of making, distributing, or using economic and social measure-
    ments; using measurements when that use is innovative. Provides an
    outlet for the reporting of results, including the use of computers
    for data storage, distribution and analysis.

REVIEW INFORMATION

REFEREED: Yes (I-A)   .   ACCEPTANCE RATE: 30%
NUMBER OF REVIEWER(S)/MS., EXCLUDING IN-HOUSE EDITOR(S): 2
REVIEWER(S): External   ARTICLES/AVG. ISSUE: 8-9
REVIEWING CRITERIA USED: BLIND REVIEW: Yes (Board
  MANUSCRIPT SUBMISSION AIDS: 1, 2   and external review)
  BIAS SAFEGUARDS: 3, 5, 7, 8, 9*
AVERAGE REVIEW TIME: 3-4 mos.   PUBLICATION TIME LAG: 4-6 mos.
MANUSCRIPT RETURNED WITH COMMENTS: Yes, SASE required

MANUSCRIPT INFORMATION

GUIDELINES PUBLISHED: Each issue; also available on request
STYLE REQUIREMENTS PUBLISHED: Each issue; also available on request
STYLE MANUAL USED: Chicago
PREFERRED TOPICS: Social sciences, including economics, statistics, and
    health fields

QUERY LETTER: No   SIMULTANEOUS SUBMISSION: No
ABSTRACT WITH MANUSCRIPT: 100 wds. COVER LETTER: Yes
NUMBER OF MANUSCRIPT COPIES: 3   MANUSCRIPT LENGTH: No limit

SUBMISSION FEE: No   PAGE CHARGES: No

MANUSCRIPT ACKNOWLEDGED: Yes, SASE req. EARLY PUBLICATION OPTION: Yes
COPYRIGHT OWNER: Publisher   REPRINTS: Purchase required

AUTHOR COMPENSATION: N.R.

MANUSCRIPT ADDRESS: Charles G. Renfro, Editor, Journal of Economic and
    Social Measurement, 11 East Princeton Road, Bala Cynwyd, PA 19004

Journal of Economic Behavior and Organization

FIRST PUBLISHED: 1980   FREQUENCY: 4/Yr.   CIRCULATION: 410
AFFILIATION: None

AUDIENCE: Academic/Professional
PERCENT OF UNSOLICITED ARTICLES/ISSUE: 95%   ISSN: 0167-2681
EDITORIAL POLICY: "Devoted to theoretical and empirical research concerning economic decision, organization and behavior. Its specific
  purpose is to foster an improved understanding of how human
  cognitive, computational and informational characteristics influence
  the working of economic organizations and market economies."

REVIEW INFORMATION

REFEREED: Yes (II-B)   ACCEPTANCE RATE: 20%
NUMBER OF REVIEWER(S)/MS., EXCLUDING IN-HOUSE EDITOR(S): 2
REVIEWER(S): Board and external   ARTICLES/AVG. ISSUE: 6
REVIEWING CRITERIA USED: BLIND REVIEW: No
  MANUSCRIPT SUBMISSION AIDS: 1, 2
  BIAS SAFEGUARDS: 4, 5, 6, 9
AVERAGE REVIEW TIME: 4 mos.   PUBLICATION TIME LAG: N.R.
MANUSCRIPT RETURNED WITH COMMENTS: Yes

MANUSCRIPT INFORMATION

GUIDELINES PUBLISHED: Each issue
STYLE REQUIREMENTS PUBLISHED: Each issue
STYLE MANUAL USED: In-house
PREFERRED TOPICS: Economic decision, organization and behavior

QUERY LETTER: No   SIMULTANEOUS SUBMISSION: Yes
ABSTRACT WITH MANUSCRIPT: 100 wds.   COVER LETTER: Yes
NUMBER OF MANUSCRIPT COPIES: 3   MANUSCRIPT LENGTH: No limit

SUBMISSION FEE: No   PAGE CHARGES: No

MANUSCRIPT ACKNOWLEDGED: Yes   EARLY PUBLICATION OPTION: No
COPYRIGHT OWNER: Journal   REPRINTS: Optional purchase

AUTHOR COMPENSATION: None

MANUSCRIPT ADDRESS: Richard H. Day, Editor, Journal of Economic
  Behavior and Organization, Department of Economics, University of
  Southern California, University Park, Los Angeles, CA 90089-0035

Journal of Economic Development

FIRST PUBLISHED: 1976   FREQUENCY: S-A   CIRCULATION: 1,150

AFFILIATION: Chung-Ang University, Economic Research Institute, Seoul, Korea

AUDIENCE: Academic/Professional; Business/Industrial; Government

PERCENT OF UNSOLICITED ARTICLES/ISSUE: 100%   ISSN: 0254-0372

EDITORIAL POLICY: An international academic journal which publishes papers on economic development issues and problems.

REVIEW INFORMATION

REFEREED: Yes (II-A)   ACCEPTANCE RATE: 20%

NUMBER OF REVIEWER(S)/MS., EXCLUDING IN-HOUSE EDITOR(S): 2

REVIEWER(S): Board and external   ARTICLES/AVG. ISSUE: 10

REVIEWING CRITERIA USED: BLIND REVIEW: Yes (Board
  MANUSCRIPT SUBMISSION AIDS: 1, 2   and external review)
  BIAS SAFEGUARDS: 3, 5, 6, 9*

AVERAGE REVIEW TIME: 2 mos.   PUBLICATION TIME LAG: 8 mos.

MANUSCRIPT RETURNED WITH COMMENTS: No

MANUSCRIPT INFORMATION

GUIDELINES PUBLISHED: Each issue

STYLE REQUIREMENTS PUBLISHED: Each issue

STYLE MANUAL USED: Chicago

PREFERRED TOPICS: Economic development and growth

QUERY LETTER: Yes   SIMULTANEOUS SUBMISSION: No

ABSTRACT WITH MANUSCRIPT: 100 wds.   COVER LETTER: Yes

NUMBER OF MANUSCRIPT COPIES: 3   MANUSCRIPT LENGTH: 25 pp. max.

SUBMISSION FEE: No   PAGE CHARGES: No

MANUSCRIPT ACKNOWLEDGED: Yes   EARLY PUBLICATION OPTION: No

COPYRIGHT OWNER: Publisher   REPRINTS: Optional purchase

AUTHOR COMPENSATION: One free journal

MANUSCRIPT ADDRESS: The Editor, Journal of Economic Development, Department of Economics, Virginia Commonwealth University, Richmond, VA 23284

Journal of Economic Education

FIRST PUBLISHED: 1969   FREQUENCY: Q   CIRCULATION: 2,000+

AFFILIATION: Joint Council on Economic Education, 2 Park Avenue,
New York, NY 10016

AUDIENCE: Academic/Professional

PERCENT OF UNSOLICITED ARTICLES/ISSUE: 81-100%   ISSN: 0022-0485

EDITORIAL POLICY: Directed primarily to an audience of those who
teach undergraduate economics. Articles include reports on
research in economic education; developments in economic theory
not yet incorporated into texts; useful ways to teach economics;
reviews and surveys of books, texts and software; professional
developments and opportunities.

REVIEW INFORMATION

REFEREED: Yes (I-A)   ACCEPTANCE RATE: 18-20%

NUMBER OF REVIEWER(S)/MS., EXCLUDING IN-HOUSE EDITOR(S): 2

REVIEWER(S): External   ARTICLES/AVG. ISSUE: 9

REVIEWING CRITERIA USED: BLIND REVIEW: Yes (Board
and external review)
  MANUSCRIPT SUBMISSION AIDS: 0

  BIAS SAFEGUARDS: 3, 4, 5, 6, 7, 9

AVERAGE REVIEW TIME: 12 wks.   PUBLICATION TIME LAG: 9-12 mos.

MANUSCRIPT RETURNED WITH COMMENTS: Yes

MANUSCRIPT INFORMATION

GUIDELINES PUBLISHED: No; available on request

STYLE REQUIREMENTS PUBLISHED: Summer 1986 issue; also available on request

STYLE MANUAL USED: Chicago

PREFERRED TOPICS: Economic research, theory developments and review,
  economic instruction

QUERY LETTER: No   SIMULTANEOUS SUBMISSION: No

ABSTRACT WITH MANUSCRIPT: No   COVER LETTER: No

NUMBER OF MANUSCRIPT COPIES: 3   MANUSCRIPT LENGTH: 10-20 pp.

SUBMISSION FEE: No   PAGE CHARGES: No

MANUSCRIPT ACKNOWLEDGED: Yes   EARLY PUBLICATION OPTION: No

COPYRIGHT OWNER: Publisher   REPRINTS: Optional purchase

AUTHOR COMPENSATION: None

MANUSCRIPT ADDRESS: Kalman Goldberg, Editor, Journal of Economic
  Education, Bradley University, Peoria, IL 61625

The Journal of Economic History

FIRST PUBLISHED: 1941   FREQUENCY: Q   CIRCULATION: 3,300

AFFILIATION: Economic History Association, Hagley Museum and Library, P.O. Box 3630, Wilmington, DE 19807

AUDIENCE: Academic/Professional

PERCENT OF UNSOLICITED ARTICLES/ISSUE: 100%   ISSN: 0022-0507

EDITORIAL POLICY: Publishes original, scholarly articles, reviews, comments and notes in the field of economic history without regard to geographic area or time period.

REVIEW INFORMATION

REFEREED: Yes (II-A)   ACCEPTANCE RATE: 15%

NUMBER OF REVIEWER(S)/MS., EXCLUDING IN-HOUSE EDITOR(S): 2

REVIEWER(S): Board and external   ARTICLES/AVG. ISSUE: 8-10

REVIEWING CRITERIA USED: BLIND REVIEW: Yes (All except
  MANUSCRIPT SUBMISSION AIDS: 1, 2   preliminary screening)
  BIAS SAFEGUARDS: 3, 5, 9

AVERAGE REVIEW TIME: 11 wks.   PUBLICATION TIME LAG: 10 wks.

MANUSCRIPT RETURNED WITH COMMENTS: Not necessarily

MANUSCRIPT INFORMATION

GUIDELINES PUBLISHED: Each issue

STYLE REQUIREMENTS PUBLISHED: Each issue; also available on request

STYLE MANUAL USED: In-house

PREFERRED TOPICS: Economic history

QUERY LETTER: No   SIMULTANEOUS SUBMISSION: No

ABSTRACT WITH MANUSCRIPT: 100 wds.   COVER LETTER: Yes

NUMBER OF MANUSCRIPT COPIES: 4   MANUSCRIPT LENGTH: 35 pp.

SUBMISSION FEE: Year's membership fee   PAGE CHARGES: No
  for nonmember contributors

MANUSCRIPT ACKNOWLEDGED: Yes   EARLY PUBLICATION OPTION: No

COPYRIGHT OWNER: Journal   REPRINTS: Optional purchase

AUTHOR COMPENSATION: None

MANUSCRIPT ADDRESS: The Editor, The Journal of Economic History, 3718 Locust Walk, University of Pennsylvania, Philadelphia, PA 19104-6297

Journal of Economic Issues

FIRST PUBLISHED: 1967   FREQUENCY: Q   CIRCULATION: 2,000

AFFILIATION: Association for Evolutionary Economics, University of
  Nebraska-Lincoln, and California State University-Sacramento

AUDIENCE: Academic/Professional; Government

PERCENT OF UNSOLICITED ARTICLES/ISSUE: 90%   ISSN: 0021-3624

EDITORIAL POLICY: "An international journal addressed especially to
  institutional and evolutionary economics. As such, it regularly
  publishes articles of quality dealing with basic economic problems,
  economic policy, methodology, the organization and control of
  economies, and all of the specialized fields of economics."

REVIEW INFORMATION

REFEREED: Yes (III-A)   ACCEPTANCE RATE: 10%

NUMBER OF REVIEWER(S)/MS., EXCLUDING IN-HOUSE EDITOR(S): 3

REVIEWER(S): Board   ARTICLES/AVG. ISSUE: 10

REVIEWING CRITERIA USED: BLIND REVIEW: Yes (Board
  MANUSCRIPT SUBMISSION AIDS: 1, 2   and external review)

  BIAS SAFEGUARDS: 3, 5, 9

AVERAGE REVIEW TIME: 2-3 mos.   PUBLICATION TIME LAG: 3-9 mos.

MANUSCRIPT RETURNED WITH COMMENTS: Yes

MANUSCRIPT INFORMATION

GUIDELINES PUBLISHED: Each issue

STYLE REQUIREMENTS PUBLISHED: Each issue

STYLE MANUAL USED: Chicago

PREFERRED TOPICS: Economic problems, economic policy, methodology,
  the organization and control of economies

QUERY LETTER: No   SIMULTANEOUS SUBMISSION: No

ABSTRACT WITH MANUSCRIPT: No   COVER LETTER: Yes

NUMBER OF MANUSCRIPT COPIES: 4   MANUSCRIPT LENGTH: 20-40 pp.

SUBMISSION FEE: No   PAGE CHARGES: No

MANUSCRIPT ACKNOWLEDGED: Yes   EARLY PUBLICATION OPTION: No

COPYRIGHT OWNER: Journal   REPRINTS: Optional purchase

AUTHOR COMPENSATION: 20 free reprints/tear sheets

MANUSCRIPT ADDRESS: Marc R. Tool, Editor, Journal of Economic Issues,
  Department of Economics, California State University-Sacramento,
  Sacramento, CA 95819-2694

Journal of Economic Studies

FIRST PUBLISHED: 1965   FREQUENCY: 4/Yr.   CIRCULATION: 400

AFFILIATION: University of Strathclyde, Department of Economics.
  Address same as journal's.

AUDIENCE: Academic/Professional; Business/Industrial; Government

PERCENT OF UNSOLICITED ARTICLES/ISSUE: 100%   ISSN: 0144-3585

EDITORIAL POLICY: Publishes up-to-date research within all fields

  of economics.

REVIEW INFORMATION

REFEREED: Yes (II-B)   ACCEPTANCE RATE: 40%

NUMBER OF REVIEWER(S)/MS., EXCLUDING IN-HOUSE EDITOR(S): 2

REVIEWER(S): Board and external   ARTICLES/AVG. ISSUE: 6

REVIEWING CRITERIA USED: BLIND REVIEW: No

  MANUSCRIPT SUBMISSION AIDS: 1, 2

  BIAS SAFEGUARDS: 4, 5, 9

AVERAGE REVIEW TIME: 10 wks.   PUBLICATION TIME LAG: 9 mos.

MANUSCRIPT RETURNED WITH COMMENTS: No

MANUSCRIPT INFORMATION

GUIDELINES PUBLISHED: Each issue

STYLE REQUIREMENTS PUBLISHED: Each issue

STYLE MANUAL USED: In-house

PREFERRED TOPICS: All fields of economics

QUERY LETTER: No   SIMULTANEOUS SUBMISSION: No

ABSTRACT WITH MANUSCRIPT: 100 wds.   COVER LETTER: No

NUMBER OF MANUSCRIPT COPIES: 3   MANUSCRIPT LENGTH: No limit

SUBMISSION FEE: No   PAGE CHARGES: No

MANUSCRIPT ACKNOWLEDGED: Yes   EARLY PUBLICATION OPTION: Yes

COPYRIGHT OWNER: Author   REPRINTS: Optional purchase

AUTHOR COMPENSATION: None

MANUSCRIPT ADDRESS: Dr. Frank M. Stephen, Managing Editor, Journal of
  Economic Studies, Department of Economics, University of Strathclyde,
  Glasgow, G4 OLN, U.K.

Journal of Economics / Zeitschrift für Nationalökonomie

FIRST PUBLISHED: 1929   FREQUENCY: Q   CIRCULATION: N.R.
AFFILIATION: None

AUDIENCE: Academic/Professional

PERCENT OF UNSOLICITED ARTICLES/ISSUE: 100%   ISSN: 0044-3158

EDITORIAL POLICY: The leading Austrian economic journal with a
great international reputation. Intensively read not only in
Austria and the Federal Republic of Germany, but also in Great
Britain, the USA and Japan. The journal specializes in mathematical
economic theory of both a medium and high level of difficulty.
Econometric case studies are sometimes published if they are of
general interest.

REVIEW INFORMATION

REFEREED: Yes (I-B)   ACCEPTANCE RATE: 20%

NUMBER OF REVIEWER(S)/MS., EXCLUDING IN-HOUSE EDITOR(S): 2

REVIEWER(S): External   ARTICLES/AVG. ISSUE: 6

REVIEWING CRITERIA USED: BLIND REVIEW: No

  MANUSCRIPT SUBMISSION AIDS: 0

  BIAS SAFEGUARDS: 5, 7, 9

AVERAGE REVIEW TIME: 4 mos.   PUBLICATION TIME LAG: 4 mos.

MANUSCRIPT RETURNED WITH COMMENTS: Yes, SASE required

MANUSCRIPT INFORMATION

GUIDELINES PUBLISHED: No; not available

STYLE REQUIREMENTS PUBLISHED: No; not available

STYLE MANUAL USED: In-house

PREFERRED TOPICS: Economic theory, particularly microeconomics

QUERY LETTER: No   SIMULTANEOUS SUBMISSION: Yes

ABSTRACT WITH MANUSCRIPT: 100 wds.   COVER LETTER: Yes

NUMBER OF MANUSCRIPT COPIES: 2   MANUSCRIPT LENGTH: 15-20 pp.

SUBMISSION FEE: No   PAGE CHARGES: No

MANUSCRIPT ACKNOWLEDGED: Yes   EARLY PUBLICATION OPTION: No

COPYRIGHT OWNER: Publisher   REPRINTS: Optional purchase

AUTHOR COMPENSATION: None

MANUSCRIPT ADDRESS: Dr. Dr. Dieter Bös, Managing Editor, Journal of
  Economics/ Zeitschrift für Nationalökonomie, Institute of Economics,
  University of Bonn, Adenauerallee 24-42, D-5300 Bonn, F.R.G.

Journal of Economics and Business

FIRST PUBLISHED: 1949   FREQUENCY: 4/Yr.   CIRCULATION: 950

AFFILIATION: Temple University, School of Business Administration.
  Address same as journal's.

AUDIENCE: Academic/Professional

PERCENT OF UNSOLICITED ARTICLES/ISSUE: 95%   ISSN: 0278-2294

EDITORIAL POLICY: Devoted to "professional and academic research in
  economics, finance, management, marketing, and related disciplines."

REVIEW INFORMATION

REFEREED: Yes (I-A)   ACCEPTANCE RATE: 20%

NUMBER OF REVIEWER(S)/MS., EXCLUDING IN-HOUSE EDITOR(S): 3

REVIEWER(S): 1 board, 2 external   ARTICLES/AVG. ISSUE: 7-8

REVIEWING CRITERIA USED: BLIND REVIEW: Yes (Entire
  MANUSCRIPT SUBMISSION AIDS: 1, 2   review)

  BIAS SAFEGUARDS: 3, 4, 5, 6, 7, 9*

AVERAGE REVIEW TIME: 10 wks.   PUBLICATION TIME LAG: 12 mos.

MANUSCRIPT RETURNED WITH COMMENTS: Yes

MANUSCRIPT INFORMATION

GUIDELINES PUBLISHED: Each issue

STYLE REQUIREMENTS PUBLISHED: Each issue

STYLE MANUAL USED: In-house

PREFERRED TOPICS: Finance, economics, management science

QUERY LETTER: No   SIMULTANEOUS SUBMISSION: No

ABSTRACT WITH MANUSCRIPT: 100 wds. COVER LETTER: Yes

NUMBER OF MANUSCRIPT COPIES: 4   MANUSCRIPT LENGTH: No limit

SUBMISSION FEE: $20.   PAGE CHARGES: No

MANUSCRIPT ACKNOWLEDGED: Yes   EARLY PUBLICATION OPTION: No

COPYRIGHT OWNER: Journal   REPRINTS: Optional purchase

AUTHOR COMPENSATION: None

MANUSCRIPT ADDRESS: Prof. Robert H. Deans, Executive Editor, Journal of
  Economics and Business, School of Business Administration, Temple
  University, Speakman Hall, Philadelphia, Pa 19122

The Journal of Energy and Development

FIRST PUBLISHED: 1975   FREQUENCY: S-A   CIRCULATION: 2,000
AFFILIATION: None

AUDIENCE: Academic/Professional; Business/Industrial; Government
PERCENT OF UNSOLICITED ARTICLES/ISSUE: 61-80%   ISSN: 0361-4476
EDITORIAL POLICY: "Brings together and facilitates the presentation
  of data on projects, current research, programs, critical policies,
  and concepts relevant to the fields of energy, economic development
  and growth which so often are interlocking. The Journal is largely
  economic in content but it also aims at an interdisciplinary approach."

REVIEW INFORMATION

REFEREED: No   ACCEPTANCE RATE: 65%
NUMBER OF REVIEWER(S)/MS., EXCLUDING IN-HOUSE EDITOR(S): 1
REVIEWER(S): Board or external   ARTICLES/AVG. ISSUE: 9
REVIEWING CRITERIA USED: BLIND REVIEW: Yes (Board
  MANUSCRIPT SUBMISSION AIDS: 1, 2   review only)
  BIAS SAFEGUARDS: 3, 4, 5, 6, 9*
AVERAGE REVIEW TIME: 2 wks.   PUBLICATION TIME LAG: 3-5 mos.
MANUSCRIPT RETURNED WITH COMMENTS: No

MANUSCRIPT INFORMATION

GUIDELINES PUBLISHED: Each issue
STYLE REQUIREMENTS PUBLISHED: Each issue
STYLE MANUAL USED: In-house; Chicago
PREFERRED TOPICS: Energy and resources economics, conservation,
  energy-related economic development, environment, regulatory
  issues, domestic and international energy topics
QUERY LETTER: No   SIMULTANEOUS SUBMISSION: No
ABSTRACT WITH MANUSCRIPT: No   COVER LETTER: Yes; vita helpful
NUMBER OF MANUSCRIPT COPIES: 2   MANUSCRIPT LENGTH: 20-30 pp.

SUBMISSION FEE: No   PAGE CHARGES: No

MANUSCRIPT ACKNOWLEDGED: Yes   EARLY PUBLICATION OPTION: No
COPYRIGHT OWNER: Journal   REPRINTS: Optional purchase

AUTHOR COMPENSATION: 2 free journals
MANUSCRIPT ADDRESS: Ragaei El Mallakh, Editor, The Journal of Energy
  and Development, 216 Economics Building, Box 263, University of
  Colorado, Boulder, CO 80309-0263

Journal of Environmental Economics and Management

FIRST PUBLISHED: 1975   FREQUENCY: Q   CIRCULATION: 950

AFFILIATION: Association of Environmental and Resource Economists, 1616 P Street N.W., Washington, D.C. 20036

AUDIENCE: Academic/Professional; Government

PERCENT OF UNSOLICITED ARTICLES/ISSUE: 100%   ISSN: 0095-0696

EDITORIAL POLICY: Aims to publish the best research articles in resource and environmental economics.

REVIEW INFORMATION

REFEREED: Yes (I-B)   ACCEPTANCE RATE: 21%

NUMBER OF REVIEWER(S)/MS., EXCLUDING IN-HOUSE EDITOR(S): 2

REVIEWER(S): External   ARTICLES/AVG. ISSUE: 5

REVIEWING CRITERIA USED: BLIND REVIEW: No

 MANUSCRIPT SUBMISSION AIDS: 1, 2

 BIAS SAFEGUARDS: 4, 5, 7, 9, 10

AVERAGE REVIEW TIME: 3 mos.   PUBLICATION TIME LAG: 10 mos.

MANUSCRIPT RETURNED WITH COMMENTS: Yes

MANUSCRIPT INFORMATION

GUIDELINES PUBLISHED: Each issue

STYLE REQUIREMENTS PUBLISHED: Each issue

STYLE MANUAL USED: In-house; Chicago

PREFERRED TOPICS: Resource and environmental economics

QUERY LETTER: No   SIMULTANEOUS SUBMISSION: No

ABSTRACT WITH MANUSCRIPT: No   COVER LETTER: Yes

NUMBER OF MANUSCRIPT COPIES: 3   MANUSCRIPT LENGTH: No limit

SUBMISSION FEE: $10. for nonmembers/ nonsubscribers   PAGE CHARGES: No

MANUSCRIPT ACKNOWLEDGED: Yes   EARLY PUBLICATION OPTION: Yes

COPYRIGHT OWNER: Journal   REPRINTS: Optional purchase

AUTHOR COMPENSATION: None

MANUSCRIPT ADDRESS: Ralph C. d'Arge, Managing Editor, Journal of Environmental Economics and Management, Box 3985, University Station, University of Wyoming, Laramie, WY 82071

The Journal of Finance

FIRST PUBLISHED: 1946   FREQUENCY: 5/Yr.   CIRCULATION: 9,000
AFFILIATION: American Finance Association. Address same as journal's.

AUDIENCE: Academic/Professional; Business/Industrial
PERCENT OF UNSOLICITED ARTICLES/ISSUE: 81-100%   ISSN: 0022-1082
EDITORIAL POLICY: The official publication of the American Finance
  Association. Publishes articles on all aspects of finance and the
  papers and proceedings of the annual meeting of the Association.

REVIEW INFORMATION

REFEREED: No   ACCEPTANCE RATE: 10%
NUMBER OF REVIEWER(S)/MS., EXCLUDING IN-HOUSE EDITOR(S): 1
REVIEWER(S): External   ARTICLES/AVG. ISSUE: 16
REVIEWING CRITERIA USED: BLIND REVIEW: Yes (Board
  MANUSCRIPT SUBMISSION AIDS: 1, 2   and external review)
  BIAS SAFEGUARDS: 3, 5, 9
AVERAGE REVIEW TIME: 6 wks.   PUBLICATION TIME LAG: 4 mos.
MANUSCRIPT RETURNED WITH COMMENTS: Yes

MANUSCRIPT INFORMATION

GUIDELINES PUBLISHED: Each issue
STYLE REQUIREMENTS PUBLISHED: Each issue
STYLE MANUAL USED: In-house
PREFERRED TOPICS: Finance

QUERY LETTER: No   SIMULTANEOUS SUBMISSION: No
ABSTRACT WITH MANUSCRIPT: 100 wds. max. COVER LETTER: Yes
NUMBER OF MANUSCRIPT COPIES: 3   MANUSCRIPT LENGTH: 30 pp. max.

SUBMISSION FEE: $30. for members/   PAGE CHARGES: No
  subscribers; $90. for others
MANUSCRIPT ACKNOWLEDGED: Yes   EARLY PUBLICATION OPTION: No
COPYRIGHT OWNER: Journal   REPRINTS: Optional purchase

AUTHOR COMPENSATION: None
MANUSCRIPT ADDRESS: Professors Edwin Elton and Martin Gruber, Co-
  Editors, The Journal of Finance, New York University, 100 Trinity
  Place, New York, NY 10006

Journal of Financial Economics

FIRST PUBLISHED: 1974   FREQUENCY: Q   CIRCULATION: 1,925

AFFILIATION: University of Rochester, Graduate School of Management. Address same as journal's.

AUDIENCE: Academic/Professional

PERCENT OF UNSOLICITED ARTICLES/ISSUE: 100%   ISSN: 0304-405X

EDITORIAL POLICY: "Intends to provide a specialized forum for the publication of research in the general area of financial economics, placing primary emphasis on the highest quality analytical, mathematical and empirical contributions."

REVIEW INFORMATION

REFEREED: No   ACCEPTANCE RATE: 18%

NUMBER OF REVIEWER(S)/MS., EXCLUDING IN-HOUSE EDITOR(S): 1

REVIEWER(S): Board or external   ARTICLES/AVG. ISSUE: 6

REVIEWING CRITERIA USED: BLIND REVIEW: Yes (Board

  MANUSCRIPT SUBMISSION AIDS: 1, 2   and external review)

  BIAS SAFEGUARDS: 3, 5, 6, 9, 10

AVERAGE REVIEW TIME: 5 wks.   PUBLICATION TIME LAG: 4 mos.

MANUSCRIPT RETURNED WITH COMMENTS: Yes

MANUSCRIPT INFORMATION

GUIDELINES PUBLISHED: Each issue

STYLE REQUIREMENTS PUBLISHED: Each issue

STYLE MANUAL USED: In-house

PREFERRED TOPICS: "Consumption and investment decisions under uncertainty, portfolio analysis, theories of market equilibrium, dynamic behaviour of asset prices in the financial and real sectors," etc.

QUERY LETTER: No   SIMULTANEOUS SUBMISSION: No

ABSTRACT WITH MANUSCRIPT: 100 wds.   COVER LETTER: No

NUMBER OF MANUSCRIPT COPIES: 3   MANUSCRIPT LENGTH: No limit

SUBMISSION FEE: $155. for members/sub- PAGE CHARGES: No
scribers; $190. for others

MANUSCRIPT ACKNOWLEDGED: Yes   EARLY PUBLICATION OPTION: No

COPYRIGHT OWNER: Publisher   REPRINTS: Optional purchase

AUTHOR COMPENSATION: 25 reprints/tear sheets

MANUSCRIPT ADDRESS: Prof. Clifford W. Smith, Jr., Managing Editor, Journal of Financial Economics, Graduate School of Management, University of Rochester, Rochester, NY 14627

The Journal of Financial Research

FIRST PUBLISHED: 1978   FREQUENCY: Q   CIRCULATION: 1,200

AFFILIATION: Southern Finance Association and Southwest Finance
  Association. Address same as journal's.

AUDIENCE: Academic/Professional

PERCENT OF UNSOLICITED ARTICLES/ISSUE: 100%   ISSN: 0270-2592

EDITORIAL POLICY: "It is the editorial policy of The Journal that
  'financial research' is broadly interpreted to include financial
  management, investments, financial institutions, capital market
  theory, and portfolio theory. This definition of scope is intended to include research results that infer market characteristics."

REVIEW INFORMATION

REFEREED: Yes (II-A)   ACCEPTANCE RATE: 18%

NUMBER OF REVIEWER(S)/MS., EXCLUDING IN-HOUSE EDITOR(S): 2

REVIEWER(S): Board and external   ARTICLES/AVG. ISSUE: 8

REVIEWING CRITERIA USED: BLIND REVIEW: Yes (Preliminary
  MANUSCRIPT SUBMISSION AIDS: 1, 2   screening and board review)

  BIAS SAFEGUARDS: 3, 4, 5, 9

AVERAGE REVIEW TIME: 9 wks.   PUBLICATION TIME LAG: 4 mos.

MANUSCRIPT RETURNED WITH COMMENTS: Yes

MANUSCRIPT INFORMATION

GUIDELINES PUBLISHED: Each issue

STYLE REQUIREMENTS PUBLISHED: Each issue

STYLE MANUAL USED: In-house; Chicago

PREFERRED TOPICS: Emphasis on "financial decision-making and policy-
  making of the individual unit of operation as opposed to monetary
  economics or public policy."

QUERY LETTER: No   SIMULTANEOUS SUBMISSION: No

ABSTRACT WITH MANUSCRIPT: 150 wds. COVER LETTER: Yes

NUMBER OF MANUSCRIPT COPIES: 4   MANUSCRIPT LENGTH: 20-25 pp.

SUBMISSION FEE: $15. for members/   PAGE CHARGES: No
  subscribers; $25. for others

MANUSCRIPT ACKNOWLEDGED: Yes   EARLY PUBLICATION OPTION: No

COPYRIGHT OWNER: Journal   REPRINTS: Not available

AUTHOR COMPENSATION: None

MANUSCRIPT ADDRESS: Richard L. Smith and Michael D. Joehnk, Co-
  Editors, The Journal of Financial Research, Department of Finance,
  College of Business, Arizona State University, Tempe, AZ 85287

The Journal of Futures Markets

FIRST PUBLISHED: 1981   FREQUENCY: Q   CIRCULATION: 1,600

AFFILIATION: Columbia University, Columbia Business School, Center for the Study of Futures Markets, New York, NY 10027

AUDIENCE: Academic/Professional; Business/Industry; Government

PERCENT OF UNSOLICITED ARTICLES/ISSUE: 100%   ISSN: 0270-7314

EDITORIAL POLICY: "Devoted to exploration of ideas and professional discussion of a wide range of issues affecting all aspects of futures." Serves as a "link between the academician, the practitioner, and the regulator in the sifting and winnowing process so necessary to informed discussion and decision making."

REVIEW INFORMATION

REFEREED: Yes (I-A)   ACCEPTANCE RATE: 40%

NUMBER OF REVIEWER(S)/MS., EXCLUDING IN-HOUSE EDITOR(S): 2

REVIEWER(S): External   ARTICLES/AVG. ISSUE: 5-10

REVIEWING CRITERIA USED: BLIND REVIEW: Yes (All except
  MANUSCRIPT SUBMISSION AIDS: 1, 2   preliminary screening)
  BIAS SAFEGUARDS: 3, 5, 7, 8, 9, 10

AVERAGE REVIEW TIME: Varies   PUBLICATION TIME LAG: 6 mos.

MANUSCRIPT RETURNED WITH COMMENTS: Not necessarily

MANUSCRIPT INFORMATION

GUIDELINES PUBLISHED: Each issue

STYLE REQUIREMENTS PUBLISHED: Each issue

STYLE MANUAL USED: In-house

PREFERRED TOPICS: All aspects of futures

QUERY LETTER: No   SIMULTANEOUS SUBMISSION: No

ABSTRACT WITH MANUSCRIPT: No   COVER LETTER: Yes

NUMBER OF MANUSCRIPT COPIES: 3   MANUSCRIPT LENGTH: No limit

SUBMISSION FEE: No   PAGE CHARGES: No

MANUSCRIPT ACKNOWLEDGED: Yes   EARLY PUBLICATION OPTION: No

COPYRIGHT OWNER: Publisher   REPRINTS: Optional purchase

AUTHOR COMPENSATION: 1 free journal

MANUSCRIPT ADDRESS: Mark J. Powers, Editor, The Journal of Futures Markets, 57 Glenmere Drive, Chatham, NJ 07928

Journal of Health Economics

FIRST PUBLISHED: 1982   FREQUENCY: 3/Yr.   CIRCULATION: 600
AFFILIATION: None

AUDIENCE: Academic/Professional
PERCENT OF UNSOLICITED ARTICLES/ISSUE: 100%   ISSN: 0167-6296
EDITORIAL POLICY: The journal seeks articles related to the economics
  of health and medical care.

REVIEW INFORMATION

REFEREED: Yes (I-B)   ACCEPTANCE RATE: 20%
NUMBER OF REVIEWER(S)/MS., EXCLUDING IN-HOUSE EDITOR(S): 2
REVIEWER(S): External   ARTICLES/AVG. ISSUE: 5-10
REVIEWING CRITERIA USED: BLIND REVIEW: No
  MANUSCRIPT SUBMISSION AIDS: 1, 2
  BIAS SAFEGUARDS: 4, 5, 6, 7, 9
AVERAGE REVIEW TIME: 6 wks.   PUBLICATION TIME LAG: 8 mos.
MANUSCRIPT RETURNED WITH COMMENTS: Yes

MANUSCRIPT INFORMATION

GUIDELINES PUBLISHED: Each issue
STYLE REQUIREMENTS PUBLISHED: Each issue
STYLE MANUAL USED: In-house
PREFERRED TOPICS: Economics of health

QUERY LETTER: No   SIMULTANEOUS SUBMISSION: No
ABSTRACT WITH MANUSCRIPT: 100 wds. max. COVER LETTER: Yes
NUMBER OF MANUSCRIPT COPIES: 3   MANUSCRIPT LENGTH: No limit

SUBMISSION FEE: No   PAGE CHARGES: No

MANUSCRIPT ACKNOWLEDGED: Yes   EARLY PUBLICATION OPTION: Yes
COPYRIGHT OWNER: Publisher   REPRINTS: Optional purchase

AUTHOR COMPENSATION: 25 free reprints/tear sheets
MANUSCRIPT ADDRESS: Dr. Joseph P. Newhouse, Editor, Journal of Health
  Economics, The Rand Corporation, 1700 Main Street, Santa Monica,
  CA 90406

The Journal of Human Resources

FIRST PUBLISHED: 1966   FREQUENCY: Q   CIRCULATION: 2,500

AFFILIATION: University of Wisconsin, Industrial Relations Research Institute and the Institute for Research on Poverty. Address same as journal's.

AUDIENCE: Academic/Professional

PERCENT OF UNSOLICITED ARTICLES/ISSUE: 81-100%   ISSN: 0022-166X

EDITORIAL POLICY: "Provides a forum for analysis of the role of education and training in enhancing production skills, employment opportunities, and income, as well as of manpower, health, and welfare policies as they relate to the labor market and to economic and social development. It gives priority to studies having empirical content."

REVIEW INFORMATION

REFEREED: Yes (I-A)   ACCEPTANCE RATE: less than 20%

NUMBER OF REVIEWER(S)/MS., EXCLUDING IN-HOUSE EDITOR(S): 2

REVIEWER(S): External   ARTICLES/AVG. ISSUE: 6

REVIEWING CRITERIA USED: BLIND REVIEW: Yes (Preliminary screening and external review)

  MANUSCRIPT SUBMISSION AIDS: 1, 2

  BIAS SAFEGUARDS: 3, 5, 7, 9

AVERAGE REVIEW TIME: 6 mos.   PUBLICATION TIME LAG: 8 mos.

MANUSCRIPT RETURNED WITH COMMENTS: Yes, SASE required

MANUSCRIPT INFORMATION

GUIDELINES PUBLISHED: Each issue

STYLE REQUIREMENTS PUBLISHED: Each issue

STYLE MANUAL USED: Chicago

PREFERRED TOPICS: Econometrics of Retirement policy, transfer policy, labor market studies, health, education, new methodology

QUERY LETTER: No   SIMULTANEOUS SUBMISSION: No

ABSTRACT WITH MANUSCRIPT: 100 wds.   COVER LETTER: Yes

NUMBER OF MANUSCRIPT COPIES: 4   MANUSCRIPT LENGTH: 20 pp.

SUBMISSION FEE: No   PAGE CHARGES: No

MANUSCRIPT ACKNOWLEDGED: Yes   EARLY PUBLICATION OPTION: No

COPYRIGHT OWNER: Publisher   REPRINTS: Optional purchase

AUTHOR COMPENSATION: 2 free journals

MANUSCRIPT ADDRESS: Eugene Smolensky, Editor, The Journal of Human Resources, 4315 Social Science Building, University of Wisconsin, 1180 Observatory Drive, Madison, WI 53706

The Journal of Industrial Economics

FIRST PUBLISHED: 1952   FREQUENCY: Q   CIRCULATION: 1,900
AFFILIATION: None

AUDIENCE: Academic/Professional
PERCENT OF UNSOLICITED ARTICLES/ISSUE: 100%   ISSN: 0022-1821
EDITORIAL POLICY: Publication of academic papers in the field of
  industrial organization and theory of the firm, both widely
  defined; a blend of theory and evidence, with a particular tradition of case studies; policy applications.

REVIEW INFORMATION

REFEREED: Yes (II-B)   ACCEPTANCE RATE: 16%
NUMBER OF REVIEWER(S)/MS., EXCLUDING IN-HOUSE EDITOR(S): 2
REVIEWER(S): Board and external   ARTICLES/AVG. ISSUE: 6
REVIEWING CRITERIA USED: BLIND REVIEW: No
  MANUSCRIPT SUBMISSION AIDS: 1, 2
  BIAS SAFEGUARDS: 4, 5, 6, 9
AVERAGE REVIEW TIME: 8 wks.   PUBLICATION TIME LAG: 8 mos.
MANUSCRIPT RETURNED WITH COMMENTS: Yes, SASE required

MANUSCRIPT INFORMATION

GUIDELINES PUBLISHED: Each issue
STYLE REQUIREMENTS PUBLISHED: Vol. 35, No. 1 (1987); also on request
STYLE MANUAL USED: In-house
PREFERRED TOPICS: Industrial organization, theory of the firm

QUERY LETTER: No   SIMULTANEOUS SUBMISSION: No
ABSTRACT WITH MANUSCRIPT: 100 wds. max. COVER LETTER: Yes
NUMBER OF MANUSCRIPT COPIES: 3   MANUSCRIPT LENGTH: 7,500 wds.

SUBMISSION FEE: No   PAGE CHARGES: No

MANUSCRIPT ACKNOWLEDGED: Yes   EARLY PUBLICATION OPTION: No
COPYRIGHT OWNER: Publisher   REPRINTS: Optional purchase

AUTHOR COMPENSATION: 25 free reprints/tear sheets
MANUSCRIPT ADDRESS: North American Editor, The Journal of Industrial
  Economics, Department of Public Policy and Management, The Wharton
  School, University of Pennsylvania, Philadelphia, PA 19104

Journal of Institutional and Theoretical Economics (JITE) / Zeitschrift für die Gesamte Staatswissenschaft

FIRST PUBLISHED: 1844   FREQUENCY: Q   CIRCULATION: 920
AFFILIATION: None

AUDIENCE: Academic/Professional
PERCENT OF UNSOLICITED ARTICLES/ISSUE: 81-100%   ISSN: 0044-2550
EDITORIAL POLICY: Covers the expanding field of modern institutional
  economics. Its approach is theoretical with the analytical rigor
  expected of theoretical contributions.

REVIEW INFORMATION

REFEREED: Yes (II-B)   ACCEPTANCE RATE: 22%
NUMBER OF REVIEWER(S)/MS., EXCLUDING IN-HOUSE EDITOR(S): 2
REVIEWER(S): Board and external   ARTICLES/AVG. ISSUE: 7
REVIEWING CRITERIA USED: BLIND REVIEW: No
  MANUSCRIPT SUBMISSION AIDS: 2
  BIAS SAFEGUARDS: 4, 5, 6, 9
AVERAGE REVIEW TIME: 2 mos.   PUBLICATION TIME LAG: 5 mos.
MANUSCRIPT RETURNED WITH COMMENTS: Yes, SASE required

MANUSCRIPT INFORMATION

GUIDELINES PUBLISHED: No; available on request
STYLE REQUIREMENTS PUBLISHED: Each issue (brief); also on request
STYLE MANUAL USED: In-house   (detailed)
PREFERRED TOPICS: Economics of property rights and of institutional
  evolution, transaction-cost economics, constitutional choice,
  experimental analysis of economic decision-making, etc.
QUERY LETTER: No   SIMULTANEOUS SUBMISSION: No
ABSTRACT WITH MANUSCRIPT: 100 wds.   COVER LETTER: Yes
NUMBER OF MANUSCRIPT COPIES: 3   MANUSCRIPT LENGTH: 25 pp.

SUBMISSION FEE: No   PAGE CHARGES: No

MANUSCRIPT ACKNOWLEDGED: Yes   EARLY PUBLICATION OPTION: Yes
COPYRIGHT OWNER: Publisher   REPRINTS: Not available

AUTHOR COMPENSATION: 40 free reprints/tear sheets
MANUSCRIPT ADDRESS: Prof. Dr. Rudolf Richter, Editor, Journal of
  Institutional and Theoretical Economics, D-6600 Saarbrücken 11
  Universitätsgebäude Nr. 31, West Germany

Journal of Labor Economics

FIRST PUBLISHED: 1983   FREQUENCY: Q   CIRCULATION: 1,450

AFFILIATION: National Opinion Research Center, Economics Research Center, 1155 East 60th Street, Chicago, IL 60637

AUDIENCE: Academic/Professional

PERCENT OF UNSOLICITED ARTICLES/ISSUE: 81-100%   ISSN: 0734-306X

EDITORIAL POLICY: Aims to be broadly based within the field of labor economics, publishing both theoretical and applied research on a wide range of issues which concern labor economics, including the supply and demand for labor services, compensation, labor markets, the distribution of income, labor demographics, unions and collective bargaining, and applied and policy issues.

REVIEW INFORMATION

REFEREED: No   ACCEPTANCE RATE: 24%

NUMBER OF REVIEWER(S)/MS., EXCLUDING IN-HOUSE EDITOR(S): 1

REVIEWER(S): External   ARTICLES/AVG. ISSUE: 7

REVIEWING CRITERIA USED: BLIND REVIEW: No

   MANUSCRIPT SUBMISSION AIDS: 2

   BIAS SAFEGUARDS: 4, 5, 9

AVERAGE REVIEW TIME: 4 mos.   PUBLICATION TIME LAG: 6 mos.

MANUSCRIPT RETURNED WITH COMMENTS: No

MANUSCRIPT INFORMATION

GUIDELINES PUBLISHED: No; not available

STYLE REQUIREMENTS PUBLISHED: Each issue

STYLE MANUAL USED: Chicago

PREFERRED TOPICS: Labor economics

QUERY LETTER: No   SIMULTANEOUS SUBMISSION: No

ABSTRACT WITH MANUSCRIPT: 100 wds.   COVER LETTER: No

NUMBER OF MANUSCRIPT COPIES: 4   MANUSCRIPT LENGTH: No limit

SUBMISSION FEE: No   PAGE CHARGES: No

MANUSCRIPT ACKNOWLEDGED: Yes   EARLY PUBLICATION OPTION: No

COPYRIGHT OWNER: Joint with publisher/ REPRINTS: Optional purchase sponsor

AUTHOR COMPENSATION: One-year subscription and 2 free copies of article

MANUSCRIPT ADDRESS: Editor, Journal of Labor Economics, 1101 East 58th Street, Chicago, IL 60637

Journal of Labor Research

FIRST PUBLISHED: 1980   FREQUENCY: Q   CIRCULATION: 1,100

AFFILIATION: George Mason University, Department of Economics.
  Address same as journal's.

AUDIENCE: Academic/Professional; Business/Industrial; Government

PERCENT OF UNSOLICITED ARTICLES/ISSUE: 81-100%   ISSN: 0195-3613

EDITORIAL POLICY: Publishes articles on the economic and political

  behavior of labor unions, the internal organization and operations

  of unions, and their impact on public policy.

REVIEW INFORMATION

REFEREED: Yes (II-A)   ACCEPTANCE RATE: 25%

NUMBER OF REVIEWER(S)/MS., EXCLUDING IN-HOUSE EDITOR(S): 2

REVIEWER(S): Board and external   ARTICLES/AVG. ISSUE: 8

REVIEWING CRITERIA USED: BLIND REVIEW: Yes (Board

  MANUSCRIPT SUBMISSION AIDS: 1   and external review)

  BIAS SAFEGUARDS: 3, 5, 9

AVERAGE REVIEW TIME: 6 wks.   PUBLICATION TIME LAG: 6 mos.

MANUSCRIPT RETURNED WITH COMMENTS: Yes, SASE required

MANUSCRIPT INFORMATION

GUIDELINES PUBLISHED: Each issue

STYLE REQUIREMENTS PUBLISHED: No; available on request

STYLE MANUAL USED: In-house

PREFERRED TOPICS: Labor economics, collective bargaining, labor-

  management relations, public choice

QUERY LETTER: No   SIMULTANEOUS SUBMISSION: Yes

ABSTRACT WITH MANUSCRIPT: 100 wds.   COVER LETTER: Yes

NUMBER OF MANUSCRIPT COPIES: 3   MANUSCRIPT LENGTH: 30 pp.

SUBMISSION FEE: $20. for nonmembers/   PAGE CHARGES: No
  nonsubscribers

MANUSCRIPT ACKNOWLEDGED: Yes   EARLY PUBLICATION OPTION: No

COPYRIGHT OWNER: Journal   REPRINTS: Optional purchase

AUTHOR COMPENSATION: None

MANUSCRIPT ADDRESS: James T. Bennett, Editor, Journal of Labor Research,
  George Mason University, 4400 University Drive, Fairfax, VA 22030

Journal of Macroeconomics

FIRST PUBLISHED: 1979   FREQUENCY: Q   CIRCULATION: 900

AFFILIATION: Louisiana State University, College of Business Administration. Address same as journal's.

AUDIENCE: Academic/Professional; Business/Industrial; Government

PERCENT OF UNSOLICITED ARTICLES/ISSUE: 100%   ISSN: 0164-0704

EDITORIAL POLICY: "Contains articles on macroeconomic theory, related
empirical work, and macroeconomic policy in theoretical and applied
areas. Studies dealing with countries other than the U.S. are
welcome if they are likely to appeal to a reasonable proportion of
the Journal's readership. Articles published in the Journal reflect
all schools of thought."

REVIEW INFORMATION

REFEREED: Yes (I-A)   ACCEPTANCE RATE: 65%

NUMBER OF REVIEWER(S)/MS., EXCLUDING IN-HOUSE EDITOR(S): 2

REVIEWER(S): External   ARTICLES/AVG. ISSUE: 10

REVIEWING CRITERIA USED: BLIND REVIEW: Yes (Preliminary
  MANUSCRIPT SUBMISSION AIDS: 2   screening only)

  BIAS SAFEGUARDS: 3, 5, 7, 9

AVERAGE REVIEW TIME: 2 wks.   PUBLICATION TIME LAG: 5 mos.

MANUSCRIPT RETURNED WITH COMMENTS: Yes

MANUSCRIPT INFORMATION

GUIDELINES PUBLISHED: No; available on request

STYLE REQUIREMENTS PUBLISHED: Each issue (brief); also available on request
                                                              (detailed)
STYLE MANUAL USED: Chicago

PREFERRED TOPICS: Macroeconomics

QUERY LETTER: No   SIMULTANEOUS SUBMISSION: No

ABSTRACT WITH MANUSCRIPT: 100 wds. COVER LETTER: Yes

NUMBER OF MANUSCRIPT COPIES: 3   MANUSCRIPT LENGTH: No limit

SUBMISSION FEE: No   PAGE CHARGES: No

MANUSCRIPT ACKNOWLEDGED: Yes   EARLY PUBLICATION OPTION: No

COPYRIGHT OWNER: Publisher   REPRINTS: Optional purchase

AUTHOR COMPENSATION: 25 free reprints/tear sheets

MANUSCRIPT ADDRESS: David J. Smyth, Editor, Journal of Macroeconomics,
Louisiana State University, College of Business Administration, CEBA
3139, Baton Rouge, LA 70803

Journal of Mathematical Economics

FIRST PUBLISHED: 1974   FREQUENCY: 3/Yr.   CIRCULATION: N.R.
AFFILIATION: None

AUDIENCE: Academic/Professional

PERCENT OF UNSOLICITED ARTICLES/ISSUE: 100%   ISSN: 0304-4068

EDITORIAL POLICY: Articles considered for publication include
"contributions to economic theory which are formal enough to make
them accessible to mathematicians; contributions of an essentially
mathematical nature" originating in economics or "of actual or
potential use in mathematical economics; surveys of existing work
in particular fields of mathematical economics or mathematics."

REVIEW INFORMATION

REFEREED: No   ACCEPTANCE RATE: N.R.

NUMBER OF REVIEWER(S)/MS., EXCLUDING IN-HOUSE EDITOR(S): 1

REVIEWER(S): Board or external   ARTICLES/AVG. ISSUE: 5-8

REVIEWING CRITERIA USED: BLIND REVIEW: No

   MANUSCRIPT SUBMISSION AIDS: 1, 2

   BIAS SAFEGUARDS: 5, 9

AVERAGE REVIEW TIME: N.R.   PUBLICATION TIME LAG: N.R.

MANUSCRIPT RETURNED WITH COMMENTS: No

MANUSCRIPT INFORMATION

GUIDELINES PUBLISHED: Each issue

STYLE REQUIREMENTS PUBLISHED: Each issue

STYLE MANUAL USED: In-house

PREFERRED TOPICS: Economics and mathematics

QUERY LETTER: No   SIMULTANEOUS SUBMISSION: No

ABSTRACT WITH MANUSCRIPT: 150 wds.   COVER LETTER: No

NUMBER OF MANUSCRIPT COPIES: 3   MANUSCRIPT LENGTH: No limit

SUBMISSION FEE: No   PAGE CHARGES: No

MANUSCRIPT ACKNOWLEDGED: Yes   EARLY PUBLICATION OPTION: No

COPYRIGHT OWNER: Publisher   REPRINTS: Optional purchase

AUTHOR COMPENSATION: None

MANUSCRIPT ADDRESS: Prof. Andreu Mas-Colell, Editor, Journal of
Mathematical Economics, Department of Economics, Littauer Center,
Harvard University, Cambridge, MA 02138

Journal of Monetary Economics

FIRST PUBLISHED: 1975   FREQUENCY: Bi-M   CIRCULATION: 1,500

AFFILIATION: University of Rochester, Graduate School of Management
  and Department of Economics. Address same as journal's.

AUDIENCE: Academic/Professional

PERCENT OF UNSOLICITED ARTICLES/ISSUE: 100%   ISSN: 0304-3923

EDITORIAL POLICY: Specialized forum for publication of research in
  monetary economics, including monetary analysis and the working
  and structure of financial institutions.

REVIEW INFORMATION

REFEREED: No   ACCEPTANCE RATE: 14.5%

NUMBER OF REVIEWER(S)/MS., EXCLUDING IN-HOUSE EDITOR(S): 1

REVIEWER(S): External   ARTICLES/AVG. ISSUE: 6-7

REVIEWING CRITERIA USED: BLIND REVIEW: No

  MANUSCRIPT SUBMISSION AIDS: 1, 2

  BIAS SAFEGUARDS: 4, 5, 6, 9

AVERAGE REVIEW TIME: 7 wks.   PUBLICATION TIME LAG: 4-5 mos.

MANUSCRIPT RETURNED WITH COMMENTS: No

MANUSCRIPT INFORMATION

GUIDELINES PUBLISHED: Each issue

STYLE REQUIREMENTS PUBLISHED: Each issue

STYLE MANUAL USED: In-house

PREFERRED TOPICS: Monetary analysis, banking, credit markets,
  institutional arrangements

QUERY LETTER: No   SIMULTANEOUS SUBMISSION: No

ABSTRACT WITH MANUSCRIPT: 100 wds. COVER LETTER: Yes

NUMBER OF MANUSCRIPT COPIES: 3   MANUSCRIPT LENGTH: No limit

SUBMISSION FEE: $60. for subscribers; PAGE CHARGES: None
  $75. for others

MANUSCRIPT ACKNOWLEDGED: Yes   EARLY PUBLICATION OPTION: Yes

COPYRIGHT OWNER: Publisher   REPRINTS: Optional purchase

AUTHOR COMPENSATION: None

MANUSCRIPT ADDRESS: Robert G. King and Charles I. Plosser, Editors,
  Journal of Monetary Economics, Graduate School of Management,
  University of Rochester, Rochester, NY 14627

Journal of Policy Analysis and Management

FIRST PUBLISHED: 1981   FREQUENCY: Q   CIRCULATION: 2,600

AFFILIATION: Association for Public Policy Analysis and Management, c/o
  D. Noto, Inst. of Policy Sciences, Duke University, Durham, NC 27706

AUDIENCE: Academic/Professional; Government

PERCENT OF UNSOLICITED ARTICLES/ISSUE: 81-100%   ISSN: 0276-8739

EDITORIAL POLICY: The journal seeks articles that deal with the
  methods and practice of professional policy analysis and that
  explore substantive issues of public policy from an interdisciplinary perspective.

REVIEW INFORMATION

REFEREED: Yes (I-A)   ACCEPTANCE RATE: 18%

NUMBER OF REVIEWER(S)/MS., EXCLUDING IN-HOUSE EDITOR(S): 2

REVIEWER(S): External   ARTICLES/AVG. ISSUE: 6

REVIEWING CRITERIA USED: BLIND REVIEW: Yes (External
  MANUSCRIPT SUBMISSION AIDS: 0   review only)
  BIAS SAFEGUARDS: 3, 5, 7, 9

AVERAGE REVIEW TIME: 6 wks.   PUBLICATION TIME LAG: 6 mos.

MANUSCRIPT RETURNED WITH COMMENTS: No

MANUSCRIPT INFORMATION

GUIDELINES PUBLISHED: No; available on request

STYLE REQUIREMENTS PUBLISHED: No; available on request

STYLE MANUAL USED: In-house

PREFERRED TOPICS: Public policy, public management

QUERY LETTER: No   SIMULTANEOUS SUBMISSION: No

ABSTRACT WITH MANUSCRIPT: 100-150 wds. COVER LETTER: Yes

NUMBER OF MANUSCRIPT COPIES: 3   MANUSCRIPT LENGTH: 10-40 pp.

SUBMISSION FEE: No   PAGE CHARGES: No

MANUSCRIPT ACKNOWLEDGED: Yes   EARLY PUBLICATION OPTION: No

COPYRIGHT OWNER: Publisher   REPRINTS: Optional purchase

AUTHOR COMPENSATION: None

MANUSCRIPT ADDRESS: Prof. David L. Weimer, Editor, Journal of Policy
  Analysis and Management , Public Policy Analysis Program, Harkness
  Hall 320, University of Rochester, Rochester, NY 14627

Journal of Policy Modeling

FIRST PUBLISHED: 1979   FREQUENCY: Q   CIRCULATION: 2,300

AFFILIATION: Society for Policy Modeling, c/o Dr. Douglas O. Walker, 543 Kings Highway East, Leonardo, NJ   07737

AUDIENCE: Academic/Professional; Business/Industrial; Government

PERCENT OF UNSOLICITED ARTICLES/ISSUE: 21-40%   ISSN: 0161-8938

EDITORIAL POLICY: Provides "a forum for analysis and debate concerning international policy issues. The Journal addresses questions of critical import to the world community as a whole, and it focuses upon the economic, social, and political interdependencies between national and regional systems. . . . [It] emphasizes formal modeling techniques serving the purposes of decision making."

REVIEW INFORMATION

REFEREED: Yes (I-B)   ACCEPTANCE RATE: 12%

NUMBER OF REVIEWER(S)/MS., EXCLUDING IN-HOUSE EDITOR(S): 3-4

REVIEWER(S): 2 board, 2 external   ARTICLES/AVG. ISSUE: 7

REVIEWING CRITERIA USED: BLIND REVIEW: No

  MANUSCRIPT SUBMISSION AIDS: 1, 2

  BIAS SAFEGUARDS: 4, 5, 6, 7, 9

AVERAGE REVIEW TIME: 6-8 wks.   PUBLICATION TIME LAG: 6-8 wks.

MANUSCRIPT RETURNED WITH COMMENTS: Yes

MANUSCRIPT INFORMATION

GUIDELINES PUBLISHED: Each issue

STYLE REQUIREMENTS PUBLISHED: Each issue

STYLE MANUAL USED: In-house

PREFERRED TOPICS: International policy issues

QUERY LETTER: No   SIMULTANEOUS SUBMISSION: No

ABSTRACT WITH MANUSCRIPT: Yes   COVER LETTER: Yes

NUMBER OF MANUSCRIPT COPIES: 3   MANUSCRIPT LENGTH: 25-30 pp.

SUBMISSION FEE: No   PAGE CHARGES: No

MANUSCRIPT ACKNOWLEDGED: Yes   EARLY PUBLICATION OPTION: Yes

COPYRIGHT OWNER: Journal   REPRINTS: Purchase required

AUTHOR COMPENSATION: None

MANUSCRIPT ADDRESS: Antonio M. Costa, Editor, Journal of Policy Modeling, OECD, 2, rue Andre-Pascal, 75775 Paris Cedex 16, France

Journal of Political Economy

FIRST PUBLISHED: 1892 FREQUENCY: Bi-M CIRCULATION: 7,000

AFFILIATION: University of Chicago, Department of Economics and
the Graduate School of Business. Address same as journal's.

AUDIENCE: Academic/Professional

PERCENT OF UNSOLICITED ARTICLES/ISSUE: 100% ISSN: 0022-3808

EDITORIAL POLICY: Articles of a general nature rather than highly
specialized are published. All areas of economics are included.

REVIEW INFORMATION

REFEREED: No ACCEPTANCE RATE: 11-20%

NUMBER OF REVIEWER(S)/MS., EXCLUDING IN-HOUSE EDITOR(S): 1

REVIEWER(S): External ARTICLES/AVG. ISSUE: 8-10

REVIEWING CRITERIA USED: BLIND REVIEW: No

  MANUSCRIPT SUBMISSION AIDS: 0

  BIAS SAFEGUARDS: 5, 6, 9

AVERAGE REVIEW TIME: 3-6 mos. PUBLICATION TIME LAG: 6 mos.

MANUSCRIPT RETURNED WITH COMMENTS: No

MANUSCRIPT INFORMATION

GUIDELINES PUBLISHED: No; not available

STYLE REQUIREMENTS PUBLISHED: No; available on request

STYLE MANUAL USED: Chicago

PREFERRED TOPICS: Economics

QUERY LETTER: No SIMULTANEOUS SUBMISSION: No

ABSTRACT WITH MANUSCRIPT: 100 wds. COVER LETTER: Yes

NUMBER OF MANUSCRIPT COPIES: 3 MANUSCRIPT LENGTH: N.R.

SUBMISSION FEE: $40. PAGE CHARGES: No

MANUSCRIPT ACKNOWLEDGED: Yes EARLY PUBLICATION OPTION: No

COPYRIGHT OWNER: Publisher REPRINTS: Optional purchase

AUTHOR COMPENSATION: 2 free journals

MANUSCRIPT ADDRESS: Editor of the Journal of Political Economy,
1126 East 59th Street, Chicago, IL 60637

Journal of Portfolio Management

FIRST PUBLISHED: 1975   FREQUENCY: Q   CIRCULATION: 2,500
AFFILIATION: None

AUDIENCE: Academic/Professional; Business/Industrial
PERCENT OF UNSOLICITED ARTICLES/ISSUE: 90%   ISSN: 0095-4918
EDITORIAL POLICY: Publishes current developments in investment
    management.

REVIEW INFORMATION

REFEREED: Yes (II-A)   ACCEPTANCE RATE: 12-14%
NUMBER OF REVIEWER(S)/MS., EXCLUDING IN-HOUSE EDITOR(S): 2
REVIEWER(S): Board and external   ARTICLES/AVG. ISSUE: 12
REVIEWING CRITERIA USED: BLIND REVIEW: Yes (Board
  MANUSCRIPT SUBMISSION AIDS: 2   and external review)
  BIAS SAFEGUARDS: 3, 4, 5, 9
AVERAGE REVIEW TIME: 6 wks.   PUBLICATION TIME LAG: 9 mos.
MANUSCRIPT RETURNED WITH COMMENTS: Yes

MANUSCRIPT INFORMATION

GUIDELINES PUBLISHED: No; not available
STYLE REQUIREMENTS PUBLISHED: Each issue
STYLE MANUAL USED: In-house
PREFERRED TOPICS: Portfolio management

QUERY LETTER: No   SIMULTANEOUS SUBMISSION: No
ABSTRACT WITH MANUSCRIPT: No   COVER LETTER: Yes
NUMBER OF MANUSCRIPT COPIES: 3   MANUSCRIPT LENGTH: No limit

SUBMISSION FEE: No   PAGE CHARGES: No

MANUSCRIPT ACKNOWLEDGED: Yes   EARLY PUBLICATION OPTION: No
COPYRIGHT OWNER: Publisher   REPRINTS: Optional purchase

AUTHOR COMPENSATION: One-year subscription and 5 free journals
MANUSCRIPT ADDRESS: Frank J. Fabozzi, Managing Editor, Journal of
    Portfolio Management, 29 Valley Spring Road, Newton, MA 02158

Journal of Post Keynesian Economics / JPKE

FIRST PUBLISHED: 1978   FREQUENCY: Q   CIRCULATION: 1,850
AFFILIATION: None

AUDIENCE: Academic/Professional

PERCENT OF UNSOLICITED ARTICLES/ISSUE: 100%   ISSN: 0160-3477

EDITORIAL POLICY: "A general scholarly journal receptive to innovative
  theoretical work that can shed fresh light on contemporary economic
  problems. . . . Committed to the principle that the cumulative development of economic theory is possible only when the theory is con-
  tinuously subject to challenge, in terms of its ability both to
  explain the real world and to provide a reliable guide to public
  policy."

REVIEW INFORMATION

REFEREED: No   ACCEPTANCE RATE: 24%

NUMBER OF REVIEWER(S)/MS., EXCLUDING IN-HOUSE EDITOR(S): 1

REVIEWER(S): External   ARTICLES/AVG. ISSUE: 12

REVIEWING CRITERIA USED: BLIND REVIEW: No

  MANUSCRIPT SUBMISSION AIDS: 0

  BIAS SAFEGUARDS: 5, 9

AVERAGE REVIEW TIME: 4-6 wks.   PUBLICATION TIME LAG: 3-9 mos.

MANUSCRIPT RETURNED WITH COMMENTS: No

MANUSCRIPT INFORMATION

GUIDELINES PUBLISHED: No; not available

STYLE REQUIREMENTS PUBLISHED: No; available on request

STYLE MANUAL USED: In-house

PREFERRED TOPICS: Economics

QUERY LETTER: No   SIMULTANEOUS SUBMISSION: No

ABSTRACT WITH MANUSCRIPT: No   COVER LETTER: Yes

NUMBER OF MANUSCRIPT COPIES: 3   MANUSCRIPT LENGTH: 20 pp.

SUBMISSION FEE: $26. for nonmembers/   PAGE CHARGES: None
  nonsubscribers

MANUSCRIPT ACKNOWLEDGED: Yes   EARLY PUBLICATION OPTION: No

COPYRIGHT OWNER: Publisher   REPRINTS: Optional purchase

AUTHOR COMPENSATION: None

MANUSCRIPT ADDRESS: Prof. Paul Davidson, Editor, Journal of Post
  Keynesian Economics, Rutgers University, Winants Hall, New
  Brusnwick, NJ 08903

Journal of Public Economics

FIRST PUBLISHED: 1972   FREQUENCY: 9/Yr.   CIRCULATION: 1,440
AFFILIATION: None

AUDIENCE: Academic/Professional; Business/Industrial; Government
PERCENT OF UNSOLICITED ARTICLES/ISSUE: 100%   ISSN: 0047-2727
EDITORIAL POLICY: To provide a forum for the publication of research
  in public economics, interpreted widely to cover all aspects of
  government policy.

REVIEW INFORMATION

REFEREED: Yes (I-B)   ACCEPTANCE RATE: 15%
NUMBER OF REVIEWER(S)/MS., EXCLUDING IN-HOUSE EDITOR(S): 2
REVIEWER(S): External   ARTICLES/AVG. ISSUE: 7-8
REVIEWING CRITERIA USED: BLIND REVIEW: No
  MANUSCRIPT SUBMISSION AIDS: 1, 2
  BIAS SAFEGUARDS: 4, 5, 6, 7, 9
AVERAGE REVIEW TIME: 3 mos.   PUBLICATION TIME LAG: 4 mos.
MANUSCRIPT RETURNED WITH COMMENTS: No

MANUSCRIPT INFORMATION

GUIDELINES PUBLISHED: Each issue
STYLE REQUIREMENTS PUBLISHED: Each issue
STYLE MANUAL USED: In-house
PREFERRED TOPICS: Public economics, taxation, public spending

QUERY LETTER: No   SIMULTANEOUS SUBMISSION: No
ABSTRACT WITH MANUSCRIPT: 100 wds. max. COVER LETTER: Yes
NUMBER OF MANUSCRIPT COPIES: 4   MANUSCRIPT LENGTH: No limit

SUBMISSION FEE: No   PAGE CHARGES: No

MANUSCRIPT ACKNOWLEDGED: Yes   EARLY PUBLICATION OPTION: No
COPYRIGHT OWNER: Publisher   REPRINTS: Optional purchase

AUTHOR COMPENSATION: 25 free reprints/tear sheets
MANUSCRIPT ADDRESS: Prof. A. B. Atkinson, Editor, Journal of Public
  Economics, London School of Economics, 10 Portugal Street, London,
  WC2A 2HD, U.K.

Journal of Regional Science

FIRST PUBLISHED: 1958   FREQUENCY: Q   CIRCULATION: 2,000

AFFILIATION: Regional Science Research Institute, P.O. Box 3735,
  Peace Dale, RI   02883

AUDIENCE: Academic/Professional; Business/Industrial

PERCENT OF UNSOLICITED ARTICLES/ISSUE: 100%   ISSN: 0022-4146

EDITORIAL POLICY: "Devoted to research and studies on the structure,
  function, and operation of regions from an economical, social,
  and political standpoint."

REVIEW INFORMATION

REFEREED: Yes (II-B)   ACCEPTANCE RATE: 21%

NUMBER OF REVIEWER(S)/MS., EXCLUDING IN-HOUSE EDITOR(S): 3

REVIEWER(S): 2 board, 1 external   ARTICLES/AVG. ISSUE: 6-10

REVIEWING CRITERIA USED: BLIND REVIEW: No

  MANUSCRIPT SUBMISSION AIDS: 1

  BIAS SAFEGUARDS: 5, 9*

AVERAGE REVIEW TIME: 3-4 mos.   PUBLICATION TIME LAG: 12 mos.

MANUSCRIPT RETURNED WITH COMMENTS: Yes

MANUSCRIPT INFORMATION

GUIDELINES PUBLISHED: Each issue

STYLE REQUIREMENTS PUBLISHED: No; available on request

STYLE MANUAL USED: In-house; Chicago

PREFERRED TOPICS: Economics, geography, urban and regional studies

QUERY LETTER: No   SIMULTANEOUS SUBMISSION: No

ABSTRACT WITH MANUSCRIPT: 100 wds.   COVER LETTER: Yes

NUMBER OF MANUSCRIPT COPIES: 2   MANUSCRIPT LENGTH: 25 pp.

SUBMISSION FEE: No   PAGE CHARGES: $30. per page
                                  (voluntary)

MANUSCRIPT ACKNOWLEDGED: Yes   EARLY PUBLICATION OPTION: No

COPYRIGHT OWNER: Publisher   REPRINTS: Optional purchase

AUTHOR COMPENSATION: 25 free reprints/tear sheets

MANUSCRIPT ADDRESS: Journal of Regional Science, Regional Science
  Department, University of Pennsylvania, 3718 Locust Walk, Philadelphia, PA   19104

Journal of Research in Islamic Economics

FIRST PUBLISHED: 1983   FREQUENCY: S-A   CIRCULATION: 3,000

AFFILIATION: King Abdulaziz University, Centre for Research in
  Islamic Economics. Address same as journal's.

AUDIENCE: Academic/Professional

PERCENT OF UNSOLICITED ARTICLES/ISSUE: 41-60%   ISSN: None

EDITORIAL POLICY: "Devoted to theoretical research in Islamic Economics.
  Empirical studies that have important theoretical implications are
  included in the scope of the journal, as are research papers contain-
  ing critiques from the Islamic point of view of well known economic
  hypotheses."

REVIEW INFORMATION

REFEREED: Yes (I-A)   ACCEPTANCE RATE: 40%

NUMBER OF REVIEWER(S)/MS., EXCLUDING IN-HOUSE EDITOR(S): 2

REVIEWER(S): Board   ARTICLES/AVG. ISSUE: 5

REVIEWING CRITERIA USED: BLIND REVIEW: Yes (External
  MANUSCRIPT SUBMISSION AIDS: 1, 2   review only)
  BIAS SAFEGUARDS: 3, 4, 5, 6, 7, 9*

AVERAGE REVIEW TIME: 3 mos.   PUBLICATION TIME LAG: 6 mos.

MANUSCRIPT RETURNED WITH COMMENTS: Yes

MANUSCRIPT INFORMATION

GUIDELINES PUBLISHED: Each issue

STYLE REQUIREMENTS PUBLISHED: Each issue

STYLE MANUAL USED: Chicago

PREFERRED TOPICS: Islamic economics, Islamic banking

QUERY LETTER: No   SIMULTANEOUS SUBMISSION: No

ABSTRACT WITH MANUSCRIPT: 200 wds. COVER LETTER: Yes

NUMBER OF MANUSCRIPT COPIES: 2   MANUSCRIPT LENGTH: 30 pp.

SUBMISSION FEE: No   PAGE CHARGES: No

MANUSCRIPT ACKNOWLEDGED: Yes   EARLY PUBLICATION OPTION: No

COPYRIGHT OWNER: Journal   REPRINTS: Not available

AUTHOR COMPENSATION: None

MANUSCRIPT ADDRESS: Dr. Omar Zohair Hafiz, Chief Editor, Journal of
  Research in Islamic Economics, King Abdulaziz University, P.O. Box
  16711, Jeddah 21474, Saudi Arabia

The Journal of Risk and Insurance

FIRST PUBLISHED: 1933   FREQUENCY: Q   CIRCULATION: 2,000

AFFILIATION: American Risk and Insurance Association, College of Business
  Administration, University of Central Florida, Orlando, Florida 32816

AUDIENCE: Academic/Professional; Business/Industrial

PERCENT OF UNSOLICITED ARTICLES/ISSUE: 100%   ISSN: 0022-4367

EDITORIAL POLICY: A multi-disciplinary publication with primary
  emphasis on high quality analytical, mathematical, and empirical
  research in the risk management and insurance area.

REVIEW INFORMATION

REFEREED: Yes (I-A)   ACCEPTANCE RATE: 26%

NUMBER OF REVIEWER(S)/MS., EXCLUDING IN-HOUSE EDITOR(S): 3

REVIEWER(S): 1 board, 2 external   ARTICLES/AVG. ISSUE: 6-10

REVIEWING CRITERIA USED: BLIND REVIEW: Yes (External
  MANUSCRIPT SUBMISSION AIDS: 1   review only)
  BIAS SAFEGUARDS: 3, 5, 6, 7, 9

AVERAGE REVIEW TIME: 3-4 mos.   PUBLICATION TIME LAG: 9 mos.

MANUSCRIPT RETURNED WITH COMMENTS: Yes

MANUSCRIPT INFORMATION

GUIDELINES PUBLISHED: Each issue (brief); September 1977 (detailed)

STYLE REQUIREMENTS PUBLISHED: No; available on request

STYLE MANUAL USED: In-house

PREFERRED TOPICS: Insurance (private and social), risk management

QUERY LETTER: No   SIMULTANEOUS SUBMISSION: Yes

ABSTRACT WITH MANUSCRIPT: 100 wds.   COVER LETTER: Yes

NUMBER OF MANUSCRIPT COPIES: 4   MANUSCRIPT LENGTH: 20-25 pp.

SUBMISSION FEE: No   PAGE CHARGES: No

MANUSCRIPT ACKNOWLEDGED: Yes   EARLY PUBLICATION OPTION: No

COPYRIGHT OWNER: Journal and author   REPRINTS: Optional purchase

AUTHOR COMPENSATION: One free journal

MANUSCRIPT ADDRESS: Dr. S. Travis Pritchett, Editor, The Journal of
  Risk and Insurance, Insurance Studies Center, College of Business
  Administration, University of South Carolina, Columbia, SC 29208

Journal of the Royal Statistical Society, Series A (General)

FIRST PUBLISHED: 1838   FREQUENCY: Irreg.   CIRCULATION: 1,530
AFFILIATION: Royal Statistical Society. Address same as journal's.

AUDIENCE: Academic/Professional; Business/Industrial; Government
PERCENT OF UNSOLICITED ARTICLES/ISSUE: 81-100%   ISSN: 0035-9238
EDITORIAL POLICY: Original papers of general statistical interest
  which are likely to appeal to Fellows because of their substantive
  rather than technical statistical content. Economic, social and
  governmental issues are of particular concern to Series A.

REVIEW INFORMATION

REFEREED: No   ACCEPTANCE RATE: 20%
NUMBER OF REVIEWER(S)/MS., EXCLUDING IN-HOUSE EDITOR(S): 1
REVIEWER(S): Board or external   ARTICLES/AVG. ISSUE: 4
REVIEWING CRITERIA USED: BLIND REVIEW: No
  MANUSCRIPT SUBMISSION AIDS: 1
  BIAS SAFEGUARDS: 5, 8, 9*
AVERAGE REVIEW TIME: 3 mos.   PUBLICATION TIME LAG: 6 mos.
MANUSCRIPT RETURNED WITH COMMENTS: Yes, SASE required

MANUSCRIPT INFORMATION

GUIDELINES PUBLISHED: Each issue
STYLE REQUIREMENTS PUBLISHED: No; not available
STYLE MANUAL USED: In-house
PREFERRED TOPICS: Social, economic, government

QUERY LETTER: No   SIMULTANEOUS SUBMISSION: No
ABSTRACT WITH MANUSCRIPT: Yes   COVER LETTER: No
NUMBER OF MANUSCRIPT COPIES: 2   MANUSCRIPT LENGTH: 5,000 wds.

SUBMISSION FEE: No   PAGE CHARGES: No

MANUSCRIPT ACKNOWLEDGED: Yes   EARLY PUBLICATION OPTION: No
COPYRIGHT OWNER: Royal Statistical   REPRINTS: Optional purchase
  Society
AUTHOR COMPENSATION: None
MANUSCRIPT ADDRESS: The Executive Secretary, Royal Statistical
  Society, 25 Enford Street, London W1H 2BH, U.K.

Journal of the Royal Statistical Society, Series B (Methodological)

FIRST PUBLISHED: 1934   FREQUENCY: Irreg.   CIRCULATION: 4,100
AFFILIATION: Royal Statistical Society. Address same as journal's.

AUDIENCE: Academic/Professional
PERCENT OF UNSOLICITED ARTICLES/ISSUE: 95-100%   ISSN: 0035-9246
EDITORIAL POLICY: To publish research work of methodological
   statisticians.

REVIEW INFORMATION

REFEREED: Yes (II-B)   ACCEPTANCE RATE: 20%
NUMBER OF REVIEWER(S)/MS., EXCLUDING IN-HOUSE EDITOR(S): 2
REVIEWER(S): Board and external   ARTICLES/AVG. ISSUE: 12
REVIEWING CRITERIA USED: BLIND REVIEW: No
   MANUSCRIPT SUBMISSION AIDS: 1, 2
   BIAS SAFEGUARDS: 5, 9
AVERAGE REVIEW TIME: 3 mos.   PUBLICATION TIME LAG: 6 mos.
MANUSCRIPT RETURNED WITH COMMENTS: No

MANUSCRIPT INFORMATION

GUIDELINES PUBLISHED: Each issue
STYLE REQUIREMENTS PUBLISHED: Each issue
STYLE MANUAL USED: In-house
PREFERRED TOPICS: Statistical methodology

QUERY LETTER: No   SIMULTANEOUS SUBMISSION: No
ABSTRACT WITH MANUSCRIPT: Yes   COVER LETTER: Yes
NUMBER OF MANUSCRIPT COPIES: 4   MANUSCRIPT LENGTH: Not specified

SUBMISSION FEE: No   PAGE CHARGES: No

MANUSCRIPT ACKNOWLEDGED: Yes   EARLY PUBLICATION OPTION: No
COPYRIGHT OWNER: Royal Statistical   REPRINTS: Optional purchase
   Society
AUTHOR COMPENSATION: 25 free reprints/tear sheets
MANUSCRIPT ADDRESS: The Executive Secretary, Royal Statistical Society,
   25 Enford Street, London W1H 2BH, U.K.

Journal of Transport Economics and Policy

FIRST PUBLISHED: 1967   FREQUENCY: 3/Yr.   CIRCULATION: 1,375

AFFILIATION: London School of Economics and Political Science and the University of Bath. Address same as journal's.

AUDIENCE: Academic/Professional; Business/Industrial; Government

PERCENT OF UNSOLICITED ARTICLES/ISSUE: 100%   ISSN: 0022-5258

EDITORIAL POLICY: "Covers all aspects of transport economics and policy. Articles range from fundamental studies making original contributions to analysis to those exploring innovations in policy. Contributors range from mathematicians and theoretical economists to practising consultants, administrators and people involved in business."

REVIEW INFORMATION

REFEREED: No   ACCEPTANCE RATE: 33%

NUMBER OF REVIEWER(S)/MS., EXCLUDING IN-HOUSE EDITOR(S): 1

REVIEWER(S): External   ARTICLES/AVG. ISSUE: 6

REVIEWING CRITERIA USED: BLIND REVIEW: No

  MANUSCRIPT SUBMISSION AIDS: 1, 2

  BIAS SAFEGUARDS: 5, 6, 9*

AVERAGE REVIEW TIME: 4 mos.   PUBLICATION TIME LAG: 6 mos.

MANUSCRIPT RETURNED WITH COMMENTS: No

MANUSCRIPT INFORMATION

GUIDELINES PUBLISHED: Each issue

STYLE REQUIREMENTS PUBLISHED: Each issue

STYLE MANUAL USED: In-house

PREFERRED TOPICS: Applied economics and econometrics, with direct or indirect transport applications

QUERY LETTER: No   SIMULTANEOUS SUBMISSION: No

ABSTRACT WITH MANUSCRIPT: 100 wds.   COVER LETTER: Yes

NUMBER OF MANUSCRIPT COPIES: 2   MANUSCRIPT LENGTH: No limit

SUBMISSION FEE: No   PAGE CHARGES: No

MANUSCRIPT ACKNOWLEDGED: Yes   EARLY PUBLICATION OPTION: No

COPYRIGHT OWNER: Journal   REPRINTS: Optional purchase

AUTHOR COMPENSATION: 1 free journal and 30 free reprints

MANUSCRIPT ADDRESS: The Editors, Journal of Transport Economics and Policy, University of Bath, Claverton Down, Bath BA2 7AY, U.K.

Journal of Urban Economics

FIRST PUBLISHED: 1974   FREQUENCY: Bi-M   CIRCULATION: 1,100
AFFILIATION: None

AUDIENCE: Academic/Professional
PERCENT OF UNSOLICITED ARTICLES/ISSUE: 100%   ISSN: 0094-1190
EDITORIAL POLICY: Publishes scholarly research papers on urban
  economics.

REVIEW INFORMATION

REFEREED: No   ACCEPTANCE RATE: 40%
NUMBER OF REVIEWER(S)/MS., EXCLUDING IN-HOUSE EDITOR(S): 1
REVIEWER(S): Board or external   ARTICLES/AVG. ISSUE: 10
REVIEWING CRITERIA USED: BLIND REVIEW: No
  MANUSCRIPT SUBMISSION AIDS: 1, 2
  BIAS SAFEGUARDS: 5, 9
AVERAGE REVIEW TIME: 2 mos.   PUBLICATION TIME LAG: 12 mos.
MANUSCRIPT RETURNED WITH COMMENTS: Yes

MANUSCRIPT INFORMATION

GUIDELINES PUBLISHED: Each issue
STYLE REQUIREMENTS PUBLISHED: Each issue
STYLE MANUAL USED: In-house
PREFERRED TOPICS: Urban economics

QUERY LETTER: No   SIMULTANEOUS SUBMISSION: No
ABSTRACT WITH MANUSCRIPT: 100 wds.   COVER LETTER: Yes
NUMBER OF MANUSCRIPT COPIES: 3   MANUSCRIPT LENGTH: No limit

SUBMISSION FEE: No   PAGE CHARGES: No

MANUSCRIPT ACKNOWLEDGED: Yes   EARLY PUBLICATION OPTION: No
COPYRIGHT OWNER: Journal   REPRINTS: Optional purchase

AUTHOR COMPENSATION: None
MANUSCRIPT ADDRESS: Prof. Edwin S. Mills, Editor, Journal of Urban
  Economics, Department of Economics, Princeton University, Princeton,
  NJ 08540

Konjunkturpolitik / Journal of Applied Economics

FIRST PUBLISHED: 1954   FREQUENCY: Bi-M   CIRCULATION: N.R.

AFFILIATION: Association of Friends of The German Institute for
  Economic Research. Address same as journal's.

AUDIENCE: Academic/Professional; Government

PERCENT OF UNSOLICITED ARTICLES/ISSUE: 100%   ISSN: 0023-3498

EDITORIAL POLICY: Publishes mainly results of research in macroeconomics which are directly relevant to economic policy and
  associated areas of politics.

REVIEW INFORMATION

REFEREED: No   ACCEPTANCE RATE: 40%

NUMBER OF REVIEWER(S)/MS., EXCLUDING IN-HOUSE EDITOR(S): 1

REVIEWER(S): External   ARTICLES/AVG. ISSUE: 3-4

REVIEWING CRITERIA USED: BLIND REVIEW: No

  MANUSCRIPT SUBMISSION AIDS: 0

  BIAS SAFEGUARDS: 5, 6, 9*

AVERAGE REVIEW TIME: 3 mos.   PUBLICATION TIME LAG: 5-10 mos.

MANUSCRIPT RETURNED WITH COMMENTS: No

MANUSCRIPT INFORMATION

GUIDELINES PUBLISHED: No; available on request

STYLE REQUIREMENTS PUBLISHED: No; not available

STYLE MANUAL USED: N.R.

PREFERRED TOPICS: Macroeconomics, stabilization policy, international
  economics, industrial policy, labor economics, development economics

QUERY LETTER: Yes   SIMULTANEOUS SUBMISSION: No

ABSTRACT WITH MANUSCRIPT: 100 wds. COVER LETTER: No

NUMBER OF MANUSCRIPT COPIES: 2   MANUSCRIPT LENGTH: 25 pp. max.

SUBMISSION FEE: No   PAGE CHARGES: No

MANUSCRIPT ACKNOWLEDGED: Yes   EARLY PUBLICATION OPTION: No

COPYRIGHT OWNER: Publisher   REPRINTS: Optional purchase

AUTHOR COMPENSATION: Fee

MANUSCRIPT ADDRESS: The Editor, Konjunkturpolitik, Köenigin-Luise-
  Str. 5, D-1000 Berlin 33, West Germany

Kyklos / International Review for Social Sciences

FIRST PUBLISHED: 1947   FREQUENCY: Q   CIRCULATION: 3,500

AFFILIATION: Genossenschaftlichen Zentralbank AG Basel and COOP Schweiz, Basel, Switzerland.

AUDIENCE: Academic/Professional; Business/Industrial; Government

PERCENT OF UNSOLICITED ARTICLES/ISSUE: 81-100%   ISSN: 0023-5962

EDITORIAL POLICY: Theoretically founded analyses of relevant economic problems; no "one-country" studies.

REVIEW INFORMATION

REFEREED: Yes (III-B)   ACCEPTANCE RATE: 8%

NUMBER OF REVIEWER(S)/MS., EXCLUDING IN-HOUSE EDITOR(S): 2

REVIEWER(S): Board   ARTICLES/AVG. ISSUE: 5-7

REVIEWING CRITERIA USED: BLIND REVIEW: No

  MANUSCRIPT SUBMISSION AIDS: 0

  BIAS SAFEGUARDS: 4, 5, 6, 9*

AVERAGE REVIEW TIME: 1-2 mos.   PUBLICATION TIME LAG: 4-7 mos.

MANUSCRIPT RETURNED WITH COMMENTS: No

MANUSCRIPT INFORMATION

GUIDELINES PUBLISHED: No; not available

STYLE REQUIREMENTS PUBLISHED: No; available on request

STYLE MANUAL USED: In-house

PREFERRED TOPICS: No specialization

QUERY LETTER: No   SIMULTANEOUS SUBMISSION: No

ABSTRACT WITH MANUSCRIPT: 100 wds.   COVER LETTER: Yes

NUMBER OF MANUSCRIPT COPIES: 2   MANUSCRIPT LENGTH: 25 pp.

SUBMISSION FEE: No   PAGE CHARGES: No

MANUSCRIPT ACKNOWLEDGED: Yes   EARLY PUBLICATION OPTION: N.R.

COPYRIGHT OWNER: Journal   REPRINTS: Optional purchase

AUTHOR COMPENSATION: Fee, two-year subscription, 30 reprints

MANUSCRIPT ADDRESS: Prof. Dr. René L. Frey, Managing Editor, Kyklos, Institut fur Sozialwissenschaften, Petersgraben 29, CH-4051, Basel, Switzerland

Labor History

FIRST PUBLISHED: 1960   FREQUENCY: 4/Yr.   CIRCULATION: 2,000
AFFILIATION: None

AUDIENCE: Academic/Professional

PERCENT OF UNSOLICITED ARTICLES/ISSUE: 81-100%   ISSN: 0023-626X

EDITORIAL POLICY: Publishes "original research in labor history,
   studies of specific unions and of the impact of labor problems
   upon ethnic and minority groups, the nature of work and working
   class life, theories of the labor movement, biographical portraits
   of important labor figures, comparative studies and analyses of
   foreign labor movements," etc.

REVIEW INFORMATION

REFEREED: Yes (III-A)   ACCEPTANCE RATE: 30%

NUMBER OF REVIEWER(S)/MS., EXCLUDING IN-HOUSE EDITOR(S): 2

REVIEWER(S): Board   ARTICLES/AVG. ISSUE: 3-4

REVIEWING CRITERIA USED: BLIND REVIEW: Yes (Preliminary
   MANUSCRIPT SUBMISSION AIDS: 1, 2   screening only)

   BIAS SAFEGUARDS: 3, 4, 5, 9

AVERAGE REVIEW TIME: 3 mos.   PUBLICATION TIME LAG: 12 mos.

MANUSCRIPT RETURNED WITH COMMENTS: Yes, SASE required

MANUSCRIPT INFORMATION

GUIDELINES PUBLISHED: Each issue
STYLE REQUIREMENTS PUBLISHED: Each issue
STYLE MANUAL USED: Chicago
PREFERRED TOPICS: Labor history

QUERY LETTER: No   SIMULTANEOUS SUBMISSION: No
ABSTRACT WITH MANUSCRIPT: No   COVER LETTER: Yes
NUMBER OF MANUSCRIPT COPIES: 2   MANUSCRIPT LENGTH: 25 pp.

SUBMISSION FEE: No   PAGE CHARGES: No

MANUSCRIPT ACKNOWLEDGED: Yes   EARLY PUBLICATION OPTION: No
COPYRIGHT OWNER: Journal   REPRINTS: Optional purchase

AUTHOR COMPENSATION: None

MANUSCRIPT ADDRESS: The Editor, Labor History, Bobst Library,
   Tamiment Institute, New York University, 70 Washington Square
   South, New York, NY 10012

Land Economics

FIRST PUBLISHED: 1925   FREQUENCY: Q   CIRCULATION: 2,600

AFFILIATION: University of Wisconsin, Department of Agricultural Economics. Address same as journal's.

AUDIENCE: Academic/Professional

PERCENT OF UNSOLICITED ARTICLES/ISSUE: 100%   ISSN: 0023-7639

EDITORIAL POLICY: "Devoted to the study of economic aspects of the entire spectrum of natural and environmental resources, emphasizing conceptual and/or empirical work with direct relevance for public policy. Emphasis is on articles that address the determinants and consequences of economic activity on the value and use of land, or the contribution of natural and environmental resources to economic activity."

REVIEW INFORMATION

REFEREED: Yes (II-B)   ACCEPTANCE RATE: 25%

NUMBER OF REVIEWER(S)/MS., EXCLUDING IN-HOUSE EDITOR(S): 2

REVIEWER(S): Board and external   ARTICLES/AVG. ISSUE: 12

REVIEWING CRITERIA USED: BLIND REVIEW: No

  MANUSCRIPT SUBMISSION AIDS: 1, 2

  BIAS SAFEGUARDS: 5, 9, 10

AVERAGE REVIEW TIME: 8 wks.   PUBLICATION TIME LAG: 6-9 mos.

MANUSCRIPT RETURNED WITH COMMENTS: Yes, SASE required

MANUSCRIPT INFORMATION

GUIDELINES PUBLISHED: Each issue

STYLE REQUIREMENTS PUBLISHED: Each issue

STYLE MANUAL USED: In-house

PREFERRED TOPICS: Economic aspects of natural and environmental resources

QUERY LETTER: No   SIMULTANEOUS SUBMISSION: No

ABSTRACT WITH MANUSCRIPT: No   COVER LETTER: Yes

NUMBER OF MANUSCRIPT COPIES: 3   MANUSCRIPT LENGTH: 30-40 pp.

SUBMISSION FEE: No   PAGE CHARGES: No

MANUSCRIPT ACKNOWLEDGED: Yes   EARLY PUBLICATION OPTION: No

COPYRIGHT OWNER: Publisher   REPRINTS: Optional purchase

AUTHOR COMPENSATION: None

MANUSCRIPT ADDRESS: Prof. Daniel W. Bromley, Editor, Land Economics, 427 Lorch St., Room 109, University of Wisconsin, Madison, WI 53706

Liiketaloudellinen Aikakauskirja /
The Finnish Journal of Business Economics

FIRST PUBLISHED: 1952   FREQUENCY: Q   CIRCULATION: 1,600

AFFILIATION: The Finnish Society of Business Economics. Address
  same as journal's.

AUDIENCE: Academic/Professional; Business/Industrial

PERCENT OF UNSOLICITED ARTICLES/ISSUE: 91-100%   ISSN: 0024-3469

EDITORIAL POLICY: Publishes in the research fields of economics and
  business administration. Text in English and Finnish.

REVIEW INFORMATION

REFEREED: Yes (II-B)   ACCEPTANCE RATE: 40%

NUMBER OF REVIEWER(S)/MS., EXCLUDING IN-HOUSE EDITOR(S): 2

REVIEWER(S): Board and external   ARTICLES/AVG. ISSUE: 6-8

REVIEWING CRITERIA USED: BLIND REVIEW: No

  MANUSCRIPT SUBMISSION AIDS: 0

  BIAS SAFEGUARDS: 4, 5, 6, 9*

AVERAGE REVIEW TIME: 3 mos.   PUBLICATION TIME LAG: 6 mos.

MANUSCRIPT RETURNED WITH COMMENTS: Yes

MANUSCRIPT INFORMATION

GUIDELINES PUBLISHED: No; available on request

STYLE REQUIREMENTS PUBLISHED: No; available on request

STYLE MANUAL USED: In-house

PREFERRED TOPICS: Economics and business administration

QUERY LETTER: No   SIMULTANEOUS SUBMISSION: No

ABSTRACT WITH MANUSCRIPT: Yes   COVER LETTER: No

NUMBER OF MANUSCRIPT COPIES: 2   MANUSCRIPT LENGTH: 20-30 pp.

SUBMISSION FEE: No   PAGE CHARGES: No

MANUSCRIPT ACKNOWLEDGED: Yes   EARLY PUBLICATION OPTION: Yes

COPYRIGHT OWNER: Journal   REPRINTS: Optional purchase

AUTHOR COMPENSATION: Free reprints/tear sheets

MANUSCRIPT ADDRESS: Huugo Raninen, Editor, The Finnish Journal of
  Business Economics, Runeberginkatu 22-24, 00100 Helsinki 10, Finland

Lloyds Bank Review

FIRST PUBLISHED: 1930   FREQUENCY: Q   CIRCULATION: N.R.
AFFILIATION: Lloyds Bank, Plc. Address same as journal's.

AUDIENCE: Academic/Professional; Business/Industrial; Government
PERCENT OF UNSOLICITED ARTICLES/ISSUE: 21-40%   ISSN: 0024-547X
EDITORIAL POLICY: Articles are chosen to be relevant to current
   economic issues and understandable by non-specialists.

REVIEW INFORMATION

REFEREED: No   ACCEPTANCE RATE: 40%
NUMBER OF REVIEWER(S)/MS., EXCLUDING IN-HOUSE EDITOR(S): 0
REVIEWER(S): Editor   ARTICLES/AVG. ISSUE: 3
REVIEWING CRITERIA USED: BLIND REVIEW: No
  MANUSCRIPT SUBMISSION AIDS: 0
  BIAS SAFEGUARDS: 0
AVERAGE REVIEW TIME: 4 wks.   PUBLICATION TIME LAG: 6 mos.
MANUSCRIPT RETURNED WITH COMMENTS: Yes

MANUSCRIPT INFORMATION

GUIDELINES PUBLISHED: No; available on request
STYLE REQUIREMENTS PUBLISHED: No; available on request
STYLE MANUAL USED: In-house
PREFERRED TOPICS: All areas of economics

QUERY LETTER: No   SIMULTANEOUS SUBMISSION: Yes
ABSTRACT WITH MANUSCRIPT: No   COVER LETTER: Yes
NUMBER OF MANUSCRIPT COPIES: 1   MANUSCRIPT LENGTH: 3,000 wds.

SUBMISSION FEE: No   PAGE CHARGES: No

MANUSCRIPT ACKNOWLEDGED: Yes   EARLY PUBLICATION OPTION: No
COPYRIGHT OWNER: Journal   REPRINTS: Optional purchase

AUTHOR COMPENSATION: Fee and 5 free journals
MANUSCRIPT ADDRESS: The Editor, Lloyds Bank Review, Lloyds Bank, Plc,
   71 Lombard Street, London, EC3P 3BS, U.K.

The Logistics and Transportation Review

FIRST PUBLISHED: 1965   FREQUENCY: Q   CIRCULATION: 1,000

AFFILIATION: University of British Columbia, Faculty of Commerce & Business Administration. Address same as journal's.

AUDIENCE: Academic/Professional; Business/Industrial; Government

PERCENT OF UNSOLICITED ARTICLES/ISSUE: 80%   ISSN: 0047-4991

EDITORIAL POLICY: "Readership of the Logistics and Transportation Review covers a wide geographic area and encompasses all aspects of logistics and transportation research. We seek manuscripts of a high standard drawn from across the spectrum of logistics and transportation research, preferably ones which can be understood by a knowledgeable cross-section of the transportation community."

REVIEW INFORMATION

REFEREED: Yes (I-B)   ACCEPTANCE RATE: 50%

NUMBER OF REVIEWER(S)/MS., EXCLUDING IN-HOUSE EDITOR(S): 2

REVIEWER(S): External   ARTICLES/AVG. ISSUE: 6

REVIEWING CRITERIA USED: BLIND REVIEW: No

  MANUSCRIPT SUBMISSION AIDS: 0

  BIAS SAFEGUARDS: 5, 7, 9

AVERAGE REVIEW TIME: 3 mos.   PUBLICATION TIME LAG: 3 mos.

MANUSCRIPT RETURNED WITH COMMENTS: Yes

MANUSCRIPT INFORMATION

GUIDELINES PUBLISHED: No; available on request

STYLE REQUIREMENTS PUBLISHED: No; available on request

STYLE MANUAL USED: In-house

PREFERRED TOPICS: Transport economics, policy, management logistics

QUERY LETTER: No   SIMULTANEOUS SUBMISSION: No

ABSTRACT WITH MANUSCRIPT: 50-75 wds.   COVER LETTER: Yes

NUMBER OF MANUSCRIPT COPIES: 3   MANUSCRIPT LENGTH: 10-30 pp.

SUBMISSION FEE: No   PAGE CHARGES: No

MANUSCRIPT ACKNOWLEDGED: Yes   EARLY PUBLICATION OPTION: No

COPYRIGHT OWNER: Journal   REPRINTS: Optional purchase

AUTHOR COMPENSATION: 2 free journals

MANUSCRIPT ADDRESS: Prof. W. G. Waters, II, Editor, The Logistics and Transportation Review, Faculty of Commerce, University of British Columbia, Vancouver, B.C., Canada V6T 1W5

Management Science

FIRST PUBLISHED: 1954   FREQUENCY: M   CIRCULATION: 10,000

AFFILIATION: The Institute of Management Sciences (TIMS), 290 Westminster
  Street, Providence, RI 02903

AUDIENCE: Academic/Professional

PERCENT OF UNSOLICITED ARTICLES/ISSUE: 99%   ISSN: 0025-1909

EDITORIAL POLICY: "Seeks to publish articles that identify, extend,
  or unify scientific knowledge pertaining to management. Articles
  must be readable, well-organized, and exhibit good writing style.
  Other important criteria are originality and significant contribution including the capacity to provide generalizations within
  the framework of application-oriented methods."

REVIEW INFORMATION

REFEREED: Yes (I-B)   ACCEPTANCE RATE: 20%

NUMBER OF REVIEWER(S)/MS., EXCLUDING IN-HOUSE EDITOR(S): 4

REVIEWER(S): 2 board, 2 external   ARTICLES/AVG. ISSUE: 10

REVIEWING CRITERIA USED: BLIND REVIEW: No

  MANUSCRIPT SUBMISSION AIDS: 1, 2

  BIAS SAFEGUARDS: 5, 7, 9

AVERAGE REVIEW TIME: 4 mos.   PUBLICATION TIME LAG: 8 mos.

MANUSCRIPT RETURNED WITH COMMENTS: Yes

MANUSCRIPT INFORMATION

GUIDELINES PUBLISHED: Each issue (brief); January 1985 (detailed)

STYLE REQUIREMENTS PUBLISHED: Each issue

STYLE MANUAL USED: In-house

PREFERRED TOPICS: All areas of management science, broadly defined

QUERY LETTER: No   SIMULTANEOUS SUBMISSION: No

ABSTRACT WITH MANUSCRIPT: 100-300 wds. COVER LETTER: Yes

NUMBER OF MANUSCRIPT COPIES: 4   MANUSCRIPT LENGTH: No limit

SUBMISSION FEE: No   PAGE CHARGES: No

MANUSCRIPT ACKNOWLEDGED: Yes   EARLY PUBLICATION OPTION: No

COPYRIGHT OWNER: Publisher   REPRINTS: Optional purchase

AUTHOR COMPENSATION: None

MANUSCRIPT ADDRESS: Prof. Donald G. Morrison, Editor-in-Chief,
  Management Science, Graduate School of Business, 401 Uris Hall,
  Columbia University, New York, NY 10027

Managerial and Decision Economics

FIRST PUBLISHED: 1980   FREQUENCY: Q   CIRCULATION: 950

AFFILIATION: Association of Managerial Economists. Address same
  as journal's.

AUDIENCE: Academic/Professional

PERCENT OF UNSOLICITED ARTICLES/ISSUE: 100%   ISSN: 0143-6570

EDITORIAL POLICY: Publishes highest quality manuscripts which relate
  economic theory and methodology to the solution of managerial
  problems.

REVIEW INFORMATION

REFEREED: Yes (I-A)   ACCEPTANCE RATE: 21%

NUMBER OF REVIEWER(S)/MS., EXCLUDING IN-HOUSE EDITOR(S): 2

REVIEWER(S): External   ARTICLES/AVG. ISSUE: 10

REVIEWING CRITERIA USED: BLIND REVIEW: Yes (Preliminary
  MANUSCRIPT SUBMISSION AIDS: 1, 2   screening only)
  BIAS SAFEGUARDS: 3, 4, 5, 6, 7, 9

AVERAGE REVIEW TIME: 4-6 wks.   PUBLICATION TIME LAG: 3 mos.

MANUSCRIPT RETURNED WITH COMMENTS: No

MANUSCRIPT INFORMATION

GUIDELINES PUBLISHED: Each issue

STYLE REQUIREMENTS PUBLISHED: Each issue

STYLE MANUAL USED: Chicago

PREFERRED TOPICS: Economic theory and methodology related to
  managerial problems

QUERY LETTER: No   SIMULTANEOUS SUBMISSION: No

ABSTRACT WITH MANUSCRIPT: 100 wds. COVER LETTER: Yes

NUMBER OF MANUSCRIPT COPIES: 4   MANUSCRIPT LENGTH: 25 pp.

SUBMISSION FEE: No   PAGE CHARGES: No

MANUSCRIPT ACKNOWLEDGED: Yes   EARLY PUBLICATION OPTION: No

COPYRIGHT OWNER: Journal   REPRINTS: Optional purchase

AUTHOR COMPENSATION: None

MANUSCRIPT ADDRESS: Prof. Mark Hirschey, North American Editor,
  Managerial and Decision Economics, Graduate School of Business
  Administration, University of Colorado at Denver, Denver, CO 80202

Margin

FIRST PUBLISHED: 1968   FREQUENCY: Q   CIRCULATION: 850

AFFILIATION: National Council of Applied Economic Research. Address same as journal's.

AUDIENCE: Academic/Professional; Business/Industrial; Government

PERCENT OF UNSOLICITED ARTICLES/ISSUE: 81-100%   ISSN: 0025-2921

EDITORIAL POLICY: Primarily designed to publish contributions on applied economic problems related to the Indian economy. Emphasis on analytical research-oriented and data-based papers.

REVIEW INFORMATION

REFEREED: Yes (I-A)   ACCEPTANCE RATE: 85%

NUMBER OF REVIEWER(S)/MS., EXCLUDING IN-HOUSE EDITOR(S): 2

REVIEWER(S): External   ARTICLES/AVG. ISSUE: 5

REVIEWING CRITERIA USED: BLIND REVIEW: Yes (External review only)
  MANUSCRIPT SUBMISSION AIDS: 1, 2
  BIAS SAFEGUARDS: 3, 5, 7, 9*

AVERAGE REVIEW TIME: 3 mos.   PUBLICATION TIME LAG: 3-6 mos.

MANUSCRIPT RETURNED WITH COMMENTS: No

MANUSCRIPT INFORMATION

GUIDELINES PUBLISHED: Each issue

STYLE REQUIREMENTS PUBLISHED: Each issue

STYLE MANUAL USED: In-house

PREFERRED TOPICS: Applied economic problems related to Indian economy

QUERY LETTER: No   SIMULTANEOUS SUBMISSION: No

ABSTRACT WITH MANUSCRIPT: No   COVER LETTER: Yes

NUMBER OF MANUSCRIPT COPIES: 2   MANUSCRIPT LENGTH: 3,000-12,000 wds.

SUBMISSION FEE: No   PAGE CHARGES: No

MANUSCRIPT ACKNOWLEDGED: Yes   EARLY PUBLICATION OPTION: No

COPYRIGHT OWNER: National Council of Applied Economic Research   REPRINTS: Optional purchase

AUTHOR COMPENSATION: One free journal and 50 free reprints

MANUSCRIPT ADDRESS: R. N. Varma, Editor, Margin, National Council of Applied Economic Research, 11 Indraprastha Estate, New Delhi 110002, India

Marine Resource Economics

FIRST PUBLISHED: 1969   FREQUENCY: Q   CIRCULATION: 1,000
AFFILIATION: None

AUDIENCE: Academic/Professional; Government

PERCENT OF UNSOLICITED ARTICLES/ISSUE: 100%   ISSN: 0738-1360

EDITORIAL POLICY: Serves as a global forum for scholarly research
  related to the development and management of fisheries and other
  natural resources of the sea. Published papers will present new
  theoretical and empirical developments, new techniques for practical application, and analyses of institutions and policies
  related to the economics of marine resources.

REVIEW INFORMATION

REFEREED: Yes (II-A)   ACCEPTANCE RATE: 40%

NUMBER OF REVIEWER(S)/MS., EXCLUDING IN-HOUSE EDITOR(S): 2

REVIEWER(S): Board and external   ARTICLES/AVG. ISSUE: 5

REVIEWING CRITERIA USED: BLIND REVIEW: Yes (Entire
  MANUSCRIPT SUBMISSION AIDS: 1, 2   review)

  BIAS SAFEGUARDS: 3, 5, 9, 10

AVERAGE REVIEW TIME: 8 wks.   PUBLICATION TIME LAG: 5 mos.

MANUSCRIPT RETURNED WITH COMMENTS: No

MANUSCRIPT INFORMATION

GUIDELINES PUBLISHED: Each issue

STYLE REQUIREMENTS PUBLISHED: Each issue

STYLE MANUAL USED: Chicago

PREFERRED TOPICS: Natural resources, industry studies, marketing
  and trade

QUERY LETTER: No   SIMULTANEOUS SUBMISSION: No

ABSTRACT WITH MANUSCRIPT: Yes   COVER LETTER: Yes

NUMBER OF MANUSCRIPT COPIES: 3   MANUSCRIPT LENGTH: 25 pp.

SUBMISSION FEE: No   PAGE CHARGES: No

MANUSCRIPT ACKNOWLEDGED: Yes   EARLY PUBLICATION OPTION: No

COPYRIGHT OWNER: Publisher   REPRINTS: Optional purchase

AUTHOR COMPENSATION: 25 free reprints/tear sheets

MANUSCRIPT ADDRESS: Jon G. Sutinen, Editor, Marine Resource Economics,
  Department of Resource Economics, University of Rhode Island,
  Kingston, RI   02881-0814

Marketing Science

FIRST PUBLISHED: 1982   FREQUENCY: Q   CIRCULATION: 1,800

AFFILIATION: The Institute of Management Sciences (TIMS), Providence, RI, and Operations Research Society of America, Baltimore, MD.

AUDIENCE: Academic/Professional; Business/Industrial; Government

PERCENT OF UNSOLICITED ARTICLES/ISSUE: 95%   ISSN: 0732-2399

EDITORIAL POLICY: Publishes the latest advances in the theory and practice of marketing. We seek quantitative articles dealing with marketing theory, models, applications and estimation techniques.

REVIEW INFORMATION

REFEREED: Yes (II-B)   ACCEPTANCE RATE: 20%

NUMBER OF REVIEWER(S)/MS., EXCLUDING IN-HOUSE EDITOR(S): 3

REVIEWER(S): 2 board, 1 external   ARTICLES/AVG. ISSUE: 5

REVIEWING CRITERIA USED: BLIND REVIEW: No

  MANUSCRIPT SUBMISSION AIDS: 1, 2

  BIAS SAFEGUARDS: 5, 8, 9

AVERAGE REVIEW TIME: 19 wks.   PUBLICATION TIME LAG: 3 mos.

MANUSCRIPT RETURNED WITH COMMENTS: No

MANUSCRIPT INFORMATION

GUIDELINES PUBLISHED: First issue of each volume

STYLE REQUIREMENTS PUBLISHED: Each issue

STYLE MANUAL USED: Chicago

PREFERRED TOPICS: Any topic in the area of marketing

QUERY LETTER: No   SIMULTANEOUS SUBMISSION: No

ABSTRACT WITH MANUSCRIPT: 200 wds. max.   COVER LETTER: Yes

NUMBER OF MANUSCRIPT COPIES: 5   MANUSCRIPT LENGTH: 40 pp. max.

SUBMISSION FEE: No   PAGE CHARGES: No

MANUSCRIPT ACKNOWLEDGED: Yes   EARLY PUBLICATION OPTION: No

COPYRIGHT OWNER: Publisher   REPRINTS: Optional purchase

AUTHOR COMPENSATION: None

MANUSCRIPT ADDRESS: Prof. Subrata K. Sen, Editor-in-Chief, Marketing Science, School of Organization and Management, Yale University, Box 1A, New Haven, CT 06520

Mathematical Social Sciences

FIRST PUBLISHED: 1980   FREQUENCY: Bi-M   CIRCULATION: N.R.

AFFILIATION: None

AUDIENCE: Academic/Professional; Business/Industrial; Government

PERCENT OF UNSOLICITED ARTICLES/ISSUE: 81-100%   ISSN: 0165-4896

EDITORIAL POLICY: Publishes original research as well as survey
  papers which are of broad interest in the mathematical social
  sciences.

REVIEW INFORMATION

REFEREED: Yes (I-B)   ACCEPTANCE RATE: 51%

NUMBER OF REVIEWER(S)/MS., EXCLUDING IN-HOUSE EDITOR(S): 3

REVIEWER(S): External   ARTICLES/AVG. ISSUE: 6

REVIEWING CRITERIA USED: BLIND REVIEW: No

  MANUSCRIPT SUBMISSION AIDS: 1, 2

  BIAS SAFEGUARDS: 4, 5, 6, 7, 9

AVERAGE REVIEW TIME: 9 mos.   PUBLICATION TIME LAG: 12 mos.

MANUSCRIPT RETURNED WITH COMMENTS: Yes

MANUSCRIPT INFORMATION

GUIDELINES PUBLISHED: Each issue

STYLE REQUIREMENTS PUBLISHED: Each issue

STYLE MANUAL USED: In-house

PREFERRED TOPICS: Decision theory, game theory, team theory, social
  welfare theory, voting theory and interdisciplinary mathematical
  social sciences

QUERY LETTER: No   SIMULTANEOUS SUBMISSION: No

ABSTRACT WITH MANUSCRIPT: 100 wds. COVER LETTER: Yes

NUMBER OF MANUSCRIPT COPIES: 3   MANUSCRIPT LENGTH: 20 pp.

SUBMISSION FEE: No   PAGE CHARGES: No

MANUSCRIPT ACKNOWLEDGED: Yes   EARLY PUBLICATION OPTION: No

COPYRIGHT OWNER: Publisher   REPRINTS: Optional purchase

AUTHOR COMPENSATION: None

MANUSCRIPT ADDRESS: Dr. K. H. Kim, Managing Editor, Mathematical
  Social Sciences, Department of Mathematics, Box 69, Alabama State
  University, Montgomery, AL 36195-0301

Metroeconomica / International Review of Economics

FIRST PUBLISHED: 1949   FREQUENCY: 3/Yr.   CIRCULATION: 650
AFFILIATION: None

AUDIENCE: Academic/Professional

PERCENT OF UNSOLICITED ARTICLES/ISSUE: 100%   ISSN: 0026-1386

EDITORIAL POLICY: "Aims to provide an international forum for the
theoretical debate among the major schools of economic thought on
the current issues of economic policy. . . . Priority is given to
the publication of papers which deal with problems of political
economy by means of mathematical modelling based on a clear speci-
fication of the underlying theoretical foundations."

REVIEW INFORMATION

REFEREED: Yes (I-A)   ACCEPTANCE RATE: 15%

NUMBER OF REVIEWER(S)/MS., EXCLUDING IN-HOUSE EDITOR(S): 2

REVIEWER(S): External   ARTICLES/AVG. ISSUE: 5

REVIEWING CRITERIA USED: BLIND REVIEW: Yes (External
   MANUSCRIPT SUBMISSION AIDS: 1, 2   review only)
   BIAS SAFEGUARDS: 3, 4, 5, 6, 7, 9

AVERAGE REVIEW TIME: 2 mos.   PUBLICATION TIME LAG: 3 mos.

MANUSCRIPT RETURNED WITH COMMENTS: No

MANUSCRIPT INFORMATION

GUIDELINES PUBLISHED: Vol. 30, December 1978

STYLE REQUIREMENTS PUBLISHED: Each issue

STYLE MANUAL USED: In-house

PREFERRED TOPICS: Economic theory

QUERY LETTER: Yes   SIMULTANEOUS SUBMISSION: No

ABSTRACT WITH MANUSCRIPT: No   COVER LETTER: Yes

NUMBER OF MANUSCRIPT COPIES: 2   MANUSCRIPT LENGTH: No limit

SUBMISSION FEE: No   PAGE CHARGES: No

MANUSCRIPT ACKNOWLEDGED: Yes   EARLY PUBLICATION OPTION: No

COPYRIGHT OWNER: Journal   REPRINTS: Optional purchase

AUTHOR COMPENSATION: None

MANUSCRIPT ADDRESS: Prof. Sergio Parrinello, Editor, Metroeconomica,
   Instituto di Economia Politica, Facoltà di Economia e Commercio,
   Università di Roma, Via del Castro Laurenziano 9, 00161 Roma, Italy

METU Studies in Development / ODTÜ Gelisme Dergisi

FIRST PUBLISHED: 1970   FREQUENCY: Q   CIRCULATION: 1,500

AFFILIATION: Middle East Technical University, Faculty of Economic
   and Administrative Sciences. Address same as journal's.

AUDIENCE: Academic/Professional

PERCENT OF UNSOLICITED ARTICLES/ISSUE: 81-100%   ISSN: None

EDITORIAL POLICY: Publishes articles in economics, public administration, management and related fields of social sciences. In recent
   years, increased focus on development issues.

REVIEW INFORMATION

REFEREED: Yes (I-A)   ACCEPTANCE RATE: 60%

NUMBER OF REVIEWER(S)/MS., EXCLUDING IN-HOUSE EDITOR(S): 2

REVIEWER(S): External   ARTICLES/AVG. ISSUE: 6

REVIEWING CRITERIA USED: BLIND REVIEW: Yes (Preliminary
   MANUSCRIPT SUBMISSION AIDS: 1, 2   screening only)
   BIAS SAFEGUARDS: 3, 4, 5, 6, 7, 8

AVERAGE REVIEW TIME: 2.5 mos.   PUBLICATION TIME LAG: 2.5 mos.

MANUSCRIPT RETURNED WITH COMMENTS: No

MANUSCRIPT INFORMATION

GUIDELINES PUBLISHED: Each issue

STYLE REQUIREMENTS PUBLISHED: Each issue

STYLE MANUAL USED: In-house

PREFERRED TOPICS: Economics, management, public administration

QUERY LETTER: No   SIMULTANEOUS SUBMISSION: No

ABSTRACT WITH MANUSCRIPT: 100 wds.   COVER LETTER: Yes

NUMBER OF MANUSCRIPT COPIES: 3   MANUSCRIPT LENGTH: 30 pp.

SUBMISSION FEE: No   PAGE CHARGES: No

MANUSCRIPT ACKNOWLEDGED: Yes   EARLY PUBLICATION OPTION: No

COPYRIGHT OWNER: Middle East Technical REPRINTS: Not available
   University

AUTHOR COMPENSATION: 50 free reprints/tear sheets

MANUSCRIPT ADDRESS: Fikret Şenses, Managing Editor, METU--Studies in
   Development, Middle East Technical University, Department of Economics,
   Ismet Inonu Bulvari, Ankara, Turkey

Michigan Law Review

FIRST PUBLISHED: 1902   FREQUENCY: 8/Yr.   CIRCULATION: 2,981

AFFILIATION: University of Michigan School of Law. Address same
as journal's.

AUDIENCE: Academic/Professional

PERCENT OF UNSOLICITED ARTICLES/ISSUE: 81-100%   ISSN: 0026-2234

EDITORIAL POLICY: Publishes articles of interest to legal scholars
and practitioners.

REVIEW INFORMATION

REFEREED: No   ACCEPTANCE RATE: 2%

NUMBER OF REVIEWER(S)/MS., EXCLUDING IN-HOUSE EDITOR(S): 0

REVIEWER(S): 1-4 in-house Article Eds. ARTICLES/AVG. ISSUE: 2

REVIEWING CRITERIA USED: BLIND REVIEW: No

  MANUSCRIPT SUBMISSION AIDS: 2

  BIAS SAFEGUARDS: 0

AVERAGE REVIEW TIME: 5 wks.   PUBLICATION TIME LAG: 6-8 mos.

MANUSCRIPT RETURNED WITH COMMENTS: No

MANUSCRIPT INFORMATION

GUIDELINES PUBLISHED: No; not available

STYLE REQUIREMENTS PUBLISHED: Each issue

STYLE MANUAL USED: Harvard

PREFERRED TOPICS: Law

QUERY LETTER: No   SIMULTANEOUS SUBMISSION: Yes

ABSTRACT WITH MANUSCRIPT: No   COVER LETTER: Yes

NUMBER OF MANUSCRIPT COPIES: 1   MANUSCRIPT LENGTH: No limit

SUBMISSION FEE: No   PAGE CHARGES: No

MANUSCRIPT ACKNOWLEDGED: Yes   EARLY PUBLICATION OPTION: No

COPYRIGHT OWNER: Journal or author   REPRINTS: Optional purchase

AUTHOR COMPENSATION: 1 free journal and 50 free reprints/tear sheets

MANUSCRIPT ADDRESS: Editor-in-Chief, Michigan Law Review, Law
  Review Association, Hutchins Hall, Ann Arbor, MI 48109-1215

Monthly Labor Review / MLR

FIRST PUBLISHED: 1915   FREQUENCY: M   CIRCULATION: 12,000

AFFILIATION: U.S. Department of Labor, Bureau of Labor Statistics. Address same as journal's.

AUDIENCE: Academic/Professional; Business/Industrial; Government

PERCENT OF UNSOLICITED ARTICLES/ISSUE: 11-20%   ISSN: 0098-1818

EDITORIAL POLICY: Manuscripts published must meet standards for sound research and should be related to the work of the Bureau of Labor Statistics. Data-oriented articles are preferred.

REVIEW INFORMATION

REFEREED: No   ACCEPTANCE RATE: 10-15%

NUMBER OF REVIEWER(S)/MS., EXCLUDING IN-HOUSE EDITOR(S): 1

REVIEWER(S): External   ARTICLES/AVG. ISSUE: 4

REVIEWING CRITERIA USED: BLIND REVIEW: No

  MANUSCRIPT SUBMISSION AIDS: 0

  BIAS SAFEGUARDS: 4, 5, 6

AVERAGE REVIEW TIME: 5 wks.   PUBLICATION TIME LAG: 8 wks.

MANUSCRIPT RETURNED WITH COMMENTS: No

MANUSCRIPT INFORMATION

GUIDELINES PUBLISHED: No; available on request

STYLE REQUIREMENTS PUBLISHED: No; available on request

STYLE MANUAL USED: In-house; GPO

PREFERRED TOPICS: Employment and unemployment, price analysis, productivity research, wage change and industrial relations, occupational change, safety and health, general economics bearing on labor issues

QUERY LETTER: No   SIMULTANEOUS SUBMISSION: No

ABSTRACT WITH MANUSCRIPT: 100 wds.   COVER LETTER: Yes

NUMBER OF MANUSCRIPT COPIES: 3   MANUSCRIPT LENGTH: 5,000 wds.

SUBMISSION FEE: No   PAGE CHARGES: No

MANUSCRIPT ACKNOWLEDGED: Yes   EARLY PUBLICATION OPTION: No

COPYRIGHT OWNER: None claimed   REPRINTS: Not available

AUTHOR COMPENSATION: None

MANUSCRIPT ADDRESS: The Editor-in-Chief, Monthly Labor Review, Bureau of Labor Statistics, U.S. Department of Labor, Washington, D.C. 20212

National Institute Economic Review

FIRST PUBLISHED: 1959   FREQUENCY: Q   CIRCULATION: 3,000

AFFILIATION: National Institute of Economic and Social Research. Address same as journal's.

AUDIENCE: Academic/Professional; Business/Industrial; Government

PERCENT OF UNSOLICITED ARTICLES/ISSUE: 61-80%   ISSN: 0027-9501

EDITORIAL POLICY: The main emphasis is on quantitative research. Although this may be of a technical statistical nature, we expect the reasoning and conclusions to be in a form which is intelligible to the "informed non-specialist."

REVIEW INFORMATION

REFEREED: Yes (II-B)   ACCEPTANCE RATE: 50%

NUMBER OF REVIEWER(S)/MS., EXCLUDING IN-HOUSE EDITOR(S): 2

REVIEWER(S): Board and external   ARTICLES/AVG. ISSUE: 2

REVIEWING CRITERIA USED: BLIND REVIEW: No

  MANUSCRIPT SUBMISSION AIDS: 0

  BIAS SAFEGUARDS: 5, 6, 9*

AVERAGE REVIEW TIME: 2 mos.   PUBLICATION TIME LAG: 4 wks.

MANUSCRIPT RETURNED WITH COMMENTS: No

MANUSCRIPT INFORMATION

GUIDELINES PUBLISHED: No; available on request

STYLE REQUIREMENTS PUBLISHED: No; available on request

STYLE MANUAL USED: In-house

PREFERRED TOPICS: Applied macro-economics, econometric modeling, industrial economics

QUERY LETTER: No   SIMULTANEOUS SUBMISSION: No

ABSTRACT WITH MANUSCRIPT: No   COVER LETTER: No

NUMBER OF MANUSCRIPT COPIES: 1   MANUSCRIPT LENGTH: N.R.

SUBMISSION FEE: No   PAGE CHARGES: No

MANUSCRIPT ACKNOWLEDGED: Yes   EARLY PUBLICATION OPTION: Yes

COPYRIGHT OWNER: Journal   REPRINTS: Not available

AUTHOR COMPENSATION: 6 free journals

MANUSCRIPT ADDRESS: Editor, National Institute Economic Review, National Institute of Economic and Social Research, 2 Dean Trench Street, Smith Square, London, SW1P 3HE, U.K.

National Tax Journal

FIRST PUBLISHED: 1948   FREQUENCY: 8/Yr.   CIRCULATION: 2,000

AFFILIATION: National Tax Association - Tax Institute of America,
  21 East State Street, Columbus, Ohio 43215

AUDIENCE: Academic/Professional; Business/Industrial; Government

PERCENT OF UNSOLICITED ARTICLES/ISSUE: 99%   ISSN: 0028-0283

EDITORIAL POLICY: To present a broad spectrum of papers dealing with
  government finance and taxation.

REVIEW INFORMATION

REFEREED: Yes (II-A)   ACCEPTANCE RATE: 25%

NUMBER OF REVIEWER(S)/MS., EXCLUDING IN-HOUSE EDITOR(S): 2

REVIEWER(S): Board and external   ARTICLES/AVG. ISSUE: 18

REVIEWING CRITERIA USED: BLIND REVIEW: Yes (Entire
  MANUSCRIPT SUBMISSION AIDS: 1   review)
  BIAS SAFEGUARDS: 3, 5, 9*

AVERAGE REVIEW TIME: 2 mos.   PUBLICATION TIME LAG: 2 mos.

MANUSCRIPT RETURNED WITH COMMENTS: Only if comments are on MS.

MANUSCRIPT INFORMATION

GUIDELINES PUBLISHED: Each issue

STYLE REQUIREMENTS PUBLISHED: No; not available

STYLE MANUAL USED: In-house

PREFERRED TOPICS: State and local government finance, taxation

QUERY LETTER: No   SIMULTANEOUS SUBMISSION: No

ABSTRACT WITH MANUSCRIPT: 100 wds.   COVER LETTER: Yes

NUMBER OF MANUSCRIPT COPIES: 3   MANUSCRIPT LENGTH: Varies

SUBMISSION FEE: No   PAGE CHARGES: No

MANUSCRIPT ACKNOWLEDGED: Yes   EARLY PUBLICATION OPTION: No

COPYRIGHT OWNER: Publisher   REPRINTS: Optional purchase

AUTHOR COMPENSATION: None

MANUSCRIPT ADDRESS: Daniel M. Holland, Editor, National Tax Journal,
  Room E52-445, Sloan School, Massachusetts Institute of Technology,
  50 Memorial Drive, Cambridge, MA 02139

National Westminster Bank Quarterly Review

FIRST PUBLISHED: 1968   FREQUENCY: Q   CIRCULATION: 40,000
AFFILIATION: National Westminster Bank. Address same as journal's.

AUDIENCE: Academic/Professional; Business/Industrial; Government
PERCENT OF UNSOLICITED ARTICLES/ISSUE: 81-100%   ISSN: 0028-0399
EDITORIAL POLICY: A middlebrow treatment of economic, financial
   and current affairs issues of the day.

REVIEW INFORMATION

REFEREED: No   ACCEPTANCE RATE: 25%
NUMBER OF REVIEWER(S)/MS., EXCLUDING IN-HOUSE EDITOR(S): 0
REVIEWER(S): Editor   ARTICLES/AVG. ISSUE: 4-5
REVIEWING CRITERIA USED: BLIND REVIEW: No
   MANUSCRIPT SUBMISSION AIDS: 0
   BIAS SAFEGUARDS: 0
AVERAGE REVIEW TIME: 3 wks.   PUBLICATION TIME LAG: 12 wks.
MANUSCRIPT RETURNED WITH COMMENTS: No

MANUSCRIPT INFORMATION

GUIDELINES PUBLISHED: No; available on request
STYLE REQUIREMENTS PUBLISHED: No; available on request
STYLE MANUAL USED: In-house
PREFERRED TOPICS: Applied and commercial economics, current policy
   issues

QUERY LETTER: Yes   SIMULTANEOUS SUBMISSION: No
ABSTRACT WITH MANUSCRIPT: No   COVER LETTER: Yes
NUMBER OF MANUSCRIPT COPIES: 1   MANUSCRIPT LENGTH: 4,000-
                                         5,000 wds.

SUBMISSION FEE: No   PAGE CHARGES: No

MANUSCRIPT ACKNOWLEDGED: Yes   EARLY PUBLICATION OPTION: No
COPYRIGHT OWNER: Publisher   REPRINTS: Not available

AUTHOR COMPENSATION: Fee
MANUSCRIPT ADDRESS: Dr. David F. Lomax, Editor, National Westminster
   Bank Quarterly Review, National Westminster Bank, 41 Lothburg,
   London EC2P 2BP, U.K.

Natural Resources Journal

FIRST PUBLISHED: 1961   FREQUENCY: Q   CIRCULATION: 2,000

AFFILIATION: University of New Mexico School of Law. Address same as journal's.

AUDIENCE: Academic/Professional; Government

PERCENT OF UNSOLICITED ARTICLES/ISSUE: 41–60%   ISSN: 0028–0739

EDITORIAL POLICY: Provides a forum for those disciplines concerned with natural resources policy.

REVIEW INFORMATION

REFEREED: Yes (II–B)   ACCEPTANCE RATE: 50%

NUMBER OF REVIEWER(S)/MS., EXCLUDING IN-HOUSE EDITOR(S): 2

REVIEWER(S): Board and external   ARTICLES/AVG. ISSUE: 6–10

REVIEWING CRITERIA USED: BLIND REVIEW: No

  MANUSCRIPT SUBMISSION AIDS: 1, 2

  BIAS SAFEGUARDS: 4, 5

AVERAGE REVIEW TIME: 3 mos.   PUBLICATION TIME LAG: 9 mos.

MANUSCRIPT RETURNED WITH COMMENTS: Yes, SASE required

MANUSCRIPT INFORMATION

GUIDELINES PUBLISHED: Each issue

STYLE REQUIREMENTS PUBLISHED: Each issue

STYLE MANUAL USED: Harvard

PREFERRED TOPICS: Natural resources policy

QUERY LETTER: No   SIMULTANEOUS SUBMISSION: No

ABSTRACT WITH MANUSCRIPT: 100 wds.   COVER LETTER: Yes

NUMBER OF MANUSCRIPT COPIES: 3   MANUSCRIPT LENGTH: No limit

SUBMISSION FEE: No   PAGE CHARGES: No

MANUSCRIPT ACKNOWLEDGED: Yes   EARLY PUBLICATION OPTION: Yes

COPYRIGHT OWNER: Journal   REPRINTS: Optional purchase

AUTHOR COMPENSATION: 25 free reprints/tear sheets

MANUSCRIPT ADDRESS: Prof. Albert E. Utton, Editor, Natural Resources Journal, University of New Mexico School of Law, 1117 Stanford N.E., Albuquerque, NM 87131

New England Economic Review

FIRST PUBLISHED: 1920   FREQUENCY: Bi-M   CIRCULATION: 12,000
AFFILIATION: Federal Reserve Bank of Boston. Address same as journal's.

AUDIENCE: Academic/Professional; Business/Industrial; Government; Banking
PERCENT OF UNSOLICITED ARTICLES/ISSUE: 0-10%   ISSN: 0028-4726
EDITORIAL POLICY: Focuses on national economic issues as well as
  regional questions. The Bank's economists report on their major
  research projects in the journal. Only occasionally is an article
  by an outside author included.

REVIEW INFORMATION

REFEREED: No   ACCEPTANCE RATE: N.R.
NUMBER OF REVIEWER(S)/MS., EXCLUDING IN-HOUSE EDITOR(S): 0
REVIEWER(S): Editor   ARTICLES/AVG. ISSUE: 4
REVIEWING CRITERIA USED: BLIND REVIEW: No
  MANUSCRIPT SUBMISSION AIDS: 0
  BIAS SAFEGUARDS: 4
AVERAGE REVIEW TIME: 1 mo.   PUBLICATION TIME LAG: 3 mos.
MANUSCRIPT RETURNED WITH COMMENTS: No

MANUSCRIPT INFORMATION

GUIDELINES PUBLISHED: No; not available
STYLE REQUIREMENTS PUBLISHED: No; not available
STYLE MANUAL USED: In-house; Chicago
PREFERRED TOPICS: Economics

QUERY LETTER: No   SIMULTANEOUS SUBMISSION: Yes
ABSTRACT WITH MANUSCRIPT: No   COVER LETTER: Yes
NUMBER OF MANUSCRIPT COPIES: 1   MANUSCRIPT LENGTH: N.R.

SUBMISSION FEE: No   PAGE CHARGES: No

MANUSCRIPT ACKNOWLEDGED: Yes   EARLY PUBLICATION OPTION: No
COPYRIGHT OWNER: None claimed   REPRINTS: Not available

AUTHOR COMPENSATION: None
MANUSCRIPT ADDRESS: Ms. Joan T. Poskanzer, Editor, New England Economic
  Review, Federal Reserve Bank of Boston, 600 Atlantic Avenue,
  Boston, MA 02106

Oxford Bulletin of Economics and Statistics

FIRST PUBLISHED: 1939   FREQUENCY: Q   CIRCULATION: 1,400

AFFILIATION: University of Oxford. Address same as journal's.

AUDIENCE: Academic/Professional

PERCENT OF UNSOLICITED ARTICLES/ISSUE: 81-100%   ISSN: 0305-9049

EDITORIAL POLICY: Publishes research papers covering all major
  areas of applied economics. Emphasis is placed on the practical
  importance, theoretical interest and policy relevance of their
  substantive results, as well as on the methodology and technical
  competence of the research.

REVIEW INFORMATION

REFEREED: Yes (II-B)   ACCEPTANCE RATE: 55%

NUMBER OF REVIEWER(S)/MS., EXCLUDING IN-HOUSE EDITOR(S): 3

REVIEWER(S): 2 board, 1 external   ARTICLES/AVG. ISSUE: 4-6

REVIEWING CRITERIA USED: BLIND REVIEW: No

  MANUSCRIPT SUBMISSION AIDS: 1, 2

  BIAS SAFEGUARDS: 4, 5, 6, 9*

AVERAGE REVIEW TIME: 2 mos.   PUBLICATION TIME LAG: 3 mos.

MANUSCRIPT RETURNED WITH COMMENTS: No

MANUSCRIPT INFORMATION

GUIDELINES PUBLISHED: Each issue

STYLE REQUIREMENTS PUBLISHED: Each issue

STYLE MANUAL USED: In-house

PREFERRED TOPICS: Applied economics: economic policy, testing theories,
  empirical research on OECD countries

QUERY LETTER: No   SIMULTANEOUS SUBMISSION: Yes

ABSTRACT WITH MANUSCRIPT: 100 wds.   COVER LETTER: Yes

NUMBER OF MANUSCRIPT COPIES: 3   MANUSCRIPT LENGTH: N.R.

SUBMISSION FEE: No   PAGE CHARGES: No

MANUSCRIPT ACKNOWLEDGED: Yes   EARLY PUBLICATION OPTION: Yes

COPYRIGHT OWNER: Publisher   REPRINTS: Optional purchase

AUTHOR COMPENSATION: 25 free reprints/tear sheets

MANUSCRIPT ADDRESS: The Editorial Board, Oxford Bulletin of Economics
  and Statistics, Institute of Economics and Statistics, St. Cross
  Building, Manor Road, Oxford OX1 3UL, U.K.

Oxford Economic Papers

FIRST PUBLISHED: 1938   FREQUENCY: Q   CIRCULATION: 2,600

AFFILIATION: University of Oxford, Faculty of Economics. Address same
as journal's.

AUDIENCE: Academic/Professional

PERCENT OF UNSOLICITED ARTICLES/ISSUE: 90-95%   ISSN: 0030-7653

EDITORIAL POLICY: Accepts "contributions in economic theory, applied
economics, econometrics, economic development, economic history, and
the history of economic thought. They are also prepared occasionally to publish survey articles in addition to original papers."

REVIEW INFORMATION

REFEREED: Yes (I-B)   ACCEPTANCE RATE: 12%

NUMBER OF REVIEWER(S)/MS., EXCLUDING IN-HOUSE EDITOR(S): 2

REVIEWER(S): External   ARTICLES/AVG. ISSUE: 10-12

REVIEWING CRITERIA USED: BLIND REVIEW: No

  MANUSCRIPT SUBMISSION AIDS: 1, 2

  BIAS SAFEGUARDS: 4, 5, 6, 7, 9

AVERAGE REVIEW TIME: 3 mos.   PUBLICATION TIME LAG: 9-12 mos.

MANUSCRIPT RETURNED WITH COMMENTS: Yes

MANUSCRIPT INFORMATION

GUIDELINES PUBLISHED: Each issue

STYLE REQUIREMENTS PUBLISHED: Each issue

STYLE MANUAL USED: In-house

PREFERRED TOPICS: Economics: all areas

QUERY LETTER: No   SIMULTANEOUS SUBMISSION: No

ABSTRACT WITH MANUSCRIPT: 100 wds. max. COVER LETTER: Yes

NUMBER OF MANUSCRIPT COPIES: 3   MANUSCRIPT LENGTH: 7,000 wds.

SUBMISSION FEE: No   PAGE CHARGES: No

MANUSCRIPT ACKNOWLEDGED: Yes   EARLY PUBLICATION OPTION: No

COPYRIGHT OWNER: Journal and publisher REPRINTS: Optional purchase

AUTHOR COMPENSATION: 50 free reprints

MANUSCRIPT ADDRESS: Editorial Secretary, Oxford Economic Papers,
Institute of Economics & Statistics, St. Cross Building, Manor
Road, Oxford, OX1 3UL, U.K.

The Pakistan Development Review

FIRST PUBLISHED: 1961   FREQUENCY: Q   CIRCULATION: 5,500

AFFILIATION: Pakistan Institute of Development Economics. Address
  same as journal's.

AUDIENCE: Academic/Professional

PERCENT OF UNSOLICITED ARTICLES/ISSUE: 81-100%   ISSN: 0030-9729

EDITORIAL POLICY: Papers submitted for publication should be based on
  fundamental research on development economics, with special focus on
  Pakistan. Theoretical papers dealing with aspects of development
  economics are also published. In special cases, country studies,
  particularly those which are of general interest and relate to the
  Third World countries are also accepted.

REVIEW INFORMATION

REFEREED: Yes (III-A)   ACCEPTANCE RATE: 22.2%

NUMBER OF REVIEWER(S)/MS., EXCLUDING IN-HOUSE EDITOR(S): 3

REVIEWER(S): Board   ARTICLES/AVG. ISSUE: 4-5

REVIEWING CRITERIA USED: BLIND REVIEW: Yes (Board
  MANUSCRIPT SUBMISSION AIDS: 1, 2   review only)

  BIAS SAFEGUARDS: 3, 4, 9

AVERAGE REVIEW TIME: 6-12 mos.   PUBLICATION TIME LAG: 3 mos.

MANUSCRIPT RETURNED WITH COMMENTS: No

MANUSCRIPT INFORMATION

GUIDELINES PUBLISHED: Each issue

STYLE REQUIREMENTS PUBLISHED: Each issue

STYLE MANUAL USED: In-house

PREFERRED TOPICS: Development economics, economic demography,

  population dynamics

QUERY LETTER: No   SIMULTANEOUS SUBMISSION: No

ABSTRACT WITH MANUSCRIPT: 70 wds. COVER LETTER: Yes

NUMBER OF MANUSCRIPT COPIES: 3   MANUSCRIPT LENGTH: No limit

SUBMISSION FEE: No   PAGE CHARGES: No

MANUSCRIPT ACKNOWLEDGED: Yes   EARLY PUBLICATION OPTION: No

COPYRIGHT OWNER: Journal   REPRINTS: Optional purchase

AUTHOR COMPENSATION: 25 free reprints/tear sheets

MANUSCRIPT ADDRESS: Prof. Syed Nawab Haider Naqvi, Editor, The
  Pakistan Development Review, Pakistan Institute of Development
  Economics, P.O. Box 1091, Islamabad, Pakistan

Pakistan Journal of Applied Economics

FIRST PUBLISHED: 1974   FREQUENCY: S-A   CIRCULATION: 147

AFFILIATION: University of Karachi, Applied Economics Research
  Centre. Address same as journal's.

AUDIENCE: Academic/Professional; Government

PERCENT OF UNSOLICITED ARTICLES/ISSUE: 90%   ISSN: 0254-9204

EDITORIAL POLICY: To promote publications related to quantitative,
  policy-oriented research on economic and social problems of development with special reference to Pakistan. The journal is expected to
  act primarily as a vehicle for research undertaken by Pakistani
  economists both within the country and abroad.

REVIEW INFORMATION

REFEREED: Yes (III-A)   ACCEPTANCE RATE: 45%

NUMBER OF REVIEWER(S)/MS., EXCLUDING IN-HOUSE EDITOR(S): 2

REVIEWER(S): Board   ARTICLES/AVG. ISSUE: 4

REVIEWING CRITERIA USED: BLIND REVIEW: Yes (Preliminary
  MANUSCRIPT SUBMISSION AIDS: 1, 2   screening only)
  BIAS SAFEGUARDS: 3, 4, 5, 6, 9

AVERAGE REVIEW TIME: 2 wks.   PUBLICATION TIME LAG: 3 mos.

MANUSCRIPT RETURNED WITH COMMENTS: Yes, SASE required

MANUSCRIPT INFORMATION

GUIDELINES PUBLISHED: Each issue

STYLE REQUIREMENTS PUBLISHED: Each issue

STYLE MANUAL USED: In-house

PREFERRED TOPICS: Development with emphasis on such fields as
  agriculture, industry, urban and regional, health and education,
  trade, public finance

QUERY LETTER: No   SIMULTANEOUS SUBMISSION: No

ABSTRACT WITH MANUSCRIPT: 100 wds.   COVER LETTER: Yes

NUMBER OF MANUSCRIPT COPIES: 3   MANUSCRIPT LENGTH: 10,000 wds.

SUBMISSION FEE: No   PAGE CHARGES: No

MANUSCRIPT ACKNOWLEDGED: Yes   EARLY PUBLICATION OPTION: No

COPYRIGHT OWNER: Journal   REPRINTS: Not available

AUTHOR COMPENSATION: 30 free reprints

MANUSCRIPT ADDRESS: Hafiz A. Pasha, Editor, Pakistan Journal of
  Applied Economics, Applied Economics Research Centre, University
  of Karachi, Karachi-32, Pakistan

The Philippine Economic Journal

FIRST PUBLISHED: 1962   FREQUENCY: Q   CIRCULATION: 1,000

AFFILIATION: Philippine Economic Society, POB 1116, Manila, Philippines

AUDIENCE: Academic/Professional; Business/Industrial; Government

PERCENT OF UNSOLICITED ARTICLES/ISSUE: 61-80%   ISSN: 0031-7506

EDITORIAL POLICY: Publishes articles on economic issues dealing with the Philippines and the Asia-Pacific region, written by Filipino scholars and other scholars studying Philippine problems. Empirical studies receive priority, although theoretical articles are also occasionally published.

REVIEW INFORMATION

REFEREED: No   ACCEPTANCE RATE: 60%

NUMBER OF REVIEWER(S)/MS., EXCLUDING IN-HOUSE EDITOR(S): 1

REVIEWER(S): Board or external   ARTICLES/AVG. ISSUE: 5-6

REVIEWING CRITERIA USED: BLIND REVIEW: No

  MANUSCRIPT SUBMISSION AIDS: 0

  BIAS SAFEGUARDS: 4, 5, 6, 9*

AVERAGE REVIEW TIME: 6 mos.   PUBLICATION TIME LAG: 15 mos.

MANUSCRIPT RETURNED WITH COMMENTS: No

MANUSCRIPT INFORMATION

GUIDELINES PUBLISHED: No; available on request

STYLE REQUIREMENTS PUBLISHED: No; not available

STYLE MANUAL USED: In-house; Chicago

PREFERRED TOPICS: Economic issues relevant to the Philippines and the Asia-Pacific region

QUERY LETTER: No   SIMULTANEOUS SUBMISSION: No

ABSTRACT WITH MANUSCRIPT: No   COVER LETTER: Yes

NUMBER OF MANUSCRIPT COPIES: 2   MANUSCRIPT LENGTH: 30 pp.

SUBMISSION FEE: No   PAGE CHARGES: No

MANUSCRIPT ACKNOWLEDGED: Yes   EARLY PUBLICATION OPTION: Yes

COPYRIGHT OWNER: Philippine Economic Society   REPRINTS: Optional purchase

AUTHOR COMPENSATION: 1 free journal

MANUSCRIPT ADDRESS: Ruperto P. Alonzo, Editor, The Philippine Economic Journal, School of Economics, University of the Philippines, Diliman, Quezon City, Philippines 3004

The Philippine Review of Economics and Business

FIRST PUBLISHED: 1964   FREQUENCY: Q   CIRCULATION: 1,000

AFFILIATION: University of the Philippines, School of Economics and College of Business Administration. Address same as journal's.

AUDIENCE: Academic/Professional; Business/Industrial; Government

PERCENT OF UNSOLICITED ARTICLES/ISSUE: 61-80%   ISSN: 0031-7780

EDITORIAL POLICY: Serves primarily as a vehicle for the publication of research work done at the School of Economics and the College of Business Administration. Outside contributions are also welcome, especially those relating to Philippine economic and business conditions.

REVIEW INFORMATION

REFEREED: No   ACCEPTANCE RATE: 73%

NUMBER OF REVIEWER(S)/MS., EXCLUDING IN-HOUSE EDITOR(S): 0

REVIEWER(S): 2 in-house editors   ARTICLES/AVG. ISSUE: 5

REVIEWING CRITERIA USED: BLIND REVIEW: Yes (Board
  MANUSCRIPT SUBMISSION AIDS: 1   and external review,
                                          when used)
  BIAS SAFEGUARDS: 3, 4, 5, 6, 9

AVERAGE REVIEW TIME: 1 mo.   PUBLICATION TIME LAG: 4 mos.

MANUSCRIPT RETURNED WITH COMMENTS: Yes

MANUSCRIPT INFORMATION

GUIDELINES PUBLISHED: Each issue

STYLE REQUIREMENTS PUBLISHED: No; available on request

STYLE MANUAL USED: In-house

PREFERRED TOPICS: Economic and business conditions relating to the Philippines

QUERY LETTER: No   SIMULTANEOUS SUBMISSION: Yes

ABSTRACT WITH MANUSCRIPT: 30-50 wds.   COVER LETTER: Yes

NUMBER OF MANUSCRIPT COPIES: 2   MANUSCRIPT LENGTH: 15 pp.

SUBMISSION FEE: No   PAGE CHARGES: No

MANUSCRIPT ACKNOWLEDGED: Yes   EARLY PUBLICATION OPTION: No

COPYRIGHT OWNER: Journal and author   REPRINTS: N.R.

AUTHOR COMPENSATION: 2 free journals and 25 free reprints/tear sheets

MANUSCRIPT ADDRESS: Dante B. Canlas, Editor, The Philippine Review of Economics and Business, University of the Philippines, School of Economics, Quezon City, Philippines 3004

Policy Review

FIRST PUBLISHED: 1977   FREQUENCY: Q   CIRCULATION: 5,000
AFFILIATION: The Heritage Foundation. Address same as journal's.

AUDIENCE: Academic/Professional; Business/Industrial; Government
PERCENT OF UNSOLICITED ARTICLES/ISSUE: 0-10%   ISSN: 0146-5945
EDITORIAL POLICY: Seeks lively conservative journalism, and thoughtful statements by leading conservative political thinkers on the
   most important political issues of our times.

REVIEW INFORMATION

REFEREED: No   ACCEPTANCE RATE: 5%
NUMBER OF REVIEWER(S)/MS., EXCLUDING IN-HOUSE EDITOR(S): 0
REVIEWER(S): Managing Editor   ARTICLES/AVG. ISSUE: 15
REVIEWING CRITERIA USED: BLIND REVIEW: No
   MANUSCRIPT SUBMISSION AIDS: 0
   BIAS SAFEGUARDS: 0
AVERAGE REVIEW TIME: 2 wks.   PUBLICATION TIME LAG: 2 mos.
MANUSCRIPT RETURNED WITH COMMENTS: N.R.

MANUSCRIPT INFORMATION

GUIDELINES PUBLISHED: No; not available
STYLE REQUIREMENTS PUBLISHED: No; not available
STYLE MANUAL USED: Chicago
PREFERRED TOPICS: Public policy

QUERY LETTER: No   SIMULTANEOUS SUBMISSION: Yes
ABSTRACT WITH MANUSCRIPT: No   COVER LETTER: No
NUMBER OF MANUSCRIPT COPIES: 1   MANUSCRIPT LENGTH: 3,000-
                                      5,000 wds.

SUBMISSION FEE: No   PAGE CHARGES: No

MANUSCRIPT ACKNOWLEDGED: Yes   EARLY PUBLICATION OPTION: Yes
COPYRIGHT OWNER: Journal   REPRINTS: Optional purchase

AUTHOR COMPENSATION: Fee varies; 2 free tear sheets
MANUSCRIPT ADDRESS: Dinesh D'Souza, Managing Editor, Policy Review,
   The Heritage Foundation, Inc., 214 Massachusetts Avenue N.E.
   Washington, D.C. 20002

Policy Sciences

FIRST PUBLISHED: 1977   FREQUENCY: Q   CIRCULATION: 3,000
AFFILIATION: None

AUDIENCE: Academic/Professional; Government
PERCENT OF UNSOLICITED ARTICLES/ISSUE: 81-100%   ISSN: 0032-2687
EDITORIAL POLICY: Publishes contributions to the theory and practice
  of the policy sciences.

REVIEW INFORMATION

REFEREED: Yes (I-A)   ACCEPTANCE RATE: 20%
NUMBER OF REVIEWER(S)/MS., EXCLUDING IN-HOUSE EDITOR(S): 2
REVIEWER(S): External   ARTICLES/AVG. ISSUE: 5
REVIEWING CRITERIA USED: BLIND REVIEW: Yes (Board and
  MANUSCRIPT SUBMISSION AIDS: 1, 2   external review)
  BIAS SAFEGUARDS: 3, 4, 5, 6, 7, 8, 9
AVERAGE REVIEW TIME: 8 wks.   PUBLICATION TIME LAG: 6 mos.
MANUSCRIPT RETURNED WITH COMMENTS: No

MANUSCRIPT INFORMATION

GUIDELINES PUBLISHED: Each issue (brief); April 1987 (detailed)
STYLE REQUIREMENTS PUBLISHED: First issue of each volume
STYLE MANUAL USED: In-house
PREFERRED TOPICS: Policy, policy process

QUERY LETTER: No   SIMULTANEOUS SUBMISSION: No
ABSTRACT WITH MANUSCRIPT: 150 wds.   COVER LETTER: Yes
NUMBER OF MANUSCRIPT COPIES: 3   MANUSCRIPT LENGTH: 25-40 pp.

SUBMISSION FEE: No   PAGE CHARGES: No

MANUSCRIPT ACKNOWLEDGED: Yes   EARLY PUBLICATION OPTION: Yes
COPYRIGHT OWNER: Publisher   REPRINTS: Optional purchase

AUTHOR COMPENSATION: 50 free reprints
MANUSCRIPT ADDRESS: William Ascher, Editor, Policy Sciences, Institute
  of Policy Sciences and Public Affairs, Duke University, 4875 Duke
  Station, Durham, NC 27706

Population and Development Review

FIRST PUBLISHED: 1975   FREQUENCY: S-A   CIRCULATION: 6,000

AFFILIATION: Population Council, Center for Policy Studies. Address
  same as journal's.

AUDIENCE: Academic/Professional; Government

PERCENT OF UNSOLICITED ARTICLES/ISSUE: 21-40%   ISSN: 0098-7921

EDITORIAL POLICY: Seeks to advance knowledge of the interrelation-
  ships between population and socioeconomic development and provides
  a forum for discussion of related issues of public policy.

REVIEW INFORMATION

REFEREED: Yes (I-A)   ACCEPTANCE RATE: 10%

NUMBER OF REVIEWER(S)/MS., EXCLUDING IN-HOUSE EDITOR(S): 2

REVIEWER(S): External   ARTICLES/AVG. ISSUE: 6

REVIEWING CRITERIA USED: BLIND REVIEW: Yes (External
  MANUSCRIPT SUBMISSION AIDS: 0   review only)

  BIAS SAFEGUARDS: 3, 4, 5, 6, 7, 9

AVERAGE REVIEW TIME: 6 wks.   PUBLICATION TIME LAG: 4 mos.

MANUSCRIPT RETURNED WITH COMMENTS: Yes, SASE required

MANUSCRIPT INFORMATION

GUIDELINES PUBLISHED: No; available on request

STYLE REQUIREMENTS PUBLISHED: No; available on request

STYLE MANUAL USED: In-house; Chicago

PREFERRED TOPICS: Social sciences with a bearing on population
  change and/or related public policy

QUERY LETTER: No   SIMULTANEOUS SUBMISSION: No

ABSTRACT WITH MANUSCRIPT: 100 wds.   COVER LETTER: Yes

NUMBER OF MANUSCRIPT COPIES: 3   MANUSCRIPT LENGTH: 25-40 pp.

SUBMISSION FEE: No   PAGE CHARGES: No

MANUSCRIPT ACKNOWLEDGED: Yes   EARLY PUBLICATION OPTION: Yes

COPYRIGHT OWNER: Publisher   REPRINTS: Optional purchase

AUTHOR COMPENSATION: 2 free journals and 25 free reprints/tear sheets

MANUSCRIPT ADDRESS: Ms. Ethel P. Churchill, Managing Editor, Population
  and Development Review, Population Council, One Dag Hammarskjold
  Plaza, New York, NY 10017

Population Studies

FIRST PUBLISHED: 1947   FREQUENCY: 3/Yr.   CIRCULATION: 2,750

AFFILIATION: London School of Economics and Political Science,
  Population Investigation Committee. Address same as journal's.

AUDIENCE: Academic/Professional; Government

PERCENT OF UNSOLICITED ARTICLES/ISSUE: 100%   ISSN: 0032-4728

EDITORIAL POLICY: Publishes original research or review articles on all
  aspects of demography, including the biological, historical, economic,
  social, psychological and political aspects, as well as papers dealing with data collection and measurement of population growth.

REVIEW INFORMATION

REFEREED: No   ACCEPTANCE RATE: 30%

NUMBER OF REVIEWER(S)/MS., EXCLUDING IN-HOUSE EDITOR(S): 1

REVIEWER(S): External   ARTICLES/AVG. ISSUE: 9-10

REVIEWING CRITERIA USED: BLIND REVIEW: No

  MANUSCRIPT SUBMISSION AIDS: 0

  BIAS SAFEGUARDS: 4, 5, 6

AVERAGE REVIEW TIME: 3 mos.   PUBLICATION TIME LAG: 12 mos.

MANUSCRIPT RETURNED WITH COMMENTS: No

MANUSCRIPT INFORMATION

GUIDELINES PUBLISHED: No; not available

STYLE REQUIREMENTS PUBLISHED: No; available on request

STYLE MANUAL USED: In-house

PREFERRED TOPICS: All aspects of studies relating to human population

QUERY LETTER: No   SIMULTANEOUS SUBMISSION: Yes

ABSTRACT WITH MANUSCRIPT: 250 wds. COVER LETTER: Yes

NUMBER OF MANUSCRIPT COPIES: 2   MANUSCRIPT LENGTH: 25 pp.

SUBMISSION FEE: No   PAGE CHARGES: No

MANUSCRIPT ACKNOWLEDGED: Yes   EARLY PUBLICATION OPTION: No

COPYRIGHT OWNER: Journal   REPRINTS: Optional purchase

AUTHOR COMPENSATION: 25 free reprints/tear sheets

MANUSCRIPT ADDRESS: Mrs. Doreen Castle, Population Investigation
  Committee, London School of Economics and Political Science,
  Houghton Street, London, WC2A 2AE, U.K.

Problems of Communism

FIRST PUBLISHED: 1952   FREQUENCY: Bi-M   CIRCULATION: 34,000
AFFILIATION: U.S. Information Agency. Address same as journal's.

AUDIENCE: Academic/Professional; Business/Industrial; Government
PERCENT OF UNSOLICITED ARTICLES/ISSUE: 41-60%   ISSN: 0032-941X
EDITORIAL POLICY: To provide analyses and significant information
  about the contemporary affairs of the Soviet Union, China, and
  comparable states and movements.

REVIEW INFORMATION

REFEREED: No   ACCEPTANCE RATE: 20%
NUMBER OF REVIEWER(S)/MS., EXCLUDING IN-HOUSE EDITOR(S): 0
REVIEWER(S): 2 in-house editors   ARTICLES/AVG. ISSUE: 2-4
REVIEWING CRITERIA USED: BLIND REVIEW: No
  MANUSCRIPT SUBMISSION AIDS: 0
  BIAS SAFEGUARDS: 4, 5
AVERAGE REVIEW TIME: 1-2 mos.   PUBLICATION TIME LAG: 2-3 mos.
MANUSCRIPT RETURNED WITH COMMENTS: No

MANUSCRIPT INFORMATION

GUIDELINES PUBLISHED: No; available with SASE
STYLE REQUIREMENTS PUBLISHED: No; available with SASE
STYLE MANUAL USED: GPO; Chicago
PREFERRED TOPICS: Social science treatments of topics in Communist
  affairs

QUERY LETTER: No   SIMULTANEOUS SUBMISSION: No
ABSTRACT WITH MANUSCRIPT: No   COVER LETTER: Yes
NUMBER OF MANUSCRIPT COPIES: 2   MANUSCRIPT LENGTH: 30-40 pp.

SUBMISSION FEE: No   PAGE CHARGES: No

MANUSCRIPT ACKNOWLEDGED: Yes   EARLY PUBLICATION OPTION: Yes
COPYRIGHT OWNER: Journal   REPRINTS: Not available

AUTHOR COMPENSATION: Fee and 30 free reprints/tear sheets
MANUSCRIPT ADDRESS: Richard Snyder, Senior Editor, Problems of Communism,
  U.S. Information Agency, 301 4th Street SW, Room 402, Washington, D.C.
  20547

Public Budgeting & Finance

FIRST PUBLISHED: 1981   FREQUENCY: Q   CIRCULATION: 2,700

AFFILIATION: AABPA, P.O. Box 1157, Falls Church, VA 22041, and budget
   section, ASPA, 1120 G St., N.W., Suite 500, Washington, D.C. 20005

AUDIENCE: Academic/Professional; Government

PERCENT OF UNSOLICITED ARTICLES/ISSUE: 61-80%   ISSN: 0275-1100

EDITORIAL POLICY: 1) To publish manuscripts on the theory and practice
   of public budgeting and financial manangment; 2) To solicit manuscripts that integrate the theory and practice of public budgeting
   and accounting.

REVIEW INFORMATION

REFEREED: Yes (I-A)   ACCEPTANCE RATE: 40%

NUMBER OF REVIEWER(S)/MS., EXCLUDING IN-HOUSE EDITOR(S): 3

REVIEWER(S): 1 board, 2 external   ARTICLES/AVG. ISSUE: 8

REVIEWING CRITERIA USED: BLIND REVIEW: Yes (Board
   MANUSCRIPT SUBMISSION AIDS: 1, 2   and external review)

   BIAS SAFEGUARDS: 3, 4, 5, 6, 7, 9

AVERAGE REVIEW TIME: 2 mos.   PUBLICATION TIME LAG: 5 mos.

MANUSCRIPT RETURNED WITH COMMENTS: Occasionally

MANUSCRIPT INFORMATION

GUIDELINES PUBLISHED: Each issue

STYLE REQUIREMENTS PUBLISHED: Each issue

STYLE MANUAL USED: Chicago

PREFERRED TOPICS: Public budgeting and financial management--federal,
   state and local

QUERY LETTER: No   SIMULTANEOUS SUBMISSION: No

ABSTRACT WITH MANUSCRIPT: No   COVER LETTER: Yes

NUMBER OF MANUSCRIPT COPIES: 3   MANUSCRIPT LENGTH: 25-30 pp.

SUBMISSION FEE: No   PAGE CHARGES: No

MANUSCRIPT ACKNOWLEDGED: Yes   EARLY PUBLICATION OPTION: Seldom

COPYRIGHT OWNER: Journal   REPRINTS: Optional purchase

AUTHOR COMPENSATION: 2 free journals

MANUSCRIPT ADDRESS: Prof. Jesse Burkhead, Editor, Public Budgeting &
   Finance, Department of Economics, The Maxwell School, Syracuse
   University, Syracuse, NY 13210

Public Choice

FIRST PUBLISHED: 1966   FREQUENCY: 9/Yr.   CIRCULATION: 1,400

AFFILIATION: Center for Study of Public Choice. Address same as
  journal's.

AUDIENCE: Academic/Professional

PERCENT OF UNSOLICITED ARTICLES/ISSUE: 99%   ISSN: 0048-5829

EDITORIAL POLICY: "Deals with the intersection between economics
  and political science. . . . Can be viewed as a field of interest
  to both economists and political scientists who are interested
  in theoretical rigor, statistical testing, and applications to
  real world problems."

REVIEW INFORMATION

REFEREED: No   ACCEPTANCE RATE: 25%

NUMBER OF REVIEWER(S)/MS., EXCLUDING IN-HOUSE EDITOR(S): 0

REVIEWER(S): Editor   ARTICLES/AVG. ISSUE: 8

REVIEWING CRITERIA USED: BLIND REVIEW: No

  MANUSCRIPT SUBMISSION AIDS: 0

  BIAS SAFEGUARDS: 5, 9

AVERAGE REVIEW TIME: 1 wk.   PUBLICATION TIME LAG: 4 mos.

MANUSCRIPT RETURNED WITH COMMENTS: Yes, SASE required

MANUSCRIPT INFORMATION

GUIDELINES PUBLISHED: No; available on request

STYLE REQUIREMENTS PUBLISHED: No; available on request

STYLE MANUAL USED: Chicago

PREFERRED TOPICS: Public choice, economics and political science

QUERY LETTER: No   SIMULTANEOUS SUBMISSION: Yes

ABSTRACT WITH MANUSCRIPT: No   COVER LETTER: Yes

NUMBER OF MANUSCRIPT COPIES: 2   MANUSCRIPT LENGTH: 20 pp.

SUBMISSION FEE: No   PAGE CHARGES: No

MANUSCRIPT ACKNOWLEDGED: Yes   EARLY PUBLICATION OPTION: Yes

COPYRIGHT OWNER: Journal   REPRINTS: Not available

AUTHOR COMPENSATION: None

MANUSCRIPT ADDRESS: Gordon Tullock, Senior Editor, Public Choice,
  Center for Study of Public Choice, St. George's Hall, George
  Mason University, 4400 University Drive, Fairfax, VA 22030

Public Finance / Finances Publiques

FIRST PUBLISHED: 1950   FREQUENCY: 3/Yr.   CIRCULATION: 1,800
AFFILIATION: None

AUDIENCE: Academic/Professional; Government
PERCENT OF UNSOLICITED ARTICLES/ISSUE: 100%   ISSN: 0033-3476
EDITORIAL POLICY: Publishes articles dealing with public finance and
   related issues, both theoretical and applied, if the papers are
   sufficiently original and improve our knowledge in the field.

REVIEW INFORMATION

REFEREED: Yes (II-B)   ACCEPTANCE RATE: 20%
NUMBER OF REVIEWER(S)/MS., EXCLUDING IN-HOUSE EDITOR(S): 2
REVIEWER(S): Board and external   ARTICLES/AVG. ISSUE: 8-12
REVIEWING CRITERIA USED: BLIND REVIEW: No
   MANUSCRIPT SUBMISSION AIDS: 1
   BIAS SAFEGUARDS: 4, 5, 6, 9
AVERAGE REVIEW TIME: 6-9 mos.   PUBLICATION TIME LAG: 3 mos.
MANUSCRIPT RETURNED WITH COMMENTS: Yes, SASE required

MANUSCRIPT INFORMATION

GUIDELINES PUBLISHED: Each issue
STYLE REQUIREMENTS PUBLISHED: No; available on request
STYLE MANUAL USED: In-house
PREFERRED TOPICS: Public finance and related issues

QUERY LETTER: No   SIMULTANEOUS SUBMISSION: No
ABSTRACT WITH MANUSCRIPT: 100 wds.   COVER LETTER: Yes
NUMBER OF MANUSCRIPT COPIES: 4   MANUSCRIPT LENGTH: Varies

SUBMISSION FEE: No   PAGE CHARGES: No

MANUSCRIPT ACKNOWLEDGED: Yes   EARLY PUBLICATION OPTION: No
COPYRIGHT OWNER: Journal   REPRINTS: Optional purchase

AUTHOR COMPENSATION: 25 free reprints/tear sheets
MANUSCRIPT ADDRESS: Prof. Dr. Dieter Biehl, Editor, Public Finance/
   Finances Publiques, Johann Wolfgang Goethe-Universität, Postfach
   111932, D-6000 Frankfurt am Main 11, Federal Republic of Germany

Public Finance Quarterly

FIRST PUBLISHED: 1973   FREQUENCY: Q   CIRCULATION: 1,800

AFFILIATION: None

AUDIENCE: Academic/Professional; Government

PERCENT OF UNSOLICITED ARTICLES/ISSUE: 100%   ISSN: 0048-5853

EDITORIAL POLICY: "A scholarly economics journal for the study of the
public sector of the economy. Original manuscripts are invited
that deal with positive or normative aspects of government policies
at the federal, state, or local level. Both theoretical and empirical studies are welcomed. The journal is particularly interested
in papers that analyze current issues of government policy."

REVIEW INFORMATION

REFEREED: Yes (I-A)   ACCEPTANCE RATE: 20%

NUMBER OF REVIEWER(S)/MS., EXCLUDING IN-HOUSE EDITOR(S): 2

REVIEWER(S): External   ARTICLES/AVG. ISSUE: 5-10

REVIEWING CRITERIA USED: BLIND REVIEW: Yes (Board and
  MANUSCRIPT SUBMISSION AIDS: 1   external review)

  BIAS SAFEGUARDS: 3, 5, 7, 9

AVERAGE REVIEW TIME: 4 mos.   PUBLICATION TIME LAG: 3 mos.

MANUSCRIPT RETURNED WITH COMMENTS: Yes

MANUSCRIPT INFORMATION

GUIDELINES PUBLISHED: Each issue

STYLE REQUIREMENTS PUBLISHED: No; available on request

STYLE MANUAL USED: In-house

PREFERRED TOPICS: Public finance, taxation, budgeting, public policy
  analysis

QUERY LETTER: No   SIMULTANEOUS SUBMISSION: No

ABSTRACT WITH MANUSCRIPT: Yes   COVER LETTER: Yes

NUMBER OF MANUSCRIPT COPIES: 3   MANUSCRIPT LENGTH: No limit

SUBMISSION FEE: $10.   PAGE CHARGES: No

MANUSCRIPT ACKNOWLEDGED: Yes   EARLY PUBLICATION OPTION: No

COPYRIGHT OWNER: Publisher   REPRINTS: Optional purchase

AUTHOR COMPENSATION: None

MANUSCRIPT ADDRESS: Prof. J. Ronnie Davis, Editor, Public Finance
  Quarterly, College of Business and Management Studies, University
  of South Alabama, Mobile, AL 36688

Quarterly Journal of Business and Economics

FIRST PUBLISHED: 1962   FREQUENCY: Q   CIRCULATION: 500

AFFILIATION: University of Nebraska-Lincoln, College of Business
  Administration. Address same as journal's.

AUDIENCE: Academic/Professional

PERCENT OF UNSOLICITED ARTICLES/ISSUE: 100%   ISSN: 0747-5535

EDITORIAL POLICY: Stresses articles that test the validity of
  theories, methodologies, and data of previously published work,
  especially articles that bridge several disciplines.

REVIEW INFORMATION

REFEREED: Yes (I-A)   ACCEPTANCE RATE: 20%

NUMBER OF REVIEWER(S)/MS., EXCLUDING IN-HOUSE EDITOR(S): 3

REVIEWER(S): External   ARTICLES/AVG. ISSUE: 5

REVIEWING CRITERIA USED: BLIND REVIEW: Yes (External
  MANUSCRIPT SUBMISSION AIDS: 1   review only)
  BIAS SAFEGUARDS: 3, 5, 6, 7, 9*

AVERAGE REVIEW TIME: 6 mos.   PUBLICATION TIME LAG: 6 mos.

MANUSCRIPT RETURNED WITH COMMENTS: No

MANUSCRIPT INFORMATION

GUIDELINES PUBLISHED: Each issue

STYLE REQUIREMENTS PUBLISHED: No; available on request

STYLE MANUAL USED: Chicago

PREFERRED TOPICS: Business, economics

QUERY LETTER: No   SIMULTANEOUS SUBMISSION: No

ABSTRACT WITH MANUSCRIPT: 100 wds.   COVER LETTER: Yes

NUMBER OF MANUSCRIPT COPIES: 3   MANUSCRIPT LENGTH: 25 pp.

SUBMISSION FEE: $20.   PAGE CHARGES: No

MANUSCRIPT ACKNOWLEDGED: Yes   EARLY PUBLICATION OPTION: No

COPYRIGHT OWNER: Publisher   REPRINTS: Not available

AUTHOR COMPENSATION: 2 free journals

MANUSCRIPT ADDRESS: Quarterly Journal of Business and Economics, 200
  College of Business Administration, University of Nebraska-Lincoln,
  Lincoln, NE 68588-0407

The Quarterly Journal of Economics

FIRST PUBLISHED: 1886   FREQUENCY: Q   CIRCULATION: 4,800

AFFILIATION: Harvard University, Department of Economics. Address same as journal's.

AUDIENCE: Academic/Professional

PERCENT OF UNSOLICITED ARTICLES/ISSUE: 100%   ISSN: 0033-5533

EDITORIAL POLICY: Significant advances in economic theory that appeal to a general audience; original research.

REVIEW INFORMATION

REFEREED: Yes (II-A)   ACCEPTANCE RATE: 8-9%

NUMBER OF REVIEWER(S)/MS., EXCLUDING IN-HOUSE EDITOR(S): 2

REVIEWER(S): Board and/or external   ARTICLES/AVG. ISSUE: 12

REVIEWING CRITERIA USED: BLIND REVIEW: Yes (Board
  MANUSCRIPT SUBMISSION AIDS: 0   and external review)
  BIAS SAFEGUARDS: 3, 5, 9*

AVERAGE REVIEW TIME: 3-4 mos.   PUBLICATION TIME LAG: 6 mos.

MANUSCRIPT RETURNED WITH COMMENTS: Only if comments are on manuscript; SASE required

MANUSCRIPT INFORMATION

GUIDELINES PUBLISHED: No; not available

STYLE REQUIREMENTS PUBLISHED: No; available on request

STYLE MANUAL USED: In-house; Chicago

PREFERRED TOPICS: Economics

QUERY LETTER: No   SIMULTANEOUS SUBMISSION: No

ABSTRACT WITH MANUSCRIPT: No   COVER LETTER: Yes

NUMBER OF MANUSCRIPT COPIES: 3   MANUSCRIPT LENGTH: 35 pp. max.

SUBMISSION FEE: No   PAGE CHARGES: No

MANUSCRIPT ACKNOWLEDGED: Yes   EARLY PUBLICATION OPTION: No

COPYRIGHT OWNER: Harvard University   REPRINTS: Optional purchase

AUTHOR COMPENSATION: None

MANUSCRIPT ADDRESS: The Quarterly Journal of Economics, Littauer Center, Harvard University, Cambridge, MA 02138

The Rand Journal of Economics

FIRST PUBLISHED: 1970   FREQUENCY: Q   CIRCULATION: 4,600
AFFILIATION: The Rand Corporation. Address same as journal's.

AUDIENCE: Academic/Professional; Business/Industrial; Government
PERCENT OF UNSOLICITED ARTICLES/ISSUE: 81-100%   ISSN: 0741-6261
EDITORIAL POLICY: "To support and encourage research in the behavior
  of regulated industries, the economic analysis of organizations,
  and more generally, applied microeconomics. Both theoretical and
  empirical manuscripts in economics and law are encouraged."

REVIEW INFORMATION

REFEREED: Yes (II-B)   ACCEPTANCE RATE: 11%
NUMBER OF REVIEWER(S)/MS., EXCLUDING IN-HOUSE EDITOR(S): 2
REVIEWER(S): Board and external   ARTICLES/AVG. ISSUE: 12
REVIEWING CRITERIA USED: BLIND REVIEW: No
  MANUSCRIPT SUBMISSION AIDS: 1
  BIAS SAFEGUARDS: 5, 6, 9
AVERAGE REVIEW TIME: 3 mos.   PUBLICATION TIME LAG: 3 mos.
MANUSCRIPT RETURNED WITH COMMENTS: Yes, SASE required

MANUSCRIPT INFORMATION

GUIDELINES PUBLISHED: Each issue
STYLE REQUIREMENTS PUBLISHED: No; not available
STYLE MANUAL USED: Chicago
PREFERRED TOPICS: Industrial organization, applied microeconomics

QUERY LETTER: No   SIMULTANEOUS SUBMISSION: No
ABSTRACT WITH MANUSCRIPT: 100 wds.   COVER LETTER: Yes
NUMBER OF MANUSCRIPT COPIES: 3   MANUSCRIPT LENGTH: 15-30 pp.

SUBMISSION FEE: $30.   PAGE CHARGES: No

MANUSCRIPT ACKNOWLEDGED: Yes   EARLY PUBLICATION OPTION: No
COPYRIGHT OWNER: Author and publisher   REPRINTS: Optional purchase

AUTHOR COMPENSATION: 50 free reprints/tear sheets
MANUSCRIPT ADDRESS: Dr. Stanley M. Besen, Editor, The Rand Journal
  of Economics, 2100 M Street, N.W., Washington, D.C. 20037

Regional Science and Urban Economics

FIRST PUBLISHED: 1971 FREQUENCY: 4/Yr. CIRCULATION: 1,000
AFFILIATION: None

AUDIENCE: Academic/Professional
PERCENT OF UNSOLICITED ARTICLES/ISSUE: 81-100% ISSN: 0166-9462
EDITORIAL POLICY: An interdisciplinary journal that seeks papers
 which "are theoretically oriented, i.e., analyze problems with a
 large degree of generality, employ formal methods from mathematics,
 econometrics, operations research and related fields, and have a
 focus on immediate or potential uses for regional and urban
 forecasting, planning and policy."

REVIEW INFORMATION

REFEREED: No ACCEPTANCE RATE: 55%
NUMBER OF REVIEWER(S)/MS., EXCLUDING IN-HOUSE EDITOR(S): 1
REVIEWER(S): Board or external ARTICLES/AVG. ISSUE: 10
REVIEWING CRITERIA USED: BLIND REVIEW: No
 MANUSCRIPT SUBMISSION AIDS: 1
 BIAS SAFEGUARDS: 5, 9
AVERAGE REVIEW TIME: 3 mos. PUBLICATION TIME LAG: 5-8 mos.
MANUSCRIPT RETURNED WITH COMMENTS: No

MANUSCRIPT INFORMATION

GUIDELINES PUBLISHED: Each issue
STYLE REQUIREMENTS PUBLISHED: No; not available
STYLE MANUAL USED: In-house
PREFERRED TOPICS: Regional and urban forecasting, planning and policy

QUERY LETTER: No SIMULTANEOUS SUBMISSION: No
ABSTRACT WITH MANUSCRIPT: 100 wds. COVER LETTER: Yes
NUMBER OF MANUSCRIPT COPIES: 3 MANUSCRIPT LENGTH: 10-20 pp.

SUBMISSION FEE: No PAGE CHARGES: No

MANUSCRIPT ACKNOWLEDGED: Yes EARLY PUBLICATION OPTION: No
COPYRIGHT OWNER: Publisher REPRINTS: Optional purchase

AUTHOR COMPENSATION: 25 free reprints/tear sheets
MANUSCRIPT ADDRESS: Prof. Urs Schweizer, Editor, Regional Science
 and Urban Economics, Department of Economics, University of Bonn,
 Adenaueralle 24, D-5300 Bonn 1, West Germany

Regional Science Perspectives

FIRST PUBLISHED: 1971   FREQUENCY: S-A   CIRCULATION: 390

AFFILIATION: Mid-Continent Regional Science Association, c/o Prof.
  Norman Walter, Department of Economics, Western Illinois University,
  Macomb, IL 61455, and Kansas State University, Dept. of Economics.
AUDIENCE: Academic/Professional; Government

PERCENT OF UNSOLICITED ARTICLES/ISSUE: 95%   ISSN: 0097-1197

EDITORIAL POLICY: To publish quality research on regional development.

REVIEW INFORMATION

REFEREED: Yes (II-A)   ACCEPTANCE RATE: 40%

NUMBER OF REVIEWER(S)/MS., EXCLUDING IN-HOUSE EDITOR(S): 2

REVIEWER(S): Board and/or external   ARTICLES/AVG. ISSUE: 7

REVIEWING CRITERIA USED: BLIND REVIEW: Yes (Board
  MANUSCRIPT SUBMISSION AIDS: 1, 2   and external review)

  BIAS SAFEGUARDS: 3, 5, 9

AVERAGE REVIEW TIME: 3 mos.   PUBLICATION TIME LAG: 6 mos.

MANUSCRIPT RETURNED WITH COMMENTS: Yes

MANUSCRIPT INFORMATION

GUIDELINES PUBLISHED: Each issue

STYLE REQUIREMENTS PUBLISHED: Each issue

STYLE MANUAL USED: In-house

PREFERRED TOPICS: Economics, geography, planning, political science,
  sociology, engineering

QUERY LETTER: No   SIMULTANEOUS SUBMISSION: No

ABSTRACT WITH MANUSCRIPT: No   COVER LETTER: Yes

NUMBER OF MANUSCRIPT COPIES: 3   MANUSCRIPT LENGTH: No limit

SUBMISSION FEE: No   PAGE CHARGES: No

MANUSCRIPT ACKNOWLEDGED: Yes   EARLY PUBLICATION OPTION: No

COPYRIGHT OWNER: Journal   REPRINTS: Optional purchase

AUTHOR COMPENSATION: None

MANUSCRIPT ADDRESS: M. Jarvin Emerson, Editor, Regional Science
  Perspectives, Department of Economics, Kansas State University,
  320 Waters Hall, Manhattan, KS 66506

Regional Studies

FIRST PUBLISHED: 1966   FREQUENCY: Bi-M   CIRCULATION: 4,000

AFFILIATION: Regional Studies Association, 29 Great James Street, London WC1N 3ES, U.K.

AUDIENCE: Academic/Professional; Business/Industrial; Government

PERCENT OF UNSOLICITED ARTICLES/ISSUE: 61-80%   ISSN: 0034-3404

EDITORIAL POLICY: To accept high quality articles in the areas of urban and regional economics and public policy, with emphasis on applications to development planning.

REVIEW INFORMATION

REFEREED: Yes (I-B)   ACCEPTANCE RATE: 30%

NUMBER OF REVIEWER(S)/MS., EXCLUDING IN-HOUSE EDITOR(S): 2

REVIEWER(S): External   ARTICLES/AVG. ISSUE: 5

REVIEWING CRITERIA USED: BLIND REVIEW: No

  MANUSCRIPT SUBMISSION AIDS: 1, 2

  BIAS SAFEGUARDS: 5, 6, 7, 8

AVERAGE REVIEW TIME: 2 mos.   PUBLICATION TIME LAG: 10 mos.

MANUSCRIPT RETURNED WITH COMMENTS: No

MANUSCRIPT INFORMATION

GUIDELINES PUBLISHED: Each issue

STYLE REQUIREMENTS PUBLISHED: Each issue

STYLE MANUAL USED: In-house

PREFERRED TOPICS: Urban and regional economics and public policy

QUERY LETTER: No   SIMULTANEOUS SUBMISSION: No

ABSTRACT WITH MANUSCRIPT: 100 wds.   COVER LETTER: Yes

NUMBER OF MANUSCRIPT COPIES: 4   MANUSCRIPT LENGTH: 30-40 pp.

SUBMISSION FEE: No   PAGE CHARGES: No

MANUSCRIPT ACKNOWLEDGED: No   EARLY PUBLICATION OPTION: No

COPYRIGHT OWNER: Publisher   REPRINTS: Optional purchase

AUTHOR COMPENSATION: None

MANUSCRIPT ADDRESS: Prof. G. L. Clark, Associate Editor, Regional Studies, School of Urban and Public Affairs, Carnegie-Mellon University, Pittsburgh, PA 15213

The Review of Black Political Economy

FIRST PUBLISHED: 1970   FREQUENCY: Q   CIRCULATION: 1,500

AFFILIATION: National Economic Association, c/o Dr. Gus T. Rigel,
   Southern University, Baton Rouge, LA 70813, and Clark College,
   SCSPP, 240 Chestnut St. SW, Atlanta, GA 30314
AUDIENCE: Academic/Professional; Government

PERCENT OF UNSOLICITED ARTICLES/ISSUE: 41-60%   ISSN: 0034-6446

EDITORIAL POLICY: "A scholarly journal devoted to the examination
   of issues related to the economic status of black and Third World
   peoples. Its aim is to encourage and promote the analysis and
   empirical study of inequality in economic status and opportunity
   based on race and ethnic origin."

REVIEW INFORMATION

REFEREED: Yes (I-A)   ACCEPTANCE RATE: 40%

NUMBER OF REVIEWER(S)/MS., EXCLUDING IN-HOUSE EDITOR(S): 2

REVIEWER(S): External   ARTICLES/AVG. ISSUE: 6

REVIEWING CRITERIA USED: BLIND REVIEW: Yes (Preliminary
   MANUSCRIPT SUBMISSION AIDS: 1, 2   screening only)

   BIAS SAFEGUARDS: 3, 5, 6, 7, 9

AVERAGE REVIEW TIME: 4 mos.   PUBLICATION TIME LAG: 3-6 mos.

MANUSCRIPT RETURNED WITH COMMENTS: If appropriate; SASE required

MANUSCRIPT INFORMATION

GUIDELINES PUBLISHED: Each issue

STYLE REQUIREMENTS PUBLISHED: Each issue

STYLE MANUAL USED: Chicago

PREFERRED TOPICS: "Practical application of policy prescriptions
   for the solution" of black economic problems

QUERY LETTER: No   SIMULTANEOUS SUBMISSION: No

ABSTRACT WITH MANUSCRIPT: 100 wds.   COVER LETTER: Yes

NUMBER OF MANUSCRIPT COPIES: 4   MANUSCRIPT LENGTH: 20-25 pp.

SUBMISSION FEE: No   PAGE CHARGES: No

MANUSCRIPT ACKNOWLEDGED: Yes   EARLY PUBLICATION OPTION: No

COPYRIGHT OWNER: Journal   REPRINTS: Not available

AUTHOR COMPENSATION: 50 free reprints/tear sheets

MANUSCRIPT ADDRESS: Dr. Margaret C. Simms, Editor, The Review of Black
   Political Economy, Suite 400, 1301 Pennsylvania Avenue N.W.,
   Washington, D.C. 20004

Review of Economic Conditions in Italy

FIRST PUBLISHED: 1947   FREQUENCY: 3/Yr.   CIRCULATION: 3,500
AFFILIATION: Banco di Roma. Address same as journal's.

AUDIENCE: Academic/Professional; Business/Industrial; Government
PERCENT OF UNSOLICITED ARTICLES/ISSUE: 0-10%   ISSN: 0034-6799
EDITORIAL POLICY: Publishes the Review "for the use of our friends
  abroad and for all those who are interested in our country, in
  an attempt to keep them informed as to the Italian economic
  situation."

REVIEW INFORMATION

REFEREED: No   ACCEPTANCE RATE: 11%
NUMBER OF REVIEWER(S)/MS., EXCLUDING IN-HOUSE EDITOR(S): 0
REVIEWER(S): Editor   ARTICLES/AVG. ISSUE: 3
REVIEWING CRITERIA USED: BLIND REVIEW: No
  MANUSCRIPT SUBMISSION AIDS: 0
  BIAS SAFEGUARDS: 9*
AVERAGE REVIEW TIME: 1 mo.   PUBLICATION TIME LAG: sevl. mos.
MANUSCRIPT RETURNED WITH COMMENTS: No

MANUSCRIPT INFORMATION

GUIDELINES PUBLISHED: No; available on request
STYLE REQUIREMENTS PUBLISHED: No; available on request
STYLE MANUAL USED: Chicago
PREFERRED TOPICS: Italian economy, finance, banking, monetary policy,
  fiscal policy, public debt

QUERY LETTER: No   SIMULTANEOUS SUBMISSION: No
ABSTRACT WITH MANUSCRIPT: 40 wds.   COVER LETTER: Yes
NUMBER OF MANUSCRIPT COPIES: 4   MANUSCRIPT LENGTH: 20-25 pp.

SUBMISSION FEE: No   PAGE CHARGES: No

MANUSCRIPT ACKNOWLEDGED: Yes   EARLY PUBLICATION OPTION: Yes
COPYRIGHT OWNER: Publisher   REPRINTS: Not available

AUTHOR COMPENSATION: Fee
MANUSCRIPT ADDRESS: Prof. Mario Arcelli, Editor, Review of Economic
  Conditions in Italy, Banco di Roma, Viale Tupini 180, 00144
  Roma, Italy

The Review of Economic Studies

FIRST PUBLISHED: 1933   FREQUENCY: Q   CIRCULATION: 2,946

AFFILIATION: The Society for Economic Analysis Ltd., c/o Tieto Ltd.,
  Bank House, 8A Hill Road, Clevedon, Avon BS21 7HH, U.K.

AUDIENCE: Academic/Professional; Government

PERCENT OF UNSOLICITED ARTICLES/ISSUE: 81-100%   ISSN: 0034-6527

EDITORIAL POLICY: Aims to publish papers in theoretical and applied
  economics and econometrics, especially by young authors.

REVIEW INFORMATION

REFEREED: Yes (II-B)   ACCEPTANCE RATE: 8.2%

NUMBER OF REVIEWER(S)/MS., EXCLUDING IN-HOUSE EDITOR(S): 2

REVIEWER(S): Board and/or external   ARTICLES/AVG. ISSUE: 11

REVIEWING CRITERIA USED: BLIND REVIEW: No

  MANUSCRIPT SUBMISSION AIDS: 2

  BIAS SAFEGUARDS: 4, 5, 6, 9

AVERAGE REVIEW TIME: 18 wks.   PUBLICATION TIME LAG: 19 wks.

MANUSCRIPT RETURNED WITH COMMENTS: Yes, SASE required

MANUSCRIPT INFORMATION

GUIDELINES PUBLISHED: No; not available

STYLE REQUIREMENTS PUBLISHED: Each issue

STYLE MANUAL USED: In-house

PREFERRED TOPICS: Economic theory, theoretical and applied econometrics

QUERY LETTER: No   SIMULTANEOUS SUBMISSION: No

ABSTRACT WITH MANUSCRIPT: 100 wds. max. COVER LETTER: Yes

NUMBER OF MANUSCRIPT COPIES: 4   MANUSCRIPT LENGTH: 5-30 pp.

SUBMISSION FEE: No   PAGE CHARGES: No

MANUSCRIPT ACKNOWLEDGED: Yes   EARLY PUBLICATION OPTION: No

COPYRIGHT OWNER: Journal   REPRINTS: Optional purchase

AUTHOR COMPENSATION: 50 free reprints/tear sheets

MANUSCRIPT ADDRESS: Dr. C. R. Bean, The Review of Economic Studies,
  Department of Economics, London School of Economics, Houghton
  Street, London WC2A 2AE, U.K.

The Review of Economics and Statistics

FIRST PUBLISHED: 1976   FREQUENCY: Q   CIRCULATION: 3,800

AFFILIATION: Harvard University, Department of Economics. Address
   same as journal's.

AUDIENCE: Academic/Professional

PERCENT OF UNSOLICITED ARTICLES/ISSUE: 100%   ISSN: 0034-6535

EDITORIAL POLICY: Publishes primarily empirical articles using
   innovative techniques of analysis. Also some articles on
   econometric methods.

REVIEW INFORMATION

REFEREED: Yes (I-B)   ACCEPTANCE RATE: 16%

NUMBER OF REVIEWER(S)/MS., EXCLUDING IN-HOUSE EDITOR(S): 2

REVIEWER(S): External   ARTICLES/AVG. ISSUE: 27

REVIEWING CRITERIA USED: BLIND REVIEW: No

   MANUSCRIPT SUBMISSION AIDS: 0

   BIAS SAFEGUARDS: 5, 7, 9, 10

AVERAGE REVIEW TIME: 2-3 mos.   PUBLICATION TIME LAG: 8-9 mos.

MANUSCRIPT RETURNED WITH COMMENTS: Yes

MANUSCRIPT INFORMATION

GUIDELINES PUBLISHED: No; available on request

STYLE REQUIREMENTS PUBLISHED: No; available on request

STYLE MANUAL USED: In-house

PREFERRED TOPICS: Economics and statistics

QUERY LETTER: No   SIMULTANEOUS SUBMISSION: No

ABSTRACT WITH MANUSCRIPT: No   COVER LETTER: Yes

NUMBER OF MANUSCRIPT COPIES: 3   MANUSCRIPT LENGTH: 6,000 wds.

SUBMISSION FEE: No   PAGE CHARGES: No

MANUSCRIPT ACKNOWLEDGED: Yes   EARLY PUBLICATION OPTION: No

COPYRIGHT OWNER: Journal   REPRINTS: Optional purchase

AUTHOR COMPENSATION: None

MANUSCRIPT ADDRESS: Editor, The Review of Economics and Statistics,
   M-8 Littauer Center, Harvard University, Cambridge, MA 02138

The Review of Income and Wealth

FIRST PUBLISHED: 1966   FREQUENCY: Q   CIRCULATION: 1,500

AFFILIATION: International Association for Research in Income and
Wealth. Address same as journal's.

AUDIENCE: Academic/Professional; Government

PERCENT OF UNSOLICITED ARTICLES/ISSUE: 41-60%   ISSN: 0034-6586

EDITORIAL POLICY: "Interested in receiving manuscripts in the area
of national accounts estimation and analysis, and related fields.
As a journal with an international readership, preference is given
to (1) studies of methodological interest, and (2) comparative
analyses of more than one country."

REVIEW INFORMATION

REFEREED: Yes (III-B)   ACCEPTANCE RATE: 20%

NUMBER OF REVIEWER(S)/MS., EXCLUDING IN-HOUSE EDITOR(S): 2

REVIEWER(S): Board   ARTICLES/AVG. ISSUE: 6

REVIEWING CRITERIA USED: BLIND REVIEW: No

  MANUSCRIPT SUBMISSION AIDS: 1

  BIAS SAFEGUARDS: 8, 9

AVERAGE REVIEW TIME: 3 mos.   PUBLICATION TIME LAG: 9 mos.

MANUSCRIPT RETURNED WITH COMMENTS: No

MANUSCRIPT INFORMATION

GUIDELINES PUBLISHED: Each issue

STYLE REQUIREMENTS PUBLISHED: No; not available

STYLE MANUAL USED: In-house

PREFERRED TOPICS: National accounting and related fields

QUERY LETTER: No   SIMULTANEOUS SUBMISSION: No

ABSTRACT WITH MANUSCRIPT: 300 wds.   COVER LETTER: No

NUMBER OF MANUSCRIPT COPIES: 3   MANUSCRIPT LENGTH: 25 pp.

SUBMISSION FEE: $15. for nonmembers   PAGE CHARGES: No

MANUSCRIPT ACKNOWLEDGED: Yes   EARLY PUBLICATION OPTION: No

COPYRIGHT OWNER: Journal   REPRINTS: Optional purchase

AUTHOR COMPENSATION: None

MANUSCRIPT ADDRESS: International Association for Research in
Income and Wealth, Box 1962, Yale Station, New Haven, CT 06520

Review of Industrial Organization

FIRST PUBLISHED: 1984   FREQUENCY: Q   CIRCULATION: 350

AFFILIATION: Industrial Organization Society, c/o Douglas F. Greer, Dept. of Economics, San Jose State Univ., San Jose, CA 95192-0114

AUDIENCE: Academic/Professional; Business/Industrial; Government

PERCENT OF UNSOLICITED ARTICLES/ISSUE: 100%   ISSN: 0889-938X

EDITORIAL POLICY: To publish contributions in the fields of micro-economics, industrial organization, public utilities and antitrust economics.

REVIEW INFORMATION

REFEREED: Yes (II-A)   ACCEPTANCE RATE: 23%

NUMBER OF REVIEWER(S)/MS., EXCLUDING IN-HOUSE EDITOR(S): 2

REVIEWER(S): Board and external   ARTICLES/AVG. ISSUE: 7

REVIEWING CRITERIA USED: BLIND REVIEW: Yes (Board and external review)
  MANUSCRIPT SUBMISSION AIDS: 0
  BIAS SAFEGUARDS: 3, 4, 5, 9

AVERAGE REVIEW TIME: 8 wks.   PUBLICATION TIME LAG: 6-8 mos.

MANUSCRIPT RETURNED WITH COMMENTS: Yes

MANUSCRIPT INFORMATION

GUIDELINES PUBLISHED: No; available on request

STYLE REQUIREMENTS PUBLISHED: No; available to authors of accepted mss.

STYLE MANUAL USED: In-house

PREFERRED TOPICS: Industrial organization and antitrust economics

QUERY LETTER: No   SIMULTANEOUS SUBMISSION: No

ABSTRACT WITH MANUSCRIPT: 150 wds.   COVER LETTER: Yes

NUMBER OF MANUSCRIPT COPIES: 3   MANUSCRIPT LENGTH: 30 pp.

SUBMISSION FEE: $15. for members/ subscribers; $25. for others   PAGE CHARGES: No

MANUSCRIPT ACKNOWLEDGED: Yes   EARLY PUBLICATION OPTION: Yes

COPYRIGHT OWNER: Publisher   REPRINTS: Optional purchase

AUTHOR COMPENSATION: None

MANUSCRIPT ADDRESS: Editor, Review of Industrial Organization, Department of Economics, 512 Business Building, University of Arkansas, Little Rock, AR 72204

Review of Marketing and Agricultural Economics

FIRST PUBLISHED: 1937   FREQUENCY: Q   CIRCULATION: 1,200

AFFILIATION: New South Wales Department of Agriculture. Address
  same as journal's.

AUDIENCE: Academic/Professional; Government

PERCENT OF UNSOLICITED ARTICLES/ISSUE: 61-80%   ISSN: 0034-6616

EDITORIAL POLICY: Submission of papers on policy issues on agricultural economics is encouraged.

REVIEW INFORMATION

REFEREED: Yes (I-B)   ACCEPTANCE RATE: 69%

NUMBER OF REVIEWER(S)/MS., EXCLUDING IN-HOUSE EDITOR(S): 2

REVIEWER(S): External   ARTICLES/AVG. ISSUE: 3

REVIEWING CRITERIA USED: BLIND REVIEW: No

  MANUSCRIPT SUBMISSION AIDS: 1, 2

  BIAS SAFEGUARDS: 5, 6, 7, 9, 10

AVERAGE REVIEW TIME: 3 mos.   PUBLICATION TIME LAG: 3 mos.

MANUSCRIPT RETURNED WITH COMMENTS: Yes

MANUSCRIPT INFORMATION

GUIDELINES PUBLISHED: Each issue (brief); also on request (detailed)

STYLE REQUIREMENTS PUBLISHED: Each issue (brief); also on request
                                                      (detailed)
STYLE MANUAL USED: Australia

PREFERRED TOPICS: Agricultural economics

QUERY LETTER: No   SIMULTANEOUS SUBMISSION: No

ABSTRACT WITH MANUSCRIPT: 100 wds.   COVER LETTER: Yes

NUMBER OF MANUSCRIPT COPIES: 3   MANUSCRIPT LENGTH: Not specified

SUBMISSION FEE: No   PAGE CHARGES: No

MANUSCRIPT ACKNOWLEDGED: Yes   EARLY PUBLICATION OPTION: No

COPYRIGHT OWNER: None claimed   REPRINTS: Not available

AUTHOR COMPENSATION: None

MANUSCRIPT ADDRESS: The Editors, Review of Marketing and Agricultural
  Economics, Division of Marketing and Economic Services, Department
  of Agriculture, P.O. Box K220, Haymarket N.S.W. 2000, Australia

The Review of Radical Political Economics

FIRST PUBLISHED: 1969   FREQUENCY: Q   CIRCULATION: 2,000

AFFILIATION: Union for Radical Political Economics, 155 West 23rd
St., 12th Floor, New York, NY 10011

AUDIENCE: Academic/Professional

PERCENT OF UNSOLICITED ARTICLES/ISSUE: 100%   ISSN: 0486-6134

EDITORIAL POLICY: "Encourages articles from all perspectives within
a broad definition of radical political economics. A non-exclusive
list in this tradition includes: Marxism, Institutionalism, the
Cambridge approach, Patriarchy, Social Democracy, Anarchy, Feminism,
and Trotskyism."

REVIEW INFORMATION

REFEREED: Yes (III-A)   ACCEPTANCE RATE: 5%

NUMBER OF REVIEWER(S)/MS., EXCLUDING IN-HOUSE EDITOR(S): 4

REVIEWER(S): Board   ARTICLES/AVG. ISSUE: 5-6

REVIEWING CRITERIA USED: BLIND REVIEW: Yes (Board
 MANUSCRIPT SUBMISSION AIDS: 1, 2   and external review)

 BIAS SAFEGUARDS: 3, 5, 9, 10

AVERAGE REVIEW TIME: 3-4 mos.   PUBLICATION TIME LAG: 6-12 mos.

MANUSCRIPT RETURNED WITH COMMENTS: No

MANUSCRIPT INFORMATION

GUIDELINES PUBLISHED: Each issue

STYLE REQUIREMENTS PUBLISHED: Each issue

STYLE MANUAL USED: Chicago

PREFERRED TOPICS: Political economy, gender, race/ethnicity, and
 international development

QUERY LETTER: No   SIMULTANEOUS SUBMISSION: No

ABSTRACT WITH MANUSCRIPT: 50-75 wds.   COVER LETTER: Yes

NUMBER OF MANUSCRIPT COPIES: 5   MANUSCRIPT LENGTH: 40 pp.

SUBMISSION FEE: No   PAGE CHARGES: No

MANUSCRIPT ACKNOWLEDGED: Yes   EARLY PUBLICATION OPTION: No

COPYRIGHT OWNER: Union for Radical   REPRINTS: Not available
 Political Economics

AUTHOR COMPENSATION: 4 free journals

MANUSCRIPT ADDRESS: Bill James, Managing Editor, The Review of
 Radical Political Economics, Department of Economics, The University
 of Utah, Salt Lake City, UT 84112

The Review of Regional Studies

FIRST PUBLISHED: 1970   FREQUENCY: 3/Yr.   CIRCULATION: 600

AFFILIATION: Clemson University, Southern Regional Science Assoc-
iation and Strom Thurmond Institute of Government and Public
Affairs. Address same as journal's.
AUDIENCE: Academic/Professional

PERCENT OF UNSOLICITED ARTICLES/ISSUE: 100%   ISSN: 0048-749X

EDITORIAL POLICY: Primarily interested in empirical studies of

regional or interregional social systems, as well as some theo-

retical and survey topics.

REVIEW INFORMATION

REFEREED: Yes (I-A)   ACCEPTANCE RATE: 35%

NUMBER OF REVIEWER(S)/MS., EXCLUDING IN-HOUSE EDITOR(S): 3

REVIEWER(S): 1 board, 2 external   ARTICLES/AVG. ISSUE: 6

REVIEWING CRITERIA USED: BLIND REVIEW: Yes (Entire
  MANUSCRIPT SUBMISSION AIDS: 1   review)

  BIAS SAFEGUARDS: 3, 4, 5, 7, 8, 9

AVERAGE REVIEW TIME: 6 wks.   PUBLICATION TIME LAG: 9 mos.

MANUSCRIPT RETURNED WITH COMMENTS: Yes, SASE required

MANUSCRIPT INFORMATION

GUIDELINES PUBLISHED: Each issue; also available on request

STYLE REQUIREMENTS PUBLISHED: No; available on request

STYLE MANUAL USED: In-house

PREFERRED TOPICS: Economic location, migration, transportation,

  regional change, and spatial interaction

QUERY LETTER: No   SIMULTANEOUS SUBMISSION: No

ABSTRACT WITH MANUSCRIPT: No   COVER LETTER: Yes

NUMBER OF MANUSCRIPT COPIES: 3   MANUSCRIPT LENGTH: 20 pp.

SUBMISSION FEE: No   PAGE CHARGES: No

MANUSCRIPT ACKNOWLEDGED: Yes   EARLY PUBLICATION OPTION: Yes

COPYRIGHT OWNER: Journal   REPRINTS: Optional purchase

AUTHOR COMPENSATION: None

MANUSCRIPT ADDRESS: James C. Hite, Editor, The Review of Regional
  Studies, 225 Barre Hall, Clemson University, Clemson, SC 29631

Review of Social Economy

FIRST PUBLISHED: 1948   FREQUENCY: 3/Yr.   CIRCULATION: 1,250

AFFILIATION: Association for Social Economics, Box 10318, Louisiana
  Tech University, Ruston, LA 71272

AUDIENCE: Academic/Professional

PERCENT OF UNSOLICITED ARTICLES/ISSUE: 95%   ISSN: 0034-6764

EDITORIAL POLICY: To foster "analysis of current socio-economic
  issues in both their theoretical and practical dimensions."

REVIEW INFORMATION

REFEREED: Yes (I-B)   ACCEPTANCE RATE: 20%

NUMBER OF REVIEWER(S)/MS., EXCLUDING IN-HOUSE EDITOR(S): 2

REVIEWER(S): External   ARTICLES/AVG. ISSUE: 7

REVIEWING CRITERIA USED: BLIND REVIEW: No

  MANUSCRIPT SUBMISSION AIDS: 0

  BIAS SAFEGUARDS: 5, 7, 9*

AVERAGE REVIEW TIME: 3 mos.   PUBLICATION TIME LAG: 6 mos.

MANUSCRIPT RETURNED WITH COMMENTS: Yes

MANUSCRIPT INFORMATION

GUIDELINES PUBLISHED: No; available on request

STYLE REQUIREMENTS PUBLISHED: No; available on request

STYLE MANUAL USED: AEA

PREFERRED TOPICS: Social economics--relation of ethics/economics

QUERY LETTER: No   SIMULTANEOUS SUBMISSION: Yes

ABSTRACT WITH MANUSCRIPT: No   COVER LETTER: Yes

NUMBER OF MANUSCRIPT COPIES: 3   MANUSCRIPT LENGTH: Varies

SUBMISSION FEE: $25. for nonmembers/ PAGE CHARGES: Yes, if excess
  nonsubscribers   of 19 pages

MANUSCRIPT ACKNOWLEDGED: Yes   EARLY PUBLICATION OPTION: No

COPYRIGHT OWNER: Publisher   REPRINTS: Not available

AUTHOR COMPENSATION: 10 free journals

MANUSCRIPT ADDRESS: William R. Waters, Editor-in-Chief, Review of
  Social Economy, De Paul University, 25 East Jackson Boulevard,
  Chicago, IL 60604

Rivista di Politica Economica

FIRST PUBLISHED: 1911   FREQUENCY: M   CIRCULATION: 1,800

AFFILIATION: Confederazione Generale dell'Industria Italiana, Viale dell'Astronomia 30, EUR, 00144, Roma, Italy.

AUDIENCE: Academic/Professional

PERCENT OF UNSOLICITED ARTICLES/ISSUE: 100%   ISSN: 0035-6468

EDITORIAL POLICY: Main purpose is to publish up-to-date articles on theoretical as well as applied economic policy problems.

REVIEW INFORMATION

REFEREED: No   ACCEPTANCE RATE: 60%

NUMBER OF REVIEWER(S)/MS., EXCLUDING IN-HOUSE EDITOR(S): 0

REVIEWER(S): Editor   ARTICLES/AVG. ISSUE: 3

REVIEWING CRITERIA USED: BLIND REVIEW: No

  MANUSCRIPT SUBMISSION AIDS: 0

  BIAS SAFEGUARDS: 4, 9

AVERAGE REVIEW TIME: 1 mo.   PUBLICATION TIME LAG: 3 mos.

MANUSCRIPT RETURNED WITH COMMENTS: Yes

MANUSCRIPT INFORMATION

GUIDELINES PUBLISHED: No; not available

STYLE REQUIREMENTS PUBLISHED: No; available on request

STYLE MANUAL USED: In-house

PREFERRED TOPICS: Economic policy

QUERY LETTER: No   SIMULTANEOUS SUBMISSION: No

ABSTRACT WITH MANUSCRIPT: 120 wds.   COVER LETTER: Yes

NUMBER OF MANUSCRIPT COPIES: 1   MANUSCRIPT LENGTH: 20-50 pp.

SUBMISSION FEE: No   PAGE CHARGES: No

MANUSCRIPT ACKNOWLEDGED: Yes   EARLY PUBLICATION OPTION: Yes

COPYRIGHT OWNER: Journal   REPRINTS: Optional purchase

AUTHOR COMPENSATION: Fee and 25 free reprints/tear sheets

MANUSCRIPT ADDRESS: Editors, Rivista di Politica Economica, Viale Pasteur 6, 00144 Roma, Italy

Rivista Internazionale di Scienze Economiche e Commerciali / International Review of Economics and Business

FIRST PUBLISHED: 1954   FREQUENCY: M   CIRCULATION: 2,500

AFFILIATION: Università Commerciale Luigi Bocconi and Università degli Studi di Milano, Milano, Italy.

AUDIENCE: Academic/Professional

PERCENT OF UNSOLICITED ARTICLES/ISSUE: 95%   ISSN: 0035-6751

EDITORIAL POLICY: Publishes original contributions to economic theory and applications. The journal aims at being an international meeting point of the economic debate.

REVIEW INFORMATION

REFEREED: No   ACCEPTANCE RATE: 60%

NUMBER OF REVIEWER(S)/MS., EXCLUDING IN-HOUSE EDITOR(S): 1

REVIEWER(S): External   ARTICLES/AVG. ISSUE: 6-7

REVIEWING CRITERIA USED: BLIND REVIEW: No

  MANUSCRIPT SUBMISSION AIDS: 0

  BIAS SAFEGUARDS: 4, 5, 9*

AVERAGE REVIEW TIME: 2-3 mos.   PUBLICATION TIME LAG: 6 mos.

MANUSCRIPT RETURNED WITH COMMENTS: No

MANUSCRIPT INFORMATION

GUIDELINES PUBLISHED: No; available on request

STYLE REQUIREMENTS PUBLISHED: No; available on request

STYLE MANUAL USED: AEA

PREFERRED TOPICS: Economics, economic policy, history of economic thought, business administration

QUERY LETTER: No   SIMULTANEOUS SUBMISSION: No

ABSTRACT WITH MANUSCRIPT: 100 wds.   COVER LETTER: No

NUMBER OF MANUSCRIPT COPIES: 2   MANUSCRIPT LENGTH: 20 pp.

SUBMISSION FEE: No   PAGE CHARGES: No

MANUSCRIPT ACKNOWLEDGED: Yes   EARLY PUBLICATION OPTION: Yes

COPYRIGHT OWNER: Journal   REPRINTS: Optional purchase

AUTHOR COMPENSATION: 1 free journal and 50 free reprints/tear sheets

MANUSCRIPT ADDRESS: Prof. Aldo Montesano, Managing Editor, Rivista Internazionale di Scienze Economiche e Commerciali, Via P. Teulie, 1, 20136 Milano, Italy

The Scandinavian Economic History Review

FIRST PUBLISHED: 1953   FREQUENCY: 3/Yr.   CIRCULATION: 700

AFFILIATION: Scandinavian Society for Economic and Social History.
Address same as journal's.

AUDIENCE: Academic/Professional

PERCENT OF UNSOLICITED ARTICLES/ISSUE: 11-20%   ISSN: 0358-5522

EDITORIAL POLICY: Publishes articles on economic and social history
by Nordic economic historians or concerning Nordic history.

REVIEW INFORMATION

REFEREED: No   ACCEPTANCE RATE: 50%

NUMBER OF REVIEWER(S)/MS., EXCLUDING IN-HOUSE EDITOR(S): 1

REVIEWER(S): Board   ARTICLES/AVG. ISSUE: 3

REVIEWING CRITERIA USED: BLIND REVIEW: Yes (Final
  MANUSCRIPT SUBMISSION AIDS: 0   selection only)
  BIAS SAFEGUARDS: 3, 9*, 10

AVERAGE REVIEW TIME: 3-24 wks.   PUBLICATION TIME LAG: 12 mos.

MANUSCRIPT RETURNED WITH COMMENTS: Yes, SASE required

MANUSCRIPT INFORMATION

GUIDELINES PUBLISHED: No; available on request

STYLE REQUIREMENTS PUBLISHED: No; available on request

STYLE MANUAL USED: In-house

PREFERRED TOPICS: Economic growth, demographic transition, social
  change

QUERY LETTER: No   SIMULTANEOUS SUBMISSION: No

ABSTRACT WITH MANUSCRIPT: No   COVER LETTER: No

NUMBER OF MANUSCRIPT COPIES: 1   MANUSCRIPT LENGTH: 30 pp.

SUBMISSION FEE: No   PAGE CHARGES: No

MANUSCRIPT ACKNOWLEDGED: Yes   EARLY PUBLICATION OPTION: Yes

COPYRIGHT OWNER: Publisher   REPRINTS: Not available

AUTHOR COMPENSATION: None

MANUSCRIPT ADDRESS: Prof. Trygve Solhaug, Editor, The Scandinavian
  Economic History Review, Institutt for Okonomish Historie,
  Norges Handelshoyskole, Helleveien 30, 5035 Bergen-Sandviken, Norway

The Scandinavian Journal of Economics

FIRST PUBLISHED: 1899   FREQUENCY: Q   CIRCULATION: 1,150

AFFILIATION: None

AUDIENCE: Academic/Professional; Government

PERCENT OF UNSOLICITED ARTICLES/ISSUE: 100%   ISSN: 0347-0520

EDITORIAL POLICY: Aims to foster original economic research of
high standard in the Nordic countries and make it known to an
international readership. Also welcomes contributions from outside the Nordic countries.

REVIEW INFORMATION

REFEREED: Yes (II-B)   ACCEPTANCE RATE: 25%

NUMBER OF REVIEWER(S)/MS., EXCLUDING IN-HOUSE EDITOR(S): 2

REVIEWER(S): Board and external   ARTICLES/AVG. ISSUE: 6

REVIEWING CRITERIA USED: BLIND REVIEW: No

  MANUSCRIPT SUBMISSION AIDS: 1, 2

  BIAS SAFEGUARDS: 5, 9*

AVERAGE REVIEW TIME: 5 mos.   PUBLICATION TIME LAG: 8 mos.

MANUSCRIPT RETURNED WITH COMMENTS: No

MANUSCRIPT INFORMATION

GUIDELINES PUBLISHED: Each issue

STYLE REQUIREMENTS PUBLISHED: Each issue

STYLE MANUAL USED: In-house

PREFERRED TOPICS: Theoretical and empirical macro- and micro-
economics

QUERY LETTER: No   SIMULTANEOUS SUBMISSION: No

ABSTRACT WITH MANUSCRIPT: 100 wds.   COVER LETTER: Yes

NUMBER OF MANUSCRIPT COPIES: 4   MANUSCRIPT LENGTH: 20 pp. max.

SUBMISSION FEE: No   PAGE CHARGES: No

MANUSCRIPT ACKNOWLEDGED: Yes   EARLY PUBLICATION OPTION: No

COPYRIGHT OWNER: Journal   REPRINTS: Optional purchase

AUTHOR COMPENSATION: 25 free reprints/tear sheets

MANUSCRIPT ADDRESS: The Editor, The Scandinavian Journal of Economics,
Department of Economics, University of Stockholm, S-106 91 Stockholm,
Sweden

Schweizerische Zeitschrift für Volkswirtschaft und Statistik / Revue Suisse d'Économie Politique et de Statistique

FIRST PUBLISHED: 1865   FREQUENCY: Q   CIRCULATION: 1,800

AFFILIATION: Swiss Association of Economics and Statistics. Address same as journal's.

AUDIENCE: Academic/Professional; Government

PERCENT OF UNSOLICITED ARTICLES/ISSUE: 100%   ISSN: 0303-9692

EDITORIAL POLICY: Publication of professional papers in theoretical and applied economics.

REVIEW INFORMATION

REFEREED: No   ACCEPTANCE RATE: 20%

NUMBER OF REVIEWER(S)/MS., EXCLUDING IN-HOUSE EDITOR(S): 1

REVIEWER(S): External   ARTICLES/AVG. ISSUE: 5-6

REVIEWING CRITERIA USED: BLIND REVIEW: No

  MANUSCRIPT SUBMISSION AIDS: 0

  BIAS SAFEGUARDS: 4, 5, 9*

AVERAGE REVIEW TIME: 2 mos.   PUBLICATION TIME LAG: 12 mos.

MANUSCRIPT RETURNED WITH COMMENTS: No

MANUSCRIPT INFORMATION

GUIDELINES PUBLISHED: No; available on request

STYLE REQUIREMENTS PUBLISHED: No; available on request

STYLE MANUAL USED: In-house

PREFERRED TOPICS: Theoretical and applied economics

QUERY LETTER: No   SIMULTANEOUS SUBMISSION: No

ABSTRACT WITH MANUSCRIPT: 100 wds.   COVER LETTER: Yes

NUMBER OF MANUSCRIPT COPIES: 1   MANUSCRIPT LENGTH: 25 pp.

SUBMISSION FEE: No   PAGE CHARGES: No

MANUSCRIPT ACKNOWLEDGED: Yes   EARLY PUBLICATION OPTION: No

COPYRIGHT OWNER: Journal   REPRINTS: Optional purchase

AUTHOR COMPENSATION: 25 free reprints/tear sheets

MANUSCRIPT ADDRESS: Prof. Dr. E. Baltensperger, Editor, Schweizerishe Zeitschrift für Volkswirtschaft und Statistik, Volkswirtschaftliches Institut, Vereinsweg 23, CH-3012 Bern, Switzerland

Science & Society

FIRST PUBLISHED: 1936   FREQUENCY: Q   CIRCULATION: 2,900

AFFILIATION: None

AUDIENCE: Academic/Professional; General

PERCENT OF UNSOLICITED ARTICLES/ISSUE: 61-80%   ISSN: 0036-8237

EDITORIAL POLICY: "An interdisciplinary journal of Marxist thought and
    analysis. It seeks original scholarship in political economy and
    the economic analysis of contemporary capitalist and socialist
    societies; in philosophy and methodology in the natural and social
    sciences; in history, labor, black and women's studies; in aesthetics,
    literature and the arts."

REVIEW INFORMATION

REFEREED: No   ACCEPTANCE RATE: 15-20%

NUMBER OF REVIEWER(S)/MS., EXCLUDING IN-HOUSE EDITOR(S): 1

REVIEWER(S): Board   ARTICLES/AVG. ISSUE: 4

REVIEWING CRITERIA USED: BLIND REVIEW: No

  MANUSCRIPT SUBMISSION AIDS: 1, 2

  BIAS SAFEGUARDS: 4, 5, 6, 9*

AVERAGE REVIEW TIME: 3 mos.   PUBLICATION TIME LAG: 6 mos.

MANUSCRIPT RETURNED WITH COMMENTS: Yes, SASE required

MANUSCRIPT INFORMATION

GUIDELINES PUBLISHED: Each issue

STYLE REQUIREMENTS PUBLISHED: Each issue

STYLE MANUAL USED: Chicago

PREFERRED TOPICS: Political economy, economic analysis of contempor-
    ary capitalist and socialist societies

QUERY LETTER: No   SIMULTANEOUS SUBMISSION: No

ABSTRACT WITH MANUSCRIPT: No   COVER LETTER: Yes

NUMBER OF MANUSCRIPT COPIES: 3   MANUSCRIPT LENGTH: 30 pp.

SUBMISSION FEE: No   PAGE CHARGES: No

MANUSCRIPT ACKNOWLEDGED: Yes   EARLY PUBLICATION OPTION: No

COPYRIGHT OWNER: Publisher   REPRINTS: Not available

AUTHOR COMPENSATION: 5 free reprints/tear sheets

MANUSCRIPT ADDRESS: The Editor, Science & Society, Room 4331,
    John Jay College, 445 West 49th Street, New York, NY 10019

Scottish Journal of Political Economy

FIRST PUBLISHED: 1954   FREQUENCY: 3/Yr.   CIRCULATION: 1,200

AFFILIATION: Scottish Economic Society, c/o P. W. Wood, Esq., PEIDA,
  10 Chester Street, Edinburgh EH3 7RA, U.K.

AUDIENCE: Academic/Professional

PERCENT OF UNSOLICITED ARTICLES/ISSUE: 100%   ISSN: 0036-9292

EDITORIAL POLICY: To maintain and develop the Scottish tradition of
  political economy by publishing papers on policy related topics,
  on the application of contemporary economic theory and statistical
  techniques to a broad range of problems, and providing a continuing
  sense of the historical development of economic analysis.

REVIEW INFORMATION

REFEREED: No   ACCEPTANCE RATE: 20%

NUMBER OF REVIEWER(S)/MS., EXCLUDING IN-HOUSE EDITOR(S): 1

REVIEWER(S): External   ARTICLES/AVG. ISSUE: 6

REVIEWING CRITERIA USED: BLIND REVIEW: No

  MANUSCRIPT SUBMISSION AIDS: 2

  BIAS SAFEGUARDS: 5, 6, 9

AVERAGE REVIEW TIME: 2 mos.   PUBLICATION TIME LAG: 6-9 mos.

MANUSCRIPT RETURNED WITH COMMENTS: On request; SASE required

MANUSCRIPT INFORMATION

GUIDELINES PUBLISHED: No; not available

STYLE REQUIREMENTS PUBLISHED: Each issue

STYLE MANUAL USED: In-house

PREFERRED TOPICS: Economic policy, theory and analysis; statistical
  techniques

QUERY LETTER: No   SIMULTANEOUS SUBMISSION: No

ABSTRACT WITH MANUSCRIPT: 100 wds.   COVER LETTER: Yes

NUMBER OF MANUSCRIPT COPIES: 2   MANUSCRIPT LENGTH: No limit

SUBMISSION FEE: No   PAGE CHARGES: No

MANUSCRIPT ACKNOWLEDGED: Yes   EARLY PUBLICATION OPTION: No

COPYRIGHT OWNER: Scottish Economic   REPRINTS: Optional purchase
  Society

AUTHOR COMPENSATION: 25 free reprints/tear sheets

MANUSCRIPT ADDRESS: Editors, Scottish Journal of Political Economy,
  Department of Social and Economic Research, Adam Smith Building,
  University of Glasgow, G12 8RT, U.K.

The Singapore Economic Review

FIRST PUBLISHED: 1956   FREQUENCY: S-A   CIRCULATION: 600

AFFILIATION: National University of Singapore, Dept. of Economics & Statistics, and the Economic Society of Singapore. Address same as journal's.

AUDIENCE: Academic/Professional

PERCENT OF UNSOLICITED ARTICLES/ISSUE: 100%   ISSN: 0217-5908

EDITORIAL POLICY: Our approach is generally ecumenical, as long as the articles are in the field of economics, although a slight preference is given to articles which deal with the Southeast Asian region.

REVIEW INFORMATION

REFEREED: No   ACCEPTANCE RATE: 20%

NUMBER OF REVIEWER(S)/MS., EXCLUDING IN-HOUSE EDITOR(S): 1

REVIEWER(S): Board or external   ARTICLES/AVG. ISSUE: 6

REVIEWING CRITERIA USED: BLIND REVIEW: Yes (Board and external review)

MANUSCRIPT SUBMISSION AIDS: 0

BIAS SAFEGUARDS: 3, 5, 9

AVERAGE REVIEW TIME: 1-3 mos.   PUBLICATION TIME LAG: 6-12 mos.

MANUSCRIPT RETURNED WITH COMMENTS: Yes

MANUSCRIPT INFORMATION

GUIDELINES PUBLISHED: No; not available

STYLE REQUIREMENTS PUBLISHED: No; not available

STYLE MANUAL USED: Chicago

PREFERRED TOPICS: Economics and related fields

QUERY LETTER: No   SIMULTANEOUS SUBMISSION: No

ABSTRACT WITH MANUSCRIPT: 100 wds.   COVER LETTER: Yes

NUMBER OF MANUSCRIPT COPIES: 2   MANUSCRIPT LENGTH: 20-30 pp.

SUBMISSION FEE: No   PAGE CHARGES: No

MANUSCRIPT ACKNOWLEDGED: Yes   EARLY PUBLICATION OPTION: No

COPYRIGHT OWNER: Publisher   REPRINTS: Optional purchase

AUTHOR COMPENSATION: 25 free reprints/tear sheets

MANUSCRIPT ADDRESS: Prof. Lim Chong-Yah, Editor, The Singapore Economic Review, Department of Economics & Statistics, National University of Singapore, Kent Ridge, Singapore 0511, Singapore

Social and Economic Studies

FIRST PUBLISHED: 1953   FREQUENCY: Q   CIRCULATION: 2,500

AFFILIATION: University of the West Indies, Institute of Social and
  Economic Research. Address same as journal's.

AUDIENCE: Academic/Professional; Business/Industrial; Government

PERCENT OF UNSOLICITED ARTICLES/ISSUE: 61-80%   ISSN: 0037-7651

EDITORIAL POLICY: "Contains reports on the work undertaken by, or
  in association with, the Institute of Social and Economic Research.
  It welcomes contributions on the social, economic and political
  problems and policy issues of the Caribbean, Latin American and
  the Third World, as well as contributions of a general theoretical
  or polemical nature."

REVIEW INFORMATION

REFEREED: Yes (I-A)   ACCEPTANCE RATE: 45-55%

NUMBER OF REVIEWER(S)/MS., EXCLUDING IN-HOUSE EDITOR(S): 2

REVIEWER(S): External   ARTICLES/AVG. ISSUE: 6

REVIEWING CRITERIA USED: BLIND REVIEW: Yes (External
  MANUSCRIPT SUBMISSION AIDS: 1, 2   review only)
  BIAS SAFEGUARDS: 3, 4, 5, 6, 7

AVERAGE REVIEW TIME: 3 mos.   PUBLICATION TIME LAG: 12 mos.

MANUSCRIPT RETURNED WITH COMMENTS: Sometimes

MANUSCRIPT INFORMATION

GUIDELINES PUBLISHED: Each issue

STYLE REQUIREMENTS PUBLISHED: Each issue

STYLE MANUAL USED: In-house

PREFERRED TOPICS: Social sciences

QUERY LETTER: No   SIMULTANEOUS SUBMISSION: No

ABSTRACT WITH MANUSCRIPT: 200 wds. COVER LETTER: No

NUMBER OF MANUSCRIPT COPIES: 3   MANUSCRIPT LENGTH: No limit

SUBMISSION FEE: No   PAGE CHARGES: No

MANUSCRIPT ACKNOWLEDGED: Yes, SASE req. EARLY PUBLICATION OPTION: Yes

COPYRIGHT OWNER: Journal   REPRINTS: Not available

AUTHOR COMPENSATION: 25 free reprints/tear sheets

MANUSCRIPT ADDRESS: Dr. J. E. Greene, General Editor, Social and Economic
  Studies, Institute of Social and Economic Research, University of
  the West Indies, Mona, Kingston 7, Jamaica, West Indies

Social Choice and Welfare

FIRST PUBLISHED: 1984   FREQUENCY: Q   CIRCULATION: N.R.
AFFILIATION: None

AUDIENCE: Academic/Professional; Business/Industrial; Government
PERCENT OF UNSOLICITED ARTICLES/ISSUE: 81-100%   ISSN: 0176-1714
EDITORIAL POLICY: Publishes original research and survey papers on
   the ethical and positive aspects of welfare economics and collective choice theory. Papers both verbal and formal in style are
   being solicited.

REVIEW INFORMATION

REFEREED: Yes (II-B)   ACCEPTANCE RATE: 40%
NUMBER OF REVIEWER(S)/MS., EXCLUDING IN-HOUSE EDITOR(S): 2
REVIEWER(S): Board and external   ARTICLES/AVG. ISSUE: 6
REVIEWING CRITERIA USED: BLIND REVIEW: No
   MANUSCRIPT SUBMISSION AIDS: 1, 2
   BIAS SAFEGUARDS: 5, 6, 9
AVERAGE REVIEW TIME: 4 mos.   PUBLICATION TIME LAG: 6 mos.
MANUSCRIPT RETURNED WITH COMMENTS: No

MANUSCRIPT INFORMATION

GUIDELINES PUBLISHED: Each issue
STYLE REQUIREMENTS PUBLISHED: Each issue
STYLE MANUAL USED: In-house
PREFERRED TOPICS: Social choice and voting theory, welfare economics

QUERY LETTER: No   SIMULTANEOUS SUBMISSION: No
ABSTRACT WITH MANUSCRIPT: 12 lines max. COVER LETTER: Yes
NUMBER OF MANUSCRIPT COPIES: 4   MANUSCRIPT LENGTH: No limit

SUBMISSION FEE: No   PAGE CHARGES: No

MANUSCRIPT ACKNOWLEDGED: Yes   EARLY PUBLICATION OPTION: No
COPYRIGHT OWNER: Publisher   REPRINTS: Optional purchase

AUTHOR COMPENSATION: 50 free reprints/tear sheets
MANUSCRIPT ADDRESS: Prof. Maurice Salles, Coordinating Editor, Social
   Choice and Welfare, CREMERC, Université de Caen, F-14032 Caen
   Cédex, France

Social Science Quarterly

FIRST PUBLISHED: 1920   FREQUENCY: Q   CIRCULATION: 3,300

AFFILIATION: Southwestern Social Science Association. Address same as journal's.

AUDIENCE: Academic/Professional

PERCENT OF UNSOLICITED ARTICLES/ISSUE: 95%   ISSN: 0038-4941

EDITORIAL POLICY: Prefers papers having an interdisciplinary approach or on topics of interest to a general social science audience.

REVIEW INFORMATION

REFEREED: Yes (I-A)   ACCEPTANCE RATE: 14%

NUMBER OF REVIEWER(S)/MS., EXCLUDING IN-HOUSE EDITOR(S): 3

REVIEWER(S): 1 board, 2 external   ARTICLES/AVG. ISSUE: 17

REVIEWING CRITERIA USED: BLIND REVIEW: Yes (Board
  MANUSCRIPT SUBMISSION AIDS: 0   and external review)
  BIAS SAFEGUARDS: 3, 5, 6, 7, 9

AVERAGE REVIEW TIME: 7 wks.   PUBLICATION TIME LAG: 7 mos.

MANUSCRIPT RETURNED WITH COMMENTS: No

MANUSCRIPT INFORMATION

GUIDELINES PUBLISHED: No; available on request

STYLE REQUIREMENTS PUBLISHED: No; available on request

STYLE MANUAL USED: In-house

PREFERRED TOPICS: All social sciences

QUERY LETTER: No   SIMULTANEOUS SUBMISSION: No

ABSTRACT WITH MANUSCRIPT: 50-70 wds.   COVER LETTER: Yes

NUMBER OF MANUSCRIPT COPIES: 4   MANUSCRIPT LENGTH: 30 pp. max.

SUBMISSION FEE: No   PAGE CHARGES: No

MANUSCRIPT ACKNOWLEDGED: Yes   EARLY PUBLICATION OPTION: No

COPYRIGHT OWNER: Journal   REPRINTS: Optional purchase

AUTHOR COMPENSATION: 25 free reprints/tear sheets

MANUSCRIPT ADDRESS: Dr. Charles M. Bonjean, Editor, Social Science Quarterly, W. C. Hogg Building, The University of Texas at Austin, Austin, TX 78712

The South African Journal of Economics /
Suid-Afrikaanse Tydskrif vir Ekonomie

FIRST PUBLISHED: 1933   FREQUENCY: Q   CIRCULATION: 1,600

AFFILIATION: Economic Society of South Africa. POB 929, Pretoria 0001, South Africa

AUDIENCE: Academic/Professional; Government

PERCENT OF UNSOLICITED ARTICLES/ISSUE: 95%   ISSN: 0038-2280

EDITORIAL POLICY: Journal of the Economic Society of South Africa, whose object is "to promote discussion of economic issues, both theoretical and applied, of South Africa or any other country. It subscribes to no ideology and welcomes contributions on any economic topic of a theoretical, applied or policy nature."

REVIEW INFORMATION

REFEREED: No   ACCEPTANCE RATE: 80%

NUMBER OF REVIEWER(S)/MS., EXCLUDING IN-HOUSE EDITOR(S): 0

REVIEWER(S): 3 in-house editors   ARTICLES/AVG. ISSUE: 5-7

REVIEWING CRITERIA USED: BLIND REVIEW: No

MANUSCRIPT SUBMISSION AIDS: 1

BIAS SAFEGUARDS: 5, 9

AVERAGE REVIEW TIME: 3-4 mos.   PUBLICATION TIME LAG: 2 mos.

MANUSCRIPT RETURNED WITH COMMENTS: Yes, SASE required

MANUSCRIPT INFORMATION

GUIDELINES PUBLISHED: Each issue

STYLE REQUIREMENTS PUBLISHED: No; available on request

STYLE MANUAL USED: In-house; Harvard

PREFERRED TOPICS: Macro-economic issues, monetary theory, economic policy, price theory, economic history

QUERY LETTER: No   SIMULTANEOUS SUBMISSION: No

ABSTRACT WITH MANUSCRIPT: 100 wds.   COVER LETTER: Yes

NUMBER OF MANUSCRIPT COPIES: 2   MANUSCRIPT LENGTH: 6,000-10,000 wds.

SUBMISSION FEE: No   PAGE CHARGES: No

MANUSCRIPT ACKNOWLEDGED: Yes   EARLY PUBLICATION OPTION: No

COPYRIGHT OWNER: Author   REPRINTS: Not available

AUTHOR COMPENSATION: None

MANUSCRIPT ADDRESS: Prof. D. J. J. Botha, Managing Editor, The South African Journal of Economics, P.O. Box 31213, Braamfontein 2017, R.S.A.

Southern Economic Journal

FIRST PUBLISHED: 1933   FREQUENCY: Q   CIRCULATION: 4,000

AFFILIATION: Southern Economic Association, College of Bus. Adm., Oklahoma State University, and the University of North Carolina.

AUDIENCE: Academic/Professional; Business/Industrial; Government

PERCENT OF UNSOLICITED ARTICLES/ISSUE: 81-100%   ISSN: 0038-4038

EDITORIAL POLICY: The journal is a primary resource for research on both theoretical and applied economics. Contains articles on technological change, prices, macroeconomics, industry studies, taxation, monetary theory, employment and spending patterns.

REVIEW INFORMATION

REFEREED: No   ACCEPTANCE RATE: 15%

NUMBER OF REVIEWER(S)/MS., EXCLUDING IN-HOUSE EDITOR(S): 1

REVIEWER(S): External   ARTICLES/AVG. ISSUE: 25-30

REVIEWING CRITERIA USED: BLIND REVIEW: Yes (External

  MANUSCRIPT SUBMISSION AIDS: 0   review only)

  BIAS SAFEGUARDS: 3, 5, 9

AVERAGE REVIEW TIME: 6 wks.   PUBLICATION TIME LAG: 6 mos.

MANUSCRIPT RETURNED WITH COMMENTS: No

MANUSCRIPT INFORMATION

GUIDELINES PUBLISHED: No; not available

STYLE REQUIREMENTS PUBLISHED: No; available on request

STYLE MANUAL USED: In-house

PREFERRED TOPICS: Theoretical and applied economics

QUERY LETTER: No   SIMULTANEOUS SUBMISSION: No

ABSTRACT WITH MANUSCRIPT: No   COVER LETTER: Yes

NUMBER OF MANUSCRIPT COPIES: 2   MANUSCRIPT LENGTH: 20-25 pp.

SUBMISSION FEE: $15. for members/   PAGE CHARGES: No
  subscribers; $35. for others

MANUSCRIPT ACKNOWLEDGED: Yes   EARLY PUBLICATION OPTION: No

COPYRIGHT OWNER: Southern Economic REPRINTS: Optional purchase
  Association

AUTHOR COMPENSATION: None

MANUSCRIPT ADDRESS: Vincent J. Tarascio, Managing Editor, Southern Economic Journal, Hanes Hall 019-A, Chapel Hill, NC 27514

Southern Journal of Agricultural Economics

FIRST PUBLISHED: 1969   FREQUENCY: S-A   CIRCULATION: 1,150

AFFILIATION: Southern Agricultural Economics Association, c/o C. L. Huang, Department of Agricultural Economics, Georgia Experiment Station, Experiment, GA 30212

AUDIENCE: Academic/Professional; Business/Industrial; Government

PERCENT OF UNSOLICITED ARTICLES/ISSUE: 100%   ISSN: 0081-3052

EDITORIAL POLICY: To provide a forum for creative and scholarly work in agricultural economics and related areas. Contributions on methodology and applications in business, extension, research and teaching phases of agricultural economics are encouraged. Preference will be given to articles addressing problems and issues of concern in the southern region of the United States.

REVIEW INFORMATION

REFEREED: Yes (II-A)   ACCEPTANCE RATE: 34%

NUMBER OF REVIEWER(S)/MS., EXCLUDING IN-HOUSE EDITOR(S): 4

REVIEWER(S): 3 board, 1 external   ARTICLES/AVG. ISSUE: 25

REVIEWING CRITERIA USED: BLIND REVIEW: Yes (Board review only)

  MANUSCRIPT SUBMISSION AIDS: 1, 2

  BIAS SAFEGUARDS: 3, 5, 6, 8, 9

AVERAGE REVIEW TIME: 7-8 wks.   PUBLICATION TIME LAG: 4 mos.

MANUSCRIPT RETURNED WITH COMMENTS: Yes

MANUSCRIPT INFORMATION

GUIDELINES PUBLISHED: Each issue

STYLE REQUIREMENTS PUBLISHED: Each issue

STYLE MANUAL USED: GPO

PREFERRED TOPICS: Agricultural economics and related areas

QUERY LETTER: No   SIMULTANEOUS SUBMISSION: No

ABSTRACT WITH MANUSCRIPT: 100 wds.   COVER LETTER: Yes

NUMBER OF MANUSCRIPT COPIES: 4   MANUSCRIPT LENGTH: 20-24 pp.

SUBMISSION FEE: No   PAGE CHARGES: $35. per page

MANUSCRIPT ACKNOWLEDGED: Yes   EARLY PUBLICATION OPTION: No

COPYRIGHT OWNER: Southern Agricultural Economics Association   REPRINTS: Not available

AUTHOR COMPENSATION: 100 free reprints

MANUSCRIPT ADDRESS: Steven Miller and Gary J. Wells, Co-Editors, Southern Journal of Agricultural Economics, Dept. of Agricultural Economics, Barre Hall, Clemson University, Clemson, SC 29631

Soviet Studies

FIRST PUBLISHED: 1949   FREQUENCY: Q   CIRCULATION: 1,800

AFFILIATION: University of Glasgow. Address same as journal's.

AUDIENCE: Academic/Professional; Government

PERCENT OF UNSOLICITED ARTICLES/ISSUE: 100%   ISSN: 0038-5859

EDITORIAL POLICY: Interdisciplinary journal publishing academic work
on the USSR and Eastern Europe in the field of social sciences.
Accessibility to readers of other disciplines is an important
criteria (in addition to quality) in acceptance decisions.

REVIEW INFORMATION

REFEREED: Yes (II-B)   ACCEPTANCE RATE: 50%

NUMBER OF REVIEWER(S)/MS., EXCLUDING IN-HOUSE EDITOR(S): 3

REVIEWER(S): 2 board, 1 external   ARTICLES/AVG. ISSUE: 6-8

REVIEWING CRITERIA USED: BLIND REVIEW: No

  MANUSCRIPT SUBMISSION AIDS: 2

  BIAS SAFEGUARDS: 5, 6, 9

AVERAGE REVIEW TIME: 3 mos.   PUBLICATION TIME LAG: 6 mos.

MANUSCRIPT RETURNED WITH COMMENTS: No

MANUSCRIPT INFORMATION

GUIDELINES PUBLISHED: No; not available

STYLE REQUIREMENTS PUBLISHED: Each issue; also available on request

STYLE MANUAL USED: In-house

PREFERRED TOPICS: Academic work on the USSR and Eastern Europe in
social sciences

QUERY LETTER: No   SIMULTANEOUS SUBMISSION: No

ABSTRACT WITH MANUSCRIPT: No   COVER LETTER: Yes

NUMBER OF MANUSCRIPT COPIES: 2   MANUSCRIPT LENGTH: 10,000 wds.
    max.

SUBMISSION FEE: No   PAGE CHARGES: No

MANUSCRIPT ACKNOWLEDGED: Yes   EARLY PUBLICATION OPTION: No

COPYRIGHT OWNER: Journal   REPRINTS: Optional purchase

AUTHOR COMPENSATION: 25 free reprints/tear sheets

MANUSCRIPT ADDRESS: The Editor, Soviet Studies, 29 Bute Gardens,
Glasgow, GS12 8RS, U.K.

Statistica

FIRST PUBLISHED: 1941 FREQUENCY: Irreg. CIRCULATION: 500

AFFILIATION: Universita degli Studi di Bologna, Via Zamboni 33, 40126 Bologna, Italy.

AUDIENCE: Academic/Professional

PERCENT OF UNSOLICITED ARTICLES/ISSUE: 61-80% ISSN: 0039-0380

EDITORIAL POLICY: Devoted to theoretical and applied problems of statistics and statistical analysis in the most varied fields of scientific research. It has become increasingly directed toward epistemological and logical developments of statistical method and to the deepening of quantitative analytical techniques for natural and social phenomena.

REVIEW INFORMATION

REFEREED: Yes (III-A) ACCEPTANCE RATE: 60%

NUMBER OF REVIEWER(S)/MS., EXCLUDING IN-HOUSE EDITOR(S): 2

REVIEWER(S): Board ARTICLES/AVG. ISSUE: 10

REVIEWING CRITERIA USED: BLIND REVIEW: Yes (Board
 MANUSCRIPT SUBMISSION AIDS: 1, 2 and external review)

 BIAS SAFEGUARDS: 3, 4, 5, 6, 8, 9*

AVERAGE REVIEW TIME: 2 wks. PUBLICATION TIME LAG: 8 mos.

MANUSCRIPT RETURNED WITH COMMENTS: No

MANUSCRIPT INFORMATION

GUIDELINES PUBLISHED: Each issue

STYLE REQUIREMENTS PUBLISHED: Each issue

STYLE MANUAL USED: N.R.

PREFERRED TOPICS: Theoretical statistics, biometry, econometry, social sciences

QUERY LETTER: No SIMULTANEOUS SUBMISSION: Yes

ABSTRACT WITH MANUSCRIPT: 90 wds. COVER LETTER: No

NUMBER OF MANUSCRIPT COPIES: 3 MANUSCRIPT LENGTH: 25 pp.

SUBMISSION FEE: No PAGE CHARGES: No

MANUSCRIPT ACKNOWLEDGED: Yes EARLY PUBLICATION OPTION: No

COPYRIGHT OWNER: Journal REPRINTS: Optional purchase

AUTHOR COMPENSATION: 50 free reprints/tear sheets

MANUSCRIPT ADDRESS: Italo Scardovi, Editor, Statistica, Via Belle Arti, 41, 40126 Bologna, Italy

Statistical Journal of the United Nations Economic Commission for Europe

FIRST PUBLISHED: 1982   FREQUENCY: Q   CIRCULATION: N.R.

AFFILIATION: United Nations Economic Commission for Europe. Address same as journal's.

AUDIENCE: Academic/Professional; Government

PERCENT OF UNSOLICITED ARTICLES/ISSUE: 61-80%   ISSN: 0167-8000

EDITORIAL POLICY: Aims "to publish contributions of high scientific quality on topics related to projects which are included in the work programs of the Conference of European Statisticians. Such contributions could be conceptual, empirical, analytical, or methodological."

REVIEW INFORMATION

REFEREED: No   ACCEPTANCE RATE: N.R.

NUMBER OF REVIEWER(S)/MS., EXCLUDING IN-HOUSE EDITOR(S): 1

REVIEWER(S): Board or external   ARTICLES/AVG. ISSUE: 7

REVIEWING CRITERIA USED: BLIND REVIEW: No

  MANUSCRIPT SUBMISSION AIDS: 1, 2

  BIAS SAFEGUARDS: 4, 5, 6

AVERAGE REVIEW TIME: 3 mos.   PUBLICATION TIME LAG: 7-9 mos.

MANUSCRIPT RETURNED WITH COMMENTS: Occasionally

MANUSCRIPT INFORMATION

GUIDELINES PUBLISHED: Each issue; also available on request

STYLE REQUIREMENTS PUBLISHED: Each issue; also available on request

STYLE MANUAL USED: In-house

PREFERRED TOPICS: Regional statistical co-operation; organization and operation of statistical services; development and harmonization of economic, social, demographic, environment, and related statistics

QUERY LETTER: No   SIMULTANEOUS SUBMISSION: Yes

ABSTRACT WITH MANUSCRIPT: 120 wds.   COVER LETTER: Yes

NUMBER OF MANUSCRIPT COPIES: 3   MANUSCRIPT LENGTH: Varies

SUBMISSION FEE: No   PAGE CHARGES: No

MANUSCRIPT ACKNOWLEDGED: No   EARLY PUBLICATION OPTION: No

COPYRIGHT OWNER: Journal   REPRINTS: Optional purchase

AUTHOR COMPENSATION: 25 free reprints

MANUSCRIPT ADDRESS: Andreas Kahnert, Editor, Statistical Journal of the United Nations Economic Commission for Europe, Palais des Nations, CH-1211, Geneva 10, Switzerland

Studi Economici

FIRST PUBLISHED: 1947   FREQUENCY: 3/Yr.   CIRCULATION: 1,000

AFFILIATION: University of Naples, Faculty of Economics. Address same as journal's.

AUDIENCE: Academic/Professional

PERCENT OF UNSOLICITED ARTICLES/ISSUE: 90%   ISSN: 0039-2938

EDITORIAL POLICY: The journal aims at developing theoretical research by giving space to materials having limited access to other journals specialised in problems of immediate practical interest. It is open to works in applied economics, provided they are analytical and not merely descriptive in content. It is specially open to contributions from young and less known authors.

REVIEW INFORMATION

REFEREED: Yes (II-B)   ACCEPTANCE RATE: 80%

NUMBER OF REVIEWER(S)/MS., EXCLUDING IN-HOUSE EDITOR(S): 2

REVIEWER(S): Board and/or external   ARTICLES/AVG. ISSUE: 5

REVIEWING CRITERIA USED: BLIND REVIEW: No

  MANUSCRIPT SUBMISSION AIDS: 2

  BIAS SAFEGUARDS: 4, 5, 6, 9

AVERAGE REVIEW TIME: 1 mo.   PUBLICATION TIME LAG: 6 mos.

MANUSCRIPT RETURNED WITH COMMENTS: Yes

MANUSCRIPT INFORMATION

GUIDELINES PUBLISHED: No; not available

STYLE REQUIREMENTS PUBLISHED: Each issue

STYLE MANUAL USED: In-house

PREFERRED TOPICS: General economics, money, history of economic thought, industrial economics

QUERY LETTER: No   SIMULTANEOUS SUBMISSION: Yes

ABSTRACT WITH MANUSCRIPT: 200 wds. max.   COVER LETTER: Yes

NUMBER OF MANUSCRIPT COPIES: 3   MANUSCRIPT LENGTH: 25-30 pp.

SUBMISSION FEE: No   PAGE CHARGES: No

MANUSCRIPT ACKNOWLEDGED: Yes   EARLY PUBLICATION OPTION: Yes

COPYRIGHT OWNER: Joint   REPRINTS: Optional purchase

AUTHOR COMPENSATION: 25 free reprints/tear sheets

MANUSCRIPT ADDRESS: Prof. Augusto Graziani, Editor, Studi Economici, Via Partenope 36, 80121 Naples, Italy

Tijdschrift voor Economie en Management

FIRST PUBLISHED: 1956   FREQUENCY: Q   CIRCULATION: 2,100
AFFILIATION: Catholic University of Leuven. Address same as journal's.

AUDIENCE: Business/Industrial; Government
PERCENT OF UNSOLICITED ARTICLES/ISSUE: 61-80%   ISSN: 0040-7461
EDITORIAL POLICY: Devoted to economic analysis on an accessible level.

REVIEW INFORMATION

REFEREED: Yes (I-B)   ACCEPTANCE RATE: 60%
NUMBER OF REVIEWER(S)/MS., EXCLUDING IN-HOUSE EDITOR(S): 2
REVIEWER(S): External   ARTICLES/AVG. ISSUE: 5
REVIEWING CRITERIA USED: BLIND REVIEW: No
  MANUSCRIPT SUBMISSION AIDS: 1, 2
  BIAS SAFEGUARDS: 5, 7, 9
AVERAGE REVIEW TIME: 2 mos.   PUBLICATION TIME LAG: 4 mos.
MANUSCRIPT RETURNED WITH COMMENTS: No

MANUSCRIPT INFORMATION

GUIDELINES PUBLISHED: Each issue
STYLE REQUIREMENTS PUBLISHED: Each issue
STYLE MANUAL USED: In-house
PREFERRED TOPICS: Economic analysis

QUERY LETTER: No   SIMULTANEOUS SUBMISSION: No
ABSTRACT WITH MANUSCRIPT: No   COVER LETTER: No
NUMBER OF MANUSCRIPT COPIES: 3   MANUSCRIPT LENGTH: 25 pp.

SUBMISSION FEE: No   PAGE CHARGES: No

MANUSCRIPT ACKNOWLEDGED: Yes   EARLY PUBLICATION OPTION: Yes
COPYRIGHT OWNER: Publisher   REPRINTS: Optional purchase

AUTHOR COMPENSATION: 5 free issues of journal
MANUSCRIPT ADDRESS: Prof. Dr. Raymond De Bondt, Editor, Tijdschrift
  voor Economie en Management, Katholieke Universiteit Leuven,
  Dekenstraat 2, 3000 Leuven, Belgium

Urban Studies

FIRST PUBLISHED: 1964   FREQUENCY: Bi-M   CIRCULATION: 1,546

AFFILIATION: University of Glasgow, Glasgow G12 8RT, U.K.

AUDIENCE: Academic/Professional; Government

PERCENT OF UNSOLICITED ARTICLES/ISSUE: 100%   ISSN: 0042-0980

EDITORIAL POLICY: Seeks to provide an international forum for economic
and social contributions to the fields of urban and regional planning.
Articles will normally be theoretical or empirical contributions which
have not been previously published; comments on articles previously
published in Urban Studies and notes on research methodology or
findings are also considered.

REVIEW INFORMATION

REFEREED: Yes (I-B)   ACCEPTANCE RATE: 38%

NUMBER OF REVIEWER(S)/MS., EXCLUDING IN-HOUSE EDITOR(S): 2

REVIEWER(S): External   ARTICLES/AVG. ISSUE: 7

REVIEWING CRITERIA USED: BLIND REVIEW: No

  MANUSCRIPT SUBMISSION AIDS: 1, 2

  BIAS SAFEGUARDS: 5, 7, 9*

AVERAGE REVIEW TIME: 18 wks.   PUBLICATION TIME LAG: 26 wks.

MANUSCRIPT RETURNED WITH COMMENTS: Yes

MANUSCRIPT INFORMATION

GUIDELINES PUBLISHED: Each issue

STYLE REQUIREMENTS PUBLISHED: Each issue

STYLE MANUAL USED: In-house

PREFERRED TOPICS: Theoretical and empirical contributions to the

  fields of urban and regional planning

QUERY LETTER: No   SIMULTANEOUS SUBMISSION: Yes

ABSTRACT WITH MANUSCRIPT: 150 wds.   COVER LETTER: Yes

NUMBER OF MANUSCRIPT COPIES: 3   MANUSCRIPT LENGTH: 4,000-
      12,000 wds.

SUBMISSION FEE: No   PAGE CHARGES: No

MANUSCRIPT ACKNOWLEDGED: Yes   EARLY PUBLICATION OPTION: No

COPYRIGHT OWNER: Journal   REPRINTS: Optional purchase

AUTHOR COMPENSATION: 25 free reprints/tear sheets

MANUSCRIPT ADDRESS: Prof. B. Chinitz, Editor, Urban Studies, Univ. of
Lowell, Lowell, MA 01854 (U.S. MSS.); Managing Editor, Urban Studies,
Adam Smith Bldg., Univ. of Glasgow, Glasgow G12 8RT, U.K. (others)

Water Resources Research

FIRST PUBLISHED: 1965   FREQUENCY: M   CIRCULATION: 4,000

AFFILIATION: American Geophysical Union, 2000 Florida Avenue, N.W., Washington, D.C. 20009

AUDIENCE: Academic/Professional; Business/Industrial; Government

PERCENT OF UNSOLICITED ARTICLES/ISSUE: 95%   ISSN: 0043-1397

EDITORIAL POLICY: "An interdisciplinary journal integrating research in the social and natural sciences of water. The editors of WRR invite original contributions in hydrology; in the physical, chemical, and biological sciences; and in the social and policy sciences including economics, systems analysis, sociology and law."

REVIEW INFORMATION

REFEREED: Yes (I-B)   ACCEPTANCE RATE: 55%

NUMBER OF REVIEWER(S)/MS., EXCLUDING IN-HOUSE EDITOR(S): 3

REVIEWER(S): 1 board, 2 external   ARTICLES/AVG. ISSUE: 10-15

REVIEWING CRITERIA USED: BLIND REVIEW: No

  MANUSCRIPT SUBMISSION AIDS: 1, 2

  BIAS SAFEGUARDS: 5, 7, 8, 9

AVERAGE REVIEW TIME: 4 mos.   PUBLICATION TIME LAG: 3-5 mos.

MANUSCRIPT RETURNED WITH COMMENTS: No

MANUSCRIPT INFORMATION

GUIDELINES PUBLISHED: Each issue

STYLE REQUIREMENTS PUBLISHED: December or January issue

STYLE MANUAL USED: In-house

PREFERRED TOPICS: All aspects of the social and natural sciences of water

QUERY LETTER: No   SIMULTANEOUS SUBMISSION: No

ABSTRACT WITH MANUSCRIPT: 150 wds. max. COVER LETTER: Yes

NUMBER OF MANUSCRIPT COPIES: 4   MANUSCRIPT LENGTH: No limit

SUBMISSION FEE: No   PAGE CHARGES: Yes, in excess of eight pages

MANUSCRIPT ACKNOWLEDGED: Yes   EARLY PUBLICATION OPTION: No

COPYRIGHT OWNER: Publisher   REPRINTS: Optional purchase

AUTHOR COMPENSATION: None

MANUSCRIPT ADDRESS: Ronald G. Cummings, Editor, Department of Economics, 1915 Roma N.E., University of New Mexico, Albuquerque, New Mexico 87131

Weltwirtschaftliches Archiv / Review of World Economics

FIRST PUBLISHED: 1914   FREQUENCY: Q   CIRCULATION: 1,800

AFFILIATION: Kiel Institute of World Economics. Address same as
  journal's.

AUDIENCE: Academic/Professional

PERCENT OF UNSOLICITED ARTICLES/ISSUE: 81-100%   ISSN: 0043-2636

EDITORIAL POLICY: Dedicated to the study of international economics
  with emphasis on empirical research.

REVIEW INFORMATION

REFEREED: No   ACCEPTANCE RATE: 25%

NUMBER OF REVIEWER(S)/MS., EXCLUDING IN-HOUSE EDITOR(S): 1

REVIEWER(S): External   ARTICLES/AVG. ISSUE: 10

REVIEWING CRITERIA USED: BLIND REVIEW: No

  MANUSCRIPT SUBMISSION AIDS: 0

  BIAS SAFEGUARDS: 4, 5, 6, 8, 9*

AVERAGE REVIEW TIME: Varies   PUBLICATION TIME LAG: 3 mos.

MANUSCRIPT RETURNED WITH COMMENTS: No

MANUSCRIPT INFORMATION

GUIDELINES PUBLISHED: No; not available

STYLE REQUIREMENTS PUBLISHED: No; not available

STYLE MANUAL USED: In-house

PREFERRED TOPICS: International trade, finance, and investment;
  economic development, especially in less developed countries

QUERY LETTER: No   SIMULTANEOUS SUBMISSION: No

ABSTRACT WITH MANUSCRIPT: 100 wds.   COVER LETTER: Yes

NUMBER OF MANUSCRIPT COPIES: 2   MANUSCRIPT LENGTH: Varies

SUBMISSION FEE: No   PAGE CHARGES: No

MANUSCRIPT ACKNOWLEDGED: Yes   EARLY PUBLICATION OPTION: No

COPYRIGHT OWNER: Journal   REPRINTS: Optional purchase

AUTHOR COMPENSATION: 25 free reprints/tear sheets

MANUSCRIPT ADDRESS: Prof. Dr. Hubertus Müller Groeling, Managing
  Editor, Weltwirtschaftliches Archiv, Institut für Weltwirtschaft,
  Düsternbrooker Weg 120, D-2300 Kiel 1, West Germany

World Development

FIRST PUBLISHED: 1973   FREQUENCY: M   CIRCULATION: 1,600
AFFILIATION: None

AUDIENCE: Academic/Professional; Business/Industrial; Government
PERCENT OF UNSOLICITED ARTICLES/ISSUE: 81-100%   ISSN: 0305-750X
EDITORIAL POLICY: "Provides a forum for international dialogue across
  national, disciplinary, and professional barriers in order to stimulate new and imaginative insights and policy proposals for tackling
  the continuing problems of development."

REVIEW INFORMATION

REFEREED: Yes (II-B)   ACCEPTANCE RATE: 15%
NUMBER OF REVIEWER(S)/MS., EXCLUDING IN-HOUSE EDITOR(S): 2
REVIEWER(S): Board and/or external   ARTICLES/AVG. ISSUE: 7-8
REVIEWING CRITERIA USED: BLIND REVIEW: No
  MANUSCRIPT SUBMISSION AIDS: 1, 2
  BIAS SAFEGUARDS: 5, 6, 9*
AVERAGE REVIEW TIME: 3-6 mos.   PUBLICATION TIME LAG: 4 mos.
MANUSCRIPT RETURNED WITH COMMENTS: No

MANUSCRIPT INFORMATION

GUIDELINES PUBLISHED: Each issue
STYLE REQUIREMENTS PUBLISHED: Each issue (brief); also on request
STYLE MANUAL USED: In-house   (detailed)
PREFERRED TOPICS: International development

QUERY LETTER: No   SIMULTANEOUS SUBMISSION: No
ABSTRACT WITH MANUSCRIPT: 100-150 wds. COVER LETTER: Yes
NUMBER OF MANUSCRIPT COPIES: 3   MANUSCRIPT LENGTH: 25-30 pp.

SUBMISSION FEE: No   PAGE CHARGES: No

MANUSCRIPT ACKNOWLEDGED: Yes   EARLY PUBLICATION OPTION: Yes
COPYRIGHT OWNER: Publisher   REPRINTS: Optional purchase

AUTHOR COMPENSATION: 1 free journal and 25 free reprints/tear sheets
MANUSCRIPT ADDRESS: Ms. Anne Gordon Drabek, Managing Editor, World
  Development, Suite 501, 1717 Massachusetts Ave., Washington,
  D.C.   20036

The World Economy

FIRST PUBLISHED: 1968   FREQUENCY: Q   CIRCULATION: 1,500

AFFILIATION: Trade Policy Research Centre. Address same as journal's.

AUDIENCE: Academic/Professional; Business/Industrial; Government

PERCENT OF UNSOLICITED ARTICLES/ISSUE: 11-20%   ISSN: 0378-5920

EDITORIAL POLICY: Aimed at readers all around the world in commerce
   and industry, the professions, academic life, government departments and international organisations, the journal endeavours to
   provide a continuous focus on the conduct of international economic
   affairs.

REVIEW INFORMATION

REFEREED: No   ACCEPTANCE RATE: 25%

NUMBER OF REVIEWER(S)/MS., EXCLUDING IN-HOUSE EDITOR(S): 1

REVIEWER(S): Board   ARTICLES/AVG. ISSUE: 6

REVIEWING CRITERIA USED: BLIND REVIEW: No

   MANUSCRIPT SUBMISSION AIDS: 0

   BIAS SAFEGUARDS: 4, 5, 6, 9*

AVERAGE REVIEW TIME: 2 mos.   PUBLICATION TIME LAG: 6 mos.

MANUSCRIPT RETURNED WITH COMMENTS: Sometimes; SASE required

MANUSCRIPT INFORMATION

GUIDELINES PUBLISHED: No; available on request

STYLE REQUIREMENTS PUBLISHED: No; available on request

STYLE MANUAL USED: In-house

PREFERRED TOPICS: Trade and economic policy, trade law, economic
   development, international finance, foreign investment, industrial
   policy, international monetary system

QUERY LETTER: Yes   SIMULTANEOUS SUBMISSION: No

ABSTRACT WITH MANUSCRIPT: No   COVER LETTER: Yes

NUMBER OF MANUSCRIPT COPIES: 2 MANUSCRIPT LENGTH: 20 pp.

SUBMISSION FEE: No   PAGE CHARGES: No

MANUSCRIPT ACKNOWLEDGED:Yes, SASE pref. EARLY PUBLICATION OPTION: N.R.

COPYRIGHT OWNER: Trade Policy Research REPRINTS: Optional purchase
   Centre

AUTHOR COMPENSATION: 2 free journals and 25 free reprints/tear sheets

MANUSCRIPT ADDRESS: Hugh Corbet, Managing Editor, The World Economy,
   Trade Policy Research Centre, 1 Gough Square, London EC4A 3DE,
   U.K.

Yale Law Journal

FIRST PUBLISHED: 1891   FREQUENCY: 8/Yr.   CIRCULATION: 4,500
AFFILIATION: Yale University Law School. Address same as journal's.

AUDIENCE: Legal community
PERCENT OF UNSOLICITED ARTICLES/ISSUE: 81-100%   ISSN: 0044-0094
EDITORIAL POLICY: General law journal.

REVIEW INFORMATION

REFEREED: No   ACCEPTANCE RATE: 1%
NUMBER OF REVIEWER(S)/MS., EXCLUDING IN-HOUSE EDITOR(S): 0
REVIEWER(S): Editor   ARTICLES/AVG. ISSUE: 2
REVIEWING CRITERIA USED: BLIND REVIEW: No
  MANUSCRIPT SUBMISSION AIDS: 0
  BIAS SAFEGUARDS: 6
AVERAGE REVIEW TIME: 4-8 wks.   PUBLICATION TIME LAG: 3-6 mos.
MANUSCRIPT RETURNED WITH COMMENTS: Sometimes; SASE required

MANUSCRIPT INFORMATION

GUIDELINES PUBLISHED: No; not available
STYLE REQUIREMENTS PUBLISHED: No; not available
STYLE MANUAL USED: Harvard
PREFERRED TOPICS: Legal

QUERY LETTER: No   SIMULTANEOUS SUBMISSION: Yes
ABSTRACT WITH MANUSCRIPT: No   COVER LETTER: Yes
NUMBER OF MANUSCRIPT COPIES: 2   MANUSCRIPT LENGTH: 50-100 pp.

SUBMISSION FEE: No   PAGE CHARGES: No

MANUSCRIPT ACKNOWLEDGED: Yes   EARLY PUBLICATION OPTION: No
COPYRIGHT OWNER: Joint   REPRINTS: Optional purchase

AUTHOR COMPENSATION: 50 free reprints/tear sheets
MANUSCRIPT ADDRESS: The Articles Editor, Yale Law Journal, 401-A
  Yale Station, New Haven, CT 06520

Zeitschrift für Wirtschafts- und Sozialwissenschaften

FIRST PUBLISHED: 1871 FREQUENCY: Bi-M CIRCULATION: 1,000
AFFILIATION: None

AUDIENCE: Academic/Professional
PERCENT OF UNSOLICITED ARTICLES/ISSUE: 100% ISSN: 0324-1783
EDITORIAL POLICY: The main purpose of the journal is the publication
  of original studies in economics.

REVIEW INFORMATION

REFEREED: No ACCEPTANCE RATE: 30%
NUMBER OF REVIEWER(S)/MS., EXCLUDING IN-HOUSE EDITOR(S): 1
REVIEWER(S): External ARTICLES/AVG. ISSUE: 3-4
REVIEWING CRITERIA USED: BLIND REVIEW: Yes (External
  MANUSCRIPT SUBMISSION AIDS: 2 review only)
  BIAS SAFEGUARDS: 3, 4, 5, 9
AVERAGE REVIEW TIME: 6 wks. PUBLICATION TIME LAG: 6-8 mos.
MANUSCRIPT RETURNED WITH COMMENTS: Yes, SASE required

MANUSCRIPT INFORMATION

GUIDELINES PUBLISHED: No; not available
STYLE REQUIREMENTS PUBLISHED: Each issue
STYLE MANUAL USED: In-house
PREFERRED TOPICS: Economics

QUERY LETTER: No SIMULTANEOUS SUBMISSION: No
ABSTRACT WITH MANUSCRIPT: 100 wds. COVER LETTER: Yes
NUMBER OF MANUSCRIPT COPIES: 4 MANUSCRIPT LENGTH: 25 pp.

SUBMISSION FEE: No PAGE CHARGES: No

MANUSCRIPT ACKNOWLEDGED: No EARLY PUBLICATION OPTION: No
COPYRIGHT OWNER: Author and publisher REPRINTS: Purchase required

AUTHOR COMPENSATION: Fee
MANUSCRIPT ADDRESS: Prof. Dr. Artur Woll, Editor, Zeitschrift für
  Wirtschafts- und Sozialwissenschaften, Universität-Gesamthochschule,
  Hölderlinstrasse 3, D-5900 Siegen, Federal Republic of Germany

Refereed Journals

CLASS I-A

CLASS I-A

CLASS I-B

CLASS II-A

CLASS II-B

CLASS II-B

CLASS III-A

CLASS III-B

Nonrefereed Journals

Journals' Reviewing Criteria

Journal Title	Manuscript Subm. Aids		Bias Safeguards								Total
	Guidelines pub.	Style reqts. pub.	Blind review	Prel. screening	Ext. reviewers	Seln. of ext. revrs.	Two(+) ext. revrs.	Reviewers use form	Comments sent auto.	Signed comments sent	
*Accounting Review	x	x	x		x		x	x			6
Acta Oeconomica			x	x	x			x		x	5
*Agricultural Econ. Research	x	x	x		x	x		x			6
*American Economic Review				x	x	x		x			4
American Economist				x				x			2
*American Historical Review	x	x	x	x	x		x	x	x	x	9
*American J. Agric. Economics	x	x	x	x	x	x	x	x			8
*American J. Econ. and Sociology				x	x			x			3
*American Political Science Rev.			x		x		x	x			4
Antitrust Bulletin			x		x	x					3
Applied Economics	x	x			x			x			4
*Applied Statistics	x	x		x	x	x	x	x			7
*AREUEA		x	x	x	x	x		x			6
Atlantic Economic Journal								x			1
*Aussenwirtschaft				x	x						2
Australian Bulletin of Labour		x		x				x			3

*Refereed journal

Journal Title	Manuscript Subm. Aids — Guidelines pub.	Style reqts. pub.	Bias Safeguards — Blind review	Prel. screening	Ext. reviewers	Seln. of ext. revrs.	Two(+) ext. revrs.	Reviewers use form	Comments sent auto.	Signed comments sent	Total
*Australian Econ. Hist. Rev.			x	x	x	x		x			5
*Australian Economic Review			x	x	x			x	x		5
*Australian J. Agric. Economics	x	x	x		x	x	x	x	x		9
Australian Tax Forum	x			x	x	x		x			5
Banca Nazionale Lavoro Q. Rev.				x	x	x		x			4
Bangladesh Development Studies	x	x	x		x	x		x			6
*British J. Industrial Rel.			x	x	x	x		x			5
*British Rev. Economic Issues	x	x			x	x	x	x			6
*Bulletin of Economic Research		x		x	x	x	x	x			6
*Bull. Indonesian Econ. Studies				x	x	x		x			4
*Business Economics	x	x	x		x			x	x		6
*Business History Review		x	x		x	x		x			5
*Cambridge Journal of Economics	x	x			x	x	x	x	x		7
*Canadian J. Agric. Economics	x	x	x		x	x		x	x	x	8
*Canadian Journal of Economics	x				x		x	x			4
*Canadian Public Policy		x			x	x	x	x			5
Cato Journal	x		x	x	x	x		x			6
CEPAL Review											0
Challenge								x			1
Comparative Economic Studies			x		x			x			3
*Conflict Mgt. and Peace Science			x		x	x	x	x			5
*Contemporary Policy Issues				x	x	x	x	x			5
Czechoslovak Economic Digest				x							1
*Demography	x	x	x	x	x	x	x	x			8
*Eastern Economic Journal			x		x		x	x			4
*Econometric Reviews	x	x						x			3
*Econometrica	x	x			x	x		x			5
Economia Internazionale	x										1
Econ. Analysis and Work. Mgt.		x	x	x	x	x		x			6

*Refereed journal

Journal Title	Manuscript Subm. Aids		Bias Safeguards								Total
	Guidelines pub.	Style reqts. pub.	Blind review	Prel. screening	Ext. reviewers	Seln. of ext. revrs.	Two(+) ext. revrs.	Reviewers use form	Comments sent auto.	Signed comments sent	
*Economic and Social Review	x	x	x	x	x		x		x		7
*Econ. Dev. and Cult. Change					x		x		x		3
*Economic Geography		x	x		x	x	x		x		6
*Economic History Review	x			x	x	x	x		x	x	7
*Economic Inquiry				x	x	x	x		x		5
*Economic Journal	x	x			x		x	x	x		6
Economic Notes					x	x			x		3
*Economic Record		x			x		x		x		4
Economic Studies Quarterly	x	x	x		x	x			x		6
*Economica	x		x		x	x	x		x		6
*Economics of Education Review	x	x	x	x	x	x			x		7
*Economics of Planning				x	x	x	x	x	x		6
*Economist, De		x			x				x		3
*Empirical Economics	x	x	x		x	x			x		6
*Energy Journal				x	x				x		3
*European Economic Review	x	x			x	x			x		5
*European Rev. Agric. Economics	x	x	x		x	x		x	x		7
*Explorations in Econ. History	x	x	x		x				x		5
*Financial Review		x	x		x			x	x		5
Fiscal Studies	x				x				x		3
Food Research Institute Studies					x	x			x		3
*Giornale Econ. Annali Econ.		x	x		x		x		x		5
*Growth and Change	x		x	x	x	x	x		x		7
*History of Political Economy		x			x	x			x		4
*Housing Finance Review	x	x			x				x		4
Indian Economic Journal				x							1
Indian Economic Review	x	x			x	x	x		x		6
*Industrial and Labor Rel. Rev.	x		x		x		x		x		5
*Industrial Relations	x	x	x	x	x	x	x		x	x	9

*Refereed journal

Journal Title	Guidelines pub.	Style reqts. pub.	Blind review	Prel. screening	Ext. reviewers	Seln. of ext revrs.	Two(+) ext. revrs.	Reviewers use form	Comments sent auto.	Signed comments sent	Total
	Manuscript Subm. Aids		Bias Safeguards								Total
*Information Econ. and Policy	x				x	x		x			4
*Inquiry	x		x		x			x	x	x	6
*International Economic Review	x			x	x	x	x	x			6
*International J. Indus. Organ.	x	x			x	x	x	x			6
*International J. Social Econ.	x			x	x	x					4
*International Labour Review	x	x									2
*International Organization	x	x	x		x				x	x	6
*International Reg. Sci. Rev.	x	x	x		x	x	x	x			7
*International Rev. Law Econ.	x	x		x	x	x	x	x			7
Jahr. Nationalökonomie Stat.	x	x		x	x	x		x			6
*J. Stud. Econ. and Economet.	x	x	x	x	x	x	x	x	x		9
J. Accounting and Economics	x	x	x		x			x			5
Journal of Accounting Research	x		x		x			x			4
*Journal of Banking and Finance	x	x	x		x	x		x			6
*Journal of Behavioral Econ.	x	x		x	x	x		x	x		7
*Journal of Business					x		x	x			3
*J. Business and Economic Stat.	x			x	x		x	x			5
*Journal of Common Market Stud.	x	x			x		x	x			5
*Journal of Comparative Econ.	x	x	x		x		x	x			6
*Journal of Consumer Research	x	x	x	x	x	x		x	x		8
*Journal of Cultural Economics	x				x			x	x		4
*Journal of Developing Areas	x	x	x		x		x	x			6
*Journal of Development Econ.		x			x	x	x	x			5
Journal of Development Studies		x		x	x	x		x	x		6
*Journal of Econometrics	x	x		x	x	x	x	x			7
*J. Econ. and Social Measure.	x	x	x		x		x	x	x		7
*J. Econ. Behavior and Organ.	x	x		x	x	x		x			6
*Journal of Economic Development	x	x	x		x	x		x			6
*Journal of Economic Education			x	x	x	x	x	x			6

*Referee journal

Journal Title	Manuscript Subm. Aids		Bias Safeguards								Total
	Guidelines pub.	Style reqts. pub.	Blind review	Prel. screening	Ext. reviewers	Seln. of ext revrs.	Two(+) ext. revrs.	Reviewers use form	Comments sent auto.	Signed comments sent	
*Journal of Economic History	x	x	x		x				x		5
*Journal of Economic Issues	x	x	x		x				x		5
*Journal of Economic Studies	x	x		x	x				x		5
*Journal of Economics					x		x		x		3
*J. Economics and Business	x	x	x	x	x	x	x		x		8
J. Energy and Development	x	x	x	x	x	x			x		7
*J. Environ. Econ. and Mgt.	x	x		x	x		x		x	x	7
Journal of Finance	x	x	x		x				x		5
Journal of Financial Economics	x	x	x		x	x			x	x	7
*Journal of Financial Research	x	x	x	x	x				x		6
*Journal of Futures Markets	x	x	x		x		x	x	x	x	8
*Journal of Health Economics	x	x		x	x	x	x		x		7
*Journal of Human Resources	x	x	x		x		x		x		6
*Journal of Industrial Economics	x	x		x	x	x			x		6
*J. Inst. and Theo. Economics		x		x	x	x			x		5
Journal of Labor Economics		x		x	x				x		4
*Journal of Labor Research	x		x		x				x		4
*Journal of Macroeconomics		x	x		x		x		x		5
Journal of Mathematical Econ.	x	x			x				x		4
Journal of Monetary Economics	x	x		x	x	x			x		6
*J. Policy Analysis and Mgt.			x		x		x		x		4
*Journal of Policy Modeling	x	x		x	x	x	x		x		7
Journal of Political Economy					x	x			x		3
*Journal of Portfolio Mgt.		x	x	x	x				x		5
J. Post Keynesian Economics					x				x		2
*Journal of Public Economics	x	x		x	x	x	x		x		7
*Journal of Regional Science	x				x				x		3
*J. Research in Islamic Econ.	x	x	x	x	x	x	x		x		8
*Journal of Risk and Insurance	x		x		x	x	x		x		6

*Refereed journal

Journal Title	Manuscript Subm. Aids		Bias Safeguards								Total
	Guidelines pub.	Style reqts. pub.	Blind review	Prel. screening	Ext. reviewers	Seln. of ext revrs.	Two(+) ext. revrs.	Reviewers use form	Comments sent auto.	Signed comments sent	
J. Royal Stat. Soc., Series A	x				x			x	x		4
*J. Royal Stat. Soc., Series B	x	x			x			x			4
J. Transport Econ. and Policy	x	x			x	x		x			5
Journal of Urban Economics	x	x			x			x			4
Konjunkturpolitik					x	x		x			3
*Kyklos				x	x	x		x			4
*Labor History	x	x	x	x	x			x			6
*Land Economics	x	x			x			x		x	5
*Liiketaloudellinen Aikakaus				x	x	x		x			4
Lloyds Bank Review											0
*Logistics and Transport. Rev.					x		x	x			3
*Management Science	x	x			x		x	x			5
*Managerial and Decision Econ.	x	x	x	x	x	x	x	x			8
*Margin	x	x	x		x		x	x			6
*Marine Resource Economics	x	x	x		x			x		x	6
*Marketing Science	x	x			x			x	x		5
*Mathematical Social Sciences	x	x		x	x	x	x	x			7
*Metroeconomica	x	x	x	x	x	x	x	x			8
*METU Studies in Development	x	x	x	x	x	x	x	x			8
Michigan Law Review		x									1
Monthly Labor Review				x	x	x					3
*National Institute Econ. Rev.					x	x		x			3
*National Tax Journal	x		x		x			x			4
Nat. Westminster Bank Q. Rev.											0
*Natural Resources Journal	x	x		x	x						4
New England Economic Review				x							1
*Oxford Bull. Econ. and Stat.	x	x		x	x	x		x			6
*Oxford Economic Papers	x	x		x	x	x	x	x			7
*Pakistan Development Review	x	x	x	x				x			5

*Refereed journal

Journal Title	Manuscript Subm. Aids		Bias Safeguards								Total
	Guidelines pub.	Style reqts. pub.	Blind review	Prel. screening	Ext. reviewers	Seln. of ext. revrs.	Two(+) ext. revrs.	Reviewers use form	Comments sent auto.	Signed comments sent	
*Pakistan J. Applied Economics	x	x	x	x	x	x			x		7
Philippine Economic Journal			x	x	x				x		4
Philippine Rev. Econ. and Bus.	x		x	x	x	x			x		6
Policy Review											0
*Policy Sciences	x	x	x	x	x	x	x	x	x		9
*Population and Development Rev.			x	x	x	x	x		x		6
Population Studies			x	x	x						3
Problems of Communism			x	x							2
*Public Budgeting & Finance	x	x	x	x	x	x	x		x		8
Public Choice				x					x		2
*Public Finance	x		x	x	x				x		5
*Public Finance Quarterly	x		x	x			x		x		5
*Quarterly J. Business and Econ.	x		x	x	x	x			x		6
*Quarterly Journal of Economics			x	x					x		3
*Rand Journal of Economics	x			x	x				x		4
Regional Sci. and Urban Econ.	x			x					x		3
*Regional Science Perspectives	x	x	x	x					x		5
*Regional Studies	x	x		x	x	x	x				6
*Rev. Black Political Economy	x	x	x		x	x	x		x		7
Rev. Econ. Conditions in Italy									x		1
*Review of Economic Studies		x		x	x	x			x		5
*Review of Economics and Stat.					x		x		x	x	4
*Review of Income and Wealth	x							x	x		3
*Rev. Industrial Organization			x	x	x				x		4
*Rev. Marketing and Agric. Econ.	x	x			x	x	x		x	x	7
*Rev. Radical Political Econ.	x	x	x	x					x	x	6
*Review of Regional Studies	x		x	x	x		x	x	x		7
*Review of Social Economy					x		x		x		3
Rivista di Politica Economica				x					x		2

*Refereed journal

Journal Title	Manuscript Subm. Aids		Bias Safeguards									Total
	Guidelines pub.	Style reqts. pub.	Blind review	Prel. screening	Ext. reviewers	Seln. of ext revrs.	Two(+) ext. revrs.	Reviewers use form	Comments sent auto.	Signed comments sent		
Rivista Int. Sci. Econ. Comm.				x	x			x				3
Scandinavian Econ. Hist. Rev.			x					x		x		3
*Scandinavian J. Economics	x	x			x			x				4
Schweiz. Zeit. Volks. Stat.				x	x			x				3
Science & Society	x	x		x	x	x		x				6
Scottish J. Political Economy		x			x	x		x				4
Singapore Economic Review			x		x			x				3
*Social and Economic Studies	x	x	x	x	x	x	x					7
*Social Choice and Welfare	x	x			x	x		x				5
*Social Science Quarterly			x		x	x	x	x				5
South African J. Economics	x				x			x				3
Southern Economic Journal			x		x			x				3
*Southern J. Agric. Economics	x	x	x		x	x	x	x				7
*Soviet Studies		x			x	x		x				4
*Statistica	x	x	x	x	x	x	x	x				8
Stat. J. UN Econ. Comm. Europe	x	x		x	x	x						5
*Studi Economici		x		x	x	x		x				5
*Tijdschrift voor Econ. en Mgt.	x	x			x		x	x				5
*Urban Studies	x	x			x		x	x				5
*Water Resources Research	x	x			x		x	x	x			6
Weltwirtschaftliches Archiv				x	x	x	x	x				5
*World Development	x	x			x	x		x				5
World Economy				x	x	x		x				4
Yale Law Journal					x							1
Zeitschrift Wirts. Sozialwiss.		x	x	x	x			x				5

*Refereed journal

Geographical Index

Journals are indexed by country or countries according to the address(es) of the journal's affiliation(s) or sponsor(s). Journals with no known affiliations are indexed under the country or countries of their manuscript submission address(es). Numbers refer to the page number of the journal entry.

Affiliations
and Keywords Index

This index includes names or acronyms of associations and institutions sponsoring journals, alternate titles, and keywords from titles, editorial policies, and preferred manuscript topics.

About the Compilers

A. CAROLYN MILLER is Associate Librarian, Heindel Library, The Pennsylvania State University at Harrisburg, Middletown, Pennsylvania. She has contributed articles to the *Journal of Academic Librarianship* and the *Journal of Higher Education*.

VICTORIA J. PUNSALAN is Senior Assistant Librarian, Heindel Library, The Pennsylvania State University at Harrisburg, Middletown, Pennsylvania.